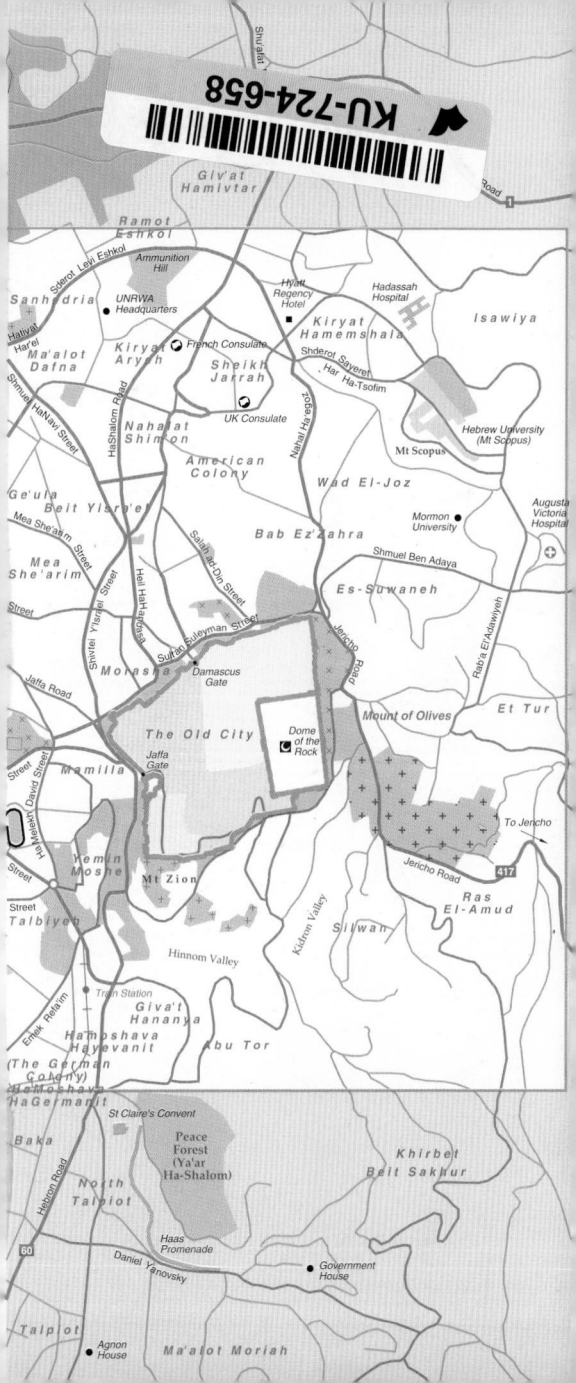

M

Jerusalem

a Lonely Planet city guide

Andrew Humphreys

Jerusalem
  1st edition

Published by
  Lonely Planet Publications
  Head Office: PO Box 617, Hawthorn, Vic 3122, Australia
  Branches: 155 Filbert St, Suite 251, Oakland,
                  CA 94607, USA
                  10 Barley Mow Passage, Chiswick,
                  London W4 4PH, UK
                  71 bis rue du Cardinal Lemoine,
                  75005 Paris, France

Printed by
  Colorcraft Ltd, Hong Kong

Photographs by
Greg Alford, Australia-Israel Chamber of Commerce, Gadi Farfour, Eddie
Gerald, Andrew Humphreys, Israeli Ministry of Tourism, Peter Jousiffe,
Leanne Logan, Mary Oliver

  Front cover: Archway, Jerusalem (Lisl Dennis, The Image Bank)
  Title page: A priest absorbed in prayer in Jerusalem's Armenian
  Quarter (Leanne Logan)

First Published
  March 1997

**Although the authors and publisher have tried to make the
information as accurate as possible, they accept no responsi-
bility for any loss, injury or inconvenience sustained by any
person using this book.**

National Library of Australia Cataloguing-in-Publication Data

Humphreys, Andrew, 1965-
  Jerusalem

  1st ed.
  Includes index.
  ISBN 0 86442 298 9.

  1. Jerusalem – Guide-books. I. Title. (Series : Lonely Planet city guide).

  915.694420454

text & maps © Lonely Planet 1997
photos © photographers as indicated 1997

Andrew Humphreys

Born in England, Andrew stayed around just long enough to complete his studies in architecture before relocating to Egypt. He spent three years in the dust and fumes, amongst other things documenting Cairo's decaying Islamic monuments, later going on to work for the country's biggest English-language periodical, *Egypt Today*. In 1991, an unexpected turn of events deposited Andrew in newly independent Estonia where he joined the staff of the *Tallinn City Paper*, before moving on to co-found a new pan-Baltic newspaper.

Whilst living in Estonia, a chance meeting with Lonely Planet led to Andrew updating the Baltic chapters of *Scandinavian & Baltic Europe on a shoestring* which earned him the dubious privilege of being despatched to Siberia to work on the mammoth *Russia, Ukraine & Belarus*. In 1995 he completed his post-Soviet trilogy by co-authoring *Central Asia*.

Returning to the Middle East, Andrew updated *Israel* and contributed a couple of chapters to Lonely Planet's shoestring guide to the region. He is now back in Cairo with no plans to move anywhere else for the time being.

From the Author

I must acknowledge my great debt to Neil Tilbury, who wrote the original text on Jerusalem as part of his first two editions of Lonely Planet's *Israel*. Significant parts of Neil's text exist within this city guide, which would be a far weaker book without them.

Thanks also to Alan Smart in Jerusalem and to my wife Gadi Farfour. Without them this book would have been completed more quickly, but then it wouldn't have been half as enjoyable to research and write.

From the Publisher

This edition of *Jerusalem* was edited at Lonely Planet's office in Melbourne, Australia, by Jane Rawson, with assistance from Michelle Coxall. The maps were drawn by Trudi Canavan, who was also responsible for the design and layout of the book. The cover was designed by Simon Bracken, with cartographic assistance from Adam McCrow.

Warning & Request

Things change – prices go up, schedules change, good places go bad and bad places go bankrupt – nothing stays the same. So, if you find things better or worse, recently opened or long since closed, please tell us and help make the next edition even more accurate and useful.

We value all of the feedback we receive from travellers. Julie Young coordinates a small team who read and acknowledge every letter, postcard and email, and ensure that every morsel of information finds its way to the appropriate authors, editors and publishers.

Everyone who writes to us will find their name in the next edition of the appropriate guide and will also receive a free subscription to our quarterly newsletter, *Planet Talk*. The very best contributions will be rewarded with a free Lonely Planet guide.

Excerpts from your correspondence may appear in new editions of this guide; in our newsletter, *Planet Talk*; or in the Postcards section of our Web site – so please let us know if you don't want your letter published or your name acknowledged.

Contents

Map Contents

Introduction

Jerusalem is as much a concept as a physical city of stone, filled with people of flesh and blood. The site of David's kingdom and of the ancient temple of the Jews, of the crucifixion of Jesus, and of Mohammed's ascent to heaven, it's a place born of childhood hymns and biblical tales. For me, as a young child Jerusalem was as fabled as Mt Olympus or Valhalla, if a little less exciting – Jesus didn't throw thunderbolts or fight trolls. It's a city that appears remarkably different to each pair of eyes; the interpretation shaped by faith and beliefs, (and the degree to which they're held), by received history, and by nationality.

It's also a city in which little tolerance has ever been shown for the opinion of one's fellow man. Over the ages it is reckoned that more people have given up their lives for some particular vision of Jerusalem than for any other city. The conflict continues today, inexhaustibly fuelled by events that took place not just years ago but centuries and even thousands of years ago. History is relentlessly evoked every day to justify actions which to the outsider seem unfathomable and uncondonable. In the words of Jerusalem-born poet Yehuda Amichai, it's the only city in the world where the vote has been given to the dead.

But it's also very much a city of the moment; history in Jerusalem is always something that is happening now. A journalist writing in London's *The Independent* recently stated that anyone wanting a crash course in the modern Middle East should start by spending 10 minutes at Jerusalem's bazaar-like central bus station. Black garbed orthodox Jews press shoulders with teenage conscripts, male and female, fooling around and only a little encumbered by their rifles. Yemenite music plays somewhere, competing with an immigrant violinist busking Yiddish folk tunes. There are one or two Palestinian Arabs. All of these peoples and their respective societies combine in Jerusalem, and all are active trying to shape the modern city in their own image. While in secular Jerusalem McDonalds and Tower Records open stores, the number of Torah schools increases elsewhere; a new Palestinian college is founded in East Jerusalem; another Russian language newspaper appears. The richness and variety of contemporary Jerusalem is every bit equal to its more celebrated collection of historically overly-revered monuments.

Of course, it is precisely because of those monuments, and to gorge themselves on that history, that most visitors do come. The important thing is not to let the concept of Jerusalem get in the way of the city of Jerusalem. Again, Yehuda Amichai has spoken most eloquently on this; sitting in the Old City and overhearing a tourist guide pointing out a Roman arch above his head, he said to himself, 'Redemption will only come if their guide tells them; You see that arch from the Roman period? It's not important, but next to it, left and down a bit, there sits a man who's bought fruit and vegetables for his family'.

Facts about Jerusalem

HISTORY

David's City

While the recorded history of Jerusalem begins in 1000 BC with David, king of the Israelites and slayer of Goliath, a settlement had already existed on the site for at least another 1000 years before the arrival of the fabled monarch. Egyptian texts recorded in 2000 BC mention the city of Ursalim, although they offer no clues as to who founded the place. At the time of David it was held by the Jebusites and took the form of a small citadel on the Ophel Ridge, the area immediately south-east of the present-day Jewish Quarter. Of little strategic significance, the citadel might well have passed from history had David not decided to conquer it and make it his capital.

The 'City of David' became the first unified Jewish city, serving to tie together the previously disparate 12 tribes of Israelites. To his city the king brought the Ark of the Covenant (2 Samuel 6), reputedly the chest built to contain the stone tablets on which the Ten Commandments were written. David died before his plans to build a house for the Ark saw fruition but the mission was taken up by his youngest son and appointed successor, Solomon.

On a hill just to the north of the city, Solomon oversaw the construction of a vast temple (referred to by historians as the First Temple) which, when dedicated in approximately 950 BC, ensured Jerusalem's status as the focus of Jewish religious life. Despite this, the kingdom failed to survive the death of Solomon 17 years later and split in two. Jerusalem remained as the capital of Judah, the kingdom comprising the two tribes that remained loyal to the lineage of David.

Fall of the First Temple Weakened by the split, first the 10 rogue tribes and then the Kingdom of Judah fell to the conquest of the Assyrians in 721 BC. Jerusalem survived intact by submitting to the suzerainty of the Assyrians until it became caught in the middle of a conflict between the Babylonians and Egyptians. The

Jerusalem Time Line

Period	Duration	Major Events	Existing Monuments
Canaanite	pre-1000 BC	City of Ursalim mentioned in Egyptian texts of 2000 BC.	
First Temple	1000 to 586 BC	David conquers Jerusalem. Solomon builds First Temple. Conquest and destruction by Nebuchadnezzar.	David's City archaeological excavations and Hezekiah's Tunnel.
Second Temple	538 BC to 70 AD	Persian rule, then conquest by Alexander and Greek rule. Romans arrive in 63 BC. Reign of King Herod. Birth of Jesus.	Western Wall and Kidron Valley tombs.
Roman	63 BC to 324 AD	Jewish revolts, resulting in destruction of Second Temple (70 AD) and Jerusalem (135 AD). Building of Aelia Capitolina.	The Cardo in the Jewish Quarter of the Old City.
Byzantine	324 to 638 AD	Spate of biblical building led by Queen Helena, mother of Emperor Constantine.	Original parts of the Church of the Holy Sepulchre.
Early Muslim	638 to 1099	Islamic conquest of Jerusalem led by Umayyad Caliph Omar.	Dome of the Rock and Al-Aqsa Mosque.

Period	Duration	Major Events	Existing Monuments
Crusader	1099 to 1187	Massacre of Jews and Muslims.	St Anne's Church and most of the Church of the Holy Sepulchre.
Ayyubid & Mamluk	1187 to 1517	Saladin conquers Jerusalem. Islamification of the city under Mamluks.	Many of the secondary structures on the Haram ash-Sharif.
Ottoman	1517 to 1917	Jerusalem falls off the map for 300 years. First waves of Jewish immigration. First settlement outside the city walls in 1860s.	Suleyman's city walls; Mea She'arim and foundations of the New City.
British Mandate	1917 to 1948	Jerusalem enters the 20th century. Palestinian Arab riots and uprisings.	Much of the central New City.
Divided Jerusalem	1948 to 1967	State of Israel proclaimed, immediately triggering war. Jerusalem partitioned.	Divided Jerusalem is commemorated in the Tourjeman Post Museum and Artillery Hill Park.
Unified Jerusalem	1967 to present	Israeli troops recapture Old City in Six Day War and annex East Jerusalem.	Western Wall plaza and Jewish Quarter of the Old City.

Jewish king, Zedekiah, backed the wrong side with the result that in 586 BC Jerusalem fell to Nebuchadnezzar, the King of Babylon. The Temple was destroyed (2 Kings 25, 2 Chronicles 36) and the Jews were driven from the city into exile.

Second Temple The period of exile lasted three years until the Babylonian empire fell to King Cyrus of Persia, who allowed the Jews to go home. He even donated money with which the Jerusalemites set about rebuilding their city, including the Temple. The Second Temple was completed around 515 BC. City walls were also added under the direction of a very able Persian-appointed governor, Nehemiah, but these proved insufficient when in 331 BC the unstoppable army of Alexander the Great rolled up against them. Alexander's rule was benevolent, as initially was that of his successors, the Syrian Greek Seleucids, but later attempts to Hellenise Jerusalem – including the rededication of the Jewish Temple to Zeus – triggered a revolt. The revolt was initiated by five brothers from the House of Hasmonean, led by the eldest, Judah the Maccabee. The fight for religious freedom ended up becoming a successful bid for political independence.

Fall of the Second Temple As seems almost inevitable in Jewish history, the victorious Hasmonean dynasty was undermined by ideological rifts and the reinvented Jewish kingdom was easily swallowed by General Pompey's Roman armies. Herod the Great, a Jew, was installed by the Romans as king. A man of excesses, he built a great palatial fortress for his residence (on the site now occupied by the Citadel); however, his major endeavour was to set 10,000 workmen to reconstructing and expanding the Temple, transforming it into 'the most wonderful edifice ever seen or spoken of' (Joseph Flavius, 1st century historian).

Following the death of Herod, the Romans governed through the person of the procurator. The most famous of these was the fifth procurator, Pontius Pilate, the man who ordered the crucifixion of Jesus of Nazareth.

Jesus had very little impact while he was alive and it wasn't until some 300 or more years after his death, with the conversion of the Roman emperor Constantine, that the ministry of the Nazarene began to spread. He was one of many orators critical of the materialism and decadence of the wealthy Jerusalemites, and contemptuous of Roman authority. His views represented those of

PETER JOUSIFFE

The Western Wall: the last remains of the Second Temple
and Judaism's most holy site

many Jews, among whom religious and political
upheaval was fermenting. When the mad Roman
empeor Caligula tried to install his image in the Temple,
extremist elements whipped up the more moderate Jews
into open revolt (the First Revolt – 66 AD). It took four
years for the Romans to quell the uprising and it was
only after a prolonged siege that, in 70 AD, the Roman
general Titus breached the walls of Jerusalem. In retali-
ation the Temple was completely destroyed and the Jews
were sold into slavery or exiled abroad (the Diaspora).

Aelia Capitolina While Jerusalem remained standing it acted as a focus for renewed Jewish nationalist

aspirations, therefore the Emperor Hadrian had the city completely razed to the ground. The action provoked the Second Revolt (132-135 AD), led by Simon Bar-Kochba. It took three years, but the Romans prevailed again. As a precaution against further rebellion they put to death Jewish leaders and elders, broke up communities and on the levelled ruins of Jerusalem they built their own Roman city of Aelia Capitolina, centre of the newly named province of Palestine.

Hadrian's city has set the street pattern for the Old City until today, with four quarters divided by two intersecting main streets, known as the Cardo and the Decumanus. The Cardo still exists as Souk Khan as-Zeit/Habad St, while the Decumanus is now David/Bab as-Silsila St.

The Holy City

In 330 AD, Constantine was inaugurated as the first Christian emperor of the newly decreed Holy Roman (or Byzantine) empire, marking the beginning of more than 300 years of uninterrupted Christian rule in Jerusalem. The Emperor's mother, Helena, initiated a wave of biblical building which resulted in structures like the Church of the Holy Sepulchre and the Church of the Nativity in nearby Bethlehem.

The Challenge of Islam Change came again in the 7th century. After weathering an invasion by the Persians, abetted by the Jews, the Byzantines were bundled out of Palestine by the sudden onslaught of a hitherto unknown force – the armies of Islam. Led by the Caliph Omar ibn Khattab, the Muslims captured Jerusalem in 638 AD. The adherents of this new religion claimed Jerusalem as a city sacred to Islam because they believed that it was from within its walls that their Prophet Mohammed had ascended to heaven. The Caliph identified the site of the ascent as the plateau on which the former temples of Solomon and Herod had stood. At that time, after centuries of neglect, the place was serving as a city rubbish tip. Omar had the plateau cleared and rededicated as a Muslim place of worship, but it was a later caliph, Abd al-Malik, who crowned the holy Islamic precinct with the magnificent Dome of the Rock (691 AD).

The first centuries of Muslim rule were marked by tolerance towards the Jews and Christians, but later Islamic dynasties were not so benevolent. In the latter part of the 11th century pilgrims were returning to Europe with stories of persecution and Muslim desecration of Jerusalem's holy sites. In 1071 the gates on the stream of pilgrims were closed altogether. Rallied by the appeal of Pope Urban II in Rome, Christians throughout western Europe responded by embarking on a crusade to liberate the holy places, thus setting in motion one of the most appalling episodes in the entire history of Jerusalem.

The Crusades On 15 June 1099 the European Crusaders breached the northern walls of the city. Under the banner of Christendom they proceeded to massacre an estimated 40,000 inhabitants, Muslims and Jews. According to a contemporary account, six months after the Crusaders' orgy of slaughter the streets still reeked of rotting bodies. Jerusalem was proclaimed the capital of the Latin Kingdom and Christian pilgrims poured in to settle the recently depopulated quarters of the city. Yet the blood-soaked victory was short-lived. In 1187 Saladin (in Arabic, Salah ad-Din), ruler of Egypt, routed the Crusaders and reinstated Islam in the Holy City. There followed a series of increasingly ill-fated campaigns by the Christian knights to recapture the city, but these finally gave out in the face of the Mamluks, a Cairo-based dynasty of former slaves that had superseded Saladin and his successors.

The Islamic City

Under the Mamluks, Jerusalem underwent a process of Islamification with the construction of large numbers of mosques and theological schools, all executed in a distinctive architectural style. Many of these buildings remain today and add much to the character of the Muslim Quarter of the Old City. The most distinctive of Jerusalem's attributes, however, was not constructed until the reign of Suleyman the Great (1520-1566), sultan of the Ottoman empire which defeated the Mamluks in 1517. It was Suleyman, Jerusalem's greatest builder since Herod, who built the massive wall which still surrounds the Old City. His solid rule returned the city to prosperity, but his death left it in the hands of petty officials, remarkable only for their corrupt and violent brand of administration.

Decline & Stagnation Off the major trade routes and of little strategic value, Jerusalem was largely ignored by the ruling powers in Constantinople and for three centuries seemed to have fallen off the map. Local warlords and Bedouins took advantage of the lack of law and order to carve out independent domains, while the physical face of the city suffered as buildings, streets and infrastructure fell into disrepair. An English visitor of 1842 described the city thus:

Nothing can be more devoid of interest than her gloomy half-ruinous streets and poverty-ridden bazaars...there is certainly no city in the world that the traveller will sooner want to leave than Jerusalem.

Despite the city's decrepit state, the end of the 17th century saw an increase in Jewish immigration as Jews sought to escape persecution elsewhere in the Diaspora. However, in the former city of David the Jews found themselves very much at the bottom of the religious pecking order. While all were obliged to defer to the Muslims, the Jews were also to a great extent at the mercy of the Christians. In 1848 a Jew who strayed into the Church of the Holy Sepulchre was almost torn apart by an enraged mob – the Greek Patriarchate claimed an official document existed which gave them the right to beat any Jews entering or even passing by the church.

The New City

Up until the mid-19th century, no-one lived outside the city walls because they were afraid of bandits and wild animals. Each evening at sunset the six great city gates were swung closed and stayed that way until sunup. It was the pressure of overcrowding in their tiny cramped quarter of the existing city (exacerbated by continued immigration) that finally forced the Jews to colonise the surrounding hills and valleys. The outside settlement began with Mishkenot Sha'ananim, a small development across the valley from Jaffa Gate, inspired and financed by an English Jewish philanthropist, Sir Moses Montefiore. However, the first residents were so afraid of attack that they would return each night to the security of their former quarters in the crowded Old City. Despite this, other experimental communities were rapidly established beyond the safety of the ramparts, such as Mea She'arim, Yemin Moshe and Nahalat Shiv'a, laying the foundations of what was to become the New City.

By this time it was apparent that the aged Ottoman empire was becoming frail and vulnerable and the major European powers began jockeying for a share of the inheritance. The first regular British consulate had opened in Jerusalem in 1838, proclaiming itself a protector of the Jewish elements in Syria and Palestine, and the diplomatic representations of other European powers were not far

ANDREW HUMPHREYS

Completed in 691, the Dome of the Rock is a unique
confection of pink-veined marble, peacock mosaics
and gold leaf

behind. As well as consulates, Jerusalem attracted many
grandiose European-originating 'missions', whose
evangelistic activities, ostensibly involving the custody
of the holy shrines, often looked suspiciously like the
manoeuvrings of international politics.

The Divided City

The European great power rivalry within Jerusalem was
effectively brought to an end when the British, led by
General Allenby, captured the city from the Turks in 1917.
As the administrative capital of the British Mandate the
city developed at a furious pace, accompanied by an

intensifying growth in the passions of Arab and Jewish nationalism. Intermittent skirmishes erupted in the streets and the British found themselves caught in the middle, the target of Jewish terrorist attacks but equally vilified by the Arabs for allowing continued Jewish immigration.

In 1948 the British withdrew and one day later the proclamation of the State of Israel triggered a war which left Jerusalem split in two. The Jordanians held the Old City and the areas immediately north and east, while the Jews held the west of Jerusalem, the New City, and proclaimed it as their 'eternal capital'. This schismatic state of affairs remained for 19 years with the city split along the line of the present-day HaShalom Rd. The scarred no-man's land where the two sides met was heavily mined and watched over by snipers from both sides. The sole official point of crossing, for the few who were permitted to pass from one side to the other, was the Mandelbaum Gate. The Gate passed into history with the Six Day War of 1967 which saw the Israelis capture the whole of Jerusalem. (The Mandelbaum Gate these days is remembered by the Tourjeman Post Museum and celebrated in a novel by Muriel Spark.)

The Schismatic City

In Jerusalem-speak, the Six Day War 'reunified' the city, but in reality this is something of a misnomer. The Israeli

Tunnel Vision

In September 1996 a little-visited tunnel running along the foot of the Western Wall hit world headlines by almost triggering a war between Israeli and Palestinian forces. Some 73 people were left dead in a week-long series of clashes. The 490m subterranean passage that allows visitors to see the foundations of Judaism's sacred Wall has been accessible for several years, but with only one opening – from the north end of the Western Wall plaza in the Jewish Quarter – serving as both entrance and exit. It was Prime Minister Netanyahu's decision to open a new Israeli-controlled exit, surfacing on the Via Dolorosa in the heart of the Muslim Quarter, that incited the violence.

While government officials claimed the opening was made solely to facilitate more traffic through the narrow passage, Palestinians saw it as an incursion into their territory and another move by the Israelis to assert control over all Jerusalem. The crux of the issue is who is the boss in the Old City. At the time of writing the new exit remains open, watched over by four heavily-armed IDF soldiers. ■

and Palestinian communities live and work apart from each other, with their own central districts, their own schools, police and fire departments, their own electricity grids, their own newspapers, and two completely opposing views on the rights of ownership of the city. The Palestinians, supported by most Arab states, want East Jerusalem to be the capital of their future state. The Israeli case was put most bluntly by their Housing Minister speaking in 1995: 'Jerusalem is ours, we will do in it what we want, and we will rule as we see fit'. The Arab-Jewish struggle for Jerusalem continues, but the methods employed are no longer guns and grenades but bricks, breezeblocks and bulldozers.

As part of what the Housing Minister referred to as 'the battle for Jerusalem', the Israelis have dedicated the last 40 years to a massive programme of settlement, ringing the core of the city with many large, new Jewish neighbourhoods. They hope that these will forestall any future suggestion of repartitioning. Most controversially, there have been large seizures of Arab land in East Jerusalem, and there are now more Jews in this sector than Palestinians.

The status of Jerusalem is one of the key issues in the ongoing peace process. Until the two sides come to an agreement over the sacred and much contested city, it is unlikely that there will ever be a firm peace in the Middle East.

CLIMATE

Jerusalem's climate is temperate, with two distinct seasons: winter, when it's cold and rainy, and summer, which tends to be long, hot and dry. You can expect July and August temperatures to range between 25°C and

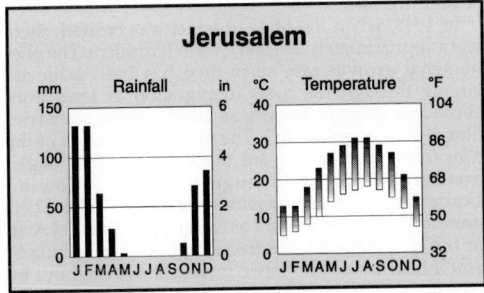

30°C (74-86°F), though low humidity makes the heat easier to bear. The city's high altitude means that by September evening temperatures have already dropped to a level where a light jacket or jumper is a good idea. Rainfall kicks in around November and usually carries on through to sometime around March. The winters can be surprisingly severe, and most years see snow. That said, even deepest winter is punctuated by many bright, sunny days and the skies tend to remain quite clear.

GOVERNMENT & POLITICS

Although Jerusalem houses the Israeli parliament, the Knesset, the real face of city politics is the mayor. The present incumbent is Ehud Olmert, but in the minds of most Jerusalemites the post will always be associated with its previous occupant, Teddy Kollek. Holding office from 1965 to 1993, the popular Kollek was devoted to Jerusalem and worked tirelessly on behalf of the city. The Israel Museum, the restoration of the Old City ramparts and Damascus Gate, the new City Hall complex – all stand as testaments to the tenacity of the former mayor. When the Israeli government wouldn't come up with the funds, he successfully rallied international Jewry and built with their donations. He earned great respect across the board for his even-handed treatment of the Arab population and refusal to bow to the demands of the more extreme political factions.

POPULATION & PEOPLE

Although it has the feel of a small provincial town, with a population of 567,100 Jerusalem is actually Israel's largest city. The majority of the population are Israeli Jews (405,000), with Palestinian Arabs numbering around 155,000.

In 1948, when the State of Israel was created, there were approximately 100,000 Jews in Jerusalem. The phenomenal growth rate since then has been achieved largely through the mass immigration of Jews from abroad (a concept known as *aliyah*, which translates literally as 'stepping up'). The most conspicuous of the *olim* (new immigrants) are the Russians, who began arriving in Israel in huge numbers following Gorbachev's *perestroiking* reforms of the late 1980s. Their presence in Jerusalem isn't as high profile as in Tel Aviv or the desert towns, but frequently on Ben Yehuda St you'll hear mournful Slavic melodies wheezed out by busking accordionists.

GADI FARFOUR

EDDIE GERALD

GADI FARFOUR

EDDIE GERALD

Jerusalem draws pilgrims and settlers from all over the world

Another slightly surprising element in the melange of Jerusalem's faces are the dark-skinned Jewish Ethiopians. They were airlifted to Israel from their famine-struck country in two massive operations in 1985 and 1991, but many Jews, especially Ashkenazim (those of European background), have found it hard to accept that these black people really share their faith. In what amounted to little more than racial prejudice, many aspersions were cast on the Ethiopians' Jewishness and it was suggested that they should go through a religious conversion ceremony, including a 'ritual' bath. The discovery in early 1996 that the Israeli authorities had been routinely throwing out blood donated by Ethiopians because of alleged AIDS fears shows that the Africans have yet to find acceptance.

ARTS

Israelis have a great enthusiasm for the arts in all forms – the country sustains several world-class orchestras, the cities and towns are crowded with art galleries, theatre performances are well attended, and bookshops are plentiful and well-stocked. By no means is it all great art, but that's not the point – the arts in Israel serve to stimulate and provoke discussion, and on that level they succeed completely.

Music

Classical Israel has long been associated with excellence in classical music. This really started in the 1930s when Jewish musicians, including the best of Europe's composers, performers and teachers, fled to Palestine to escape Nazism. The Israeli musical pedigree was further boosted by the waves of Soviet Jews who arrived during the 1980s – the joke went that if a Soviet Jew was not carrying a violin case upon arrival at Ben-Gurion airport, then they must be a pianist.

The Israel Philharmonic Orchestra (whose home is the Binyanei Ha'Umah Conference Centre) and violinist Yitzhak Perlman are world-renowned, and there are many other musicians and groups worthy of note. The major orchestras and groups perform regularly, mainly by subscription, from October to July – visitors will not always find it easy to get tickets to these concerts.

In 1986 the Nuyha/Al-Hakawati Theatre in East Jerusalem produced the first-known Arabic operetta. Its music department teaches the use of traditional Arab instruments and incorporates a recording studio.

Klezmer Klezmer is traditional Yiddish dance music, born in the Ashkenazi Jewish communities of Eastern and Central Europe – think *Fiddler on the Roof*. Centred on violins, the sound can range from weeping melancholy through to wild thigh-slapping, high-kicking exuberance. In the past 20 years klezmer has experienced something of a revival and it's no longer confined to wizened old men turning out hoary standards at wedding parties. Bands such as the New York-based Klezmatics have extended the boundaries with new compositions and eclectic fusions which draw large audiences wherever they perform. Renowned classical violinist Yitzhak Perlman recently recorded a klezmer album which was extremely well received (*In The Fiddler's House* released on EMI).

Writers on Jerusalem

Although the Bible, in its more than 700 references to the city, heralds Jerusalem variously as 'the golden', 'the sacred' and 'the holy', few writers since have shown much sympathy with the place. One early Muslim scribe did define happiness as 'eating a banana in the shadow of the Dome of the Rock,' but the 10th century Arab geographer Ibn Muqaddasi spoke more representatively when he described Jerusalem as 'a golden basin filled with scorpions'.

If anything, the image of the place had fallen even further when Europe and America began to discover Palestine in the mid-19th century. Gustave Flaubert, visiting in 1850, was of the view that Jerusalem was 'a charnel house surrounded by walls' (roughly 100 years later this sentiment was echoed by Aldous Huxley who referred to the city as 'the great slaughterhouse of the religions'). Flaubert also supplied the unnecessary information that his first reaction on entering through Jaffa Gate was to 'let out a fart'. *Moby Dick* author Herman Melville spent eight days in the city and was profoundly depressed by the 'stony tombs, stony hills and stony hearts'.

Mark Twain, though finding Jerusalem 'mournful and dreary and lifeless', at least found a wealth of targets to satirise in his *Innocents Abroad* – there will not be a second coming, he quipped, Christ had been in Jerusalem once and would not deign to come again. Twain's mocking scepticism was shared by George Bernard Shaw, who when visiting in the 1930s advised the early Zionists to erect notices at every holy site reading 'do not trouble to stop here, it isn't genuine'.

With a succinctness that, again, might have appealed to Twain, Selma Lagerlof, Nobel Prize-winning author of the international bestseller *To Jerusalem*, pinpointed a sad truth to the effect that in Jerusalem 'One hates one's fellow man to the glory of God'. ∎

Literature

Hebrew as a modern language only came into being at the very end of last century, largely through the championing of one man, Eliezer Ben Yehuda. In the very short time since then, the Israelis have created a mountain of national literature that has made its entry into libraries the world over. The best represented Israeli author in translation these days is Jerusalem-born Amos Oz, whose books appear in 22 languages. Many of his novels and stories are set in his home city and almost anything he's written is worth reading. Almost rivalling Oz in his collection of international accolades is life-long

Jerusalem resident David Grossman. The author of three novels *(The Smile of the Lamb, See Under Love* and, most recently, *The Book of Intimate Grammar)*, his work has drawn comparisons with Gunter Grass and Gabriel Garcia Marquez.

Much less well known abroad but enormously popular at home is the poet Yehuda Amichai. While the writings of Oz and Grossman often employ Jerusalem as a backdrop, in the work of life-long resident Amichai the Holy City frequently takes centre stage. He's probably the city's foremost spokesperson, and it takes only the most casual acquaintance with the place to feel the truth of his words:

The air over Jerusalem is saturated with prayers and dreams like the air over industrial cities.
It's hard to breathe.

Israeli control over Jerusalem and the subsequent hounding of any Palestinian writer whose works manifested even a hint of political involvement, has led to Beirut becoming the centre of Palestinian literary life. The best represented of Jerusalem-born Palestinians in English translation is Liana Badr, who fled to Beirut via Jordan in 1967. In recent years she has returned to live in Ramallah, just north of Jerusalem, but her first-hand experience of upheaval forms the basis of much of her work; *The Eye of the Mirror* and the short story collection *A Balcony over the Fakihani* are both available in English language editions.

Architecture

It's only this century that Jerusalem has developed anything that could be thought of as an indigenous building style. Through its millennia-long history, Jerusalem's architecture has conformed to the tastes of whatever dynasty or empire was in occupation at the time. Solomon's city was in essence Phoenician; the Jerusalem of Herod was Ptolemaic-Egyptian; the reconstructed Aelia Capitolina was Roman, which was then reshaped by the Byzantines and Crusaders. Later an Islamic spin was put on the whole thing, most notably by the Mamluks (responsible for some of the most attractive structures in the Old City today), followed up by the introduction of Ottoman Turkish elements, including the Old City walls.

Towards the end of last century a whole new series of architectural references was introduced as the great powers of Europe embarked on an unrestrained build-

ANDREW HUMPHREYS

Intricate Mamluk-era carved patterns decorate
the Tomb of Turkan Khatun

ing spree, vying for political influence in the Holy City.
The ostentatious churches, hospices and missions they
threw up were all executed in their own national styles;
as writer Amos Elon puts it, 'like flags planted in the
ground'. So it is that Jerusalem has an Italianate hospital
straight out of a Canaletto painting, an Oxford quadran-
gle on Nablus Rd, a cluster of Muscovite onion-domes
on the Mount of Olives and a Rhineland Gothic castle on
Mt Scopus.

The one mitigating factor in this Euro-Disneyfication
of the city was the predominant use of Jerusalem stone,
which did at least ensure some degree of uniformity. The
white stone, quarried locally, has been the one constant
element throughout the city's whole history of building.
In 1917 the stone's use was even made obligatory in a
law introduced by the British military governor, Sir
Ronald Storrs – this bit of enlightened legislation has
stuck.

It was also during the British Mandate that the first
steps towards formulating a 'Jerusalem architecture'
were made. The International Style, then coming into
vogue in Europe, was imported into Palestine by Jewish
architects fleeing the rise of Nazism. The functional
unadorned lines of this new architecture were adapted
to local conditions of climate, topography and materials,
and combined with local motifs, such as the dome and
arch. This is seen to best effect at the Hadassah Hospital
on Mt Scopus, designed in the 1930s by famed German
architect Erich Mendelsohn, and at St Andrew's Church
(1930), which although very modernist in design
manages to echo Crusader structures such as the Church
of St Anne in the Old City.

Another innovation at this time – seen in the Hadassah Hospital – was the attempt to break down monolithic masses into smaller units, often of different heights, echoing the hillside tumble of traditional Arab villages. It's a technique that has since been much used, most notably in the design of the Israel Museum complex (1965).

This basic, and very flexible, vocabulary has continued to serve as the blueprint for local architecture. With a few unfortunate exceptions (the Knesset building and some of the tower-block hotels come to mind), the result is an extremely cohesive cityscape with a strong awareness of historical tradition and a harmonious relation with the surrounding topography.

SOCIETY & CONDUCT

There are three distinct social elements in Jerusalem: the secular Israelis, the orthodox communities and the Pal-

---

Sorry for What?

Two recent immigrants, one from Russia and one from America, and a native Israeli are at the supermarket where they come across a sign reading 'We're sorry, but due to shortages we have no meat'. The Russian turns to the other two and says, 'What is meat?'. The American shrugs, 'What do they mean by shortages?'. The Israeli shakes his head and looks perplexed, 'What do they mean by this sorry?'.

The Israelis tell this joke about themselves, and any visitor who's been in the country for more than five minutes will nod despairingly at the punch line. The Israelis, as they'll readily agree, are not hot on the niceties of social intercourse. No official or sales assistant will acknowledge your presence until addressed directly. Dining out, a waitress will Frisbee a menu at the table, then indicate she's ready to take the order with an uninterested, 'Yeah?'. Likely-looking places to ask for directions or timetables ward off all potential enquiries with prominently displayed 'No Information' notices.

For those who perceive the difference, it's not, explains writer Stephen Brook, that the Israelis are bad-mannered but rather that they have no manners at all. Faced with a waiter who shrugs aside your complaints of cold food with 'People don't like it if it's too hot', anyone might feel that such subtleties are irrelevant. But one thing to remember is never lose your temper and start shouting, because there's nothing Israelis love more than a good row. ∎

estinians. Few, if any, concessions need to be made in the secular areas of town (which include the New City centre and areas south and west), where the inhabitants lead a style of life which very closely conforms to that enjoyed in much of Europe or the US. Elsewhere, however, large parts of Jerusalem's society revolve around religion, and as such many of the dos and don'ts you will have to consider are based on religious beliefs (for more information see the following Religion section).

The most obvious thing to be aware of is dress. In predominantly orthodox Jewish areas of town (the Jewish Quarter of the Old City and New City districts like Mea She'arim) very strict attention has to be paid to what you wear, with modesty being the watchword. This means that women should be covered from ankle to neck, with no bare shoulders or upper arm exposed, and legs must be hidden beneath a loose-fitting skirt – trousers won't do as they reveal too much of a woman's figure.

Generally speaking, the Palestinians, though they are themselves quite conservative, are far more accepting of foreigners' ways; jeans and T-shirts are OK for women visiting East Jerusalem, although shorts and revealing tops are definitely not a good idea. In the Old City, most religious sites (the Haram ash-Sharif and the Church of the Holy Sepulchre included) will refuse entrance to anyone improperly dressed.

Jewish Society

The assassination of Yitzhak Rabin by a fellow Jew in November 1995 finally dispelled the myth of the Jews of Israel as a homogenous people. The truth is that they are a deeply divided nation. Nowhere is this more evident than in Jerusalem, where 'two Jews equals three opinions' is more than just an amusing aphorism. Divisions exist along the lines of secular vs nonsecular, hawks vs doves, Oriental Jews vs European, those who use creamer vs those who don't – everything is an issue here to be debated and argued in cafes and newspaper columns, on TV talk shows and over the dining room table.

Unfortunately, in Jerusalem differences of opinion have a nasty habit of going beyond verbal arguments, especially where the city's outspoken ultraorthodox communities are concerned. There is a real attempt by the *haredim* (the general term for the ultraorthodox) to force their strict ideology on the less observant majority of society. In recent years haredim have burnt down bus stops for carrying lewd advertising, invaded football pitches hosting Shabbat fixtures, and assaulted 'improperly dressed' women – see the Modesty Squads box in the Things to See & Do chapter. (Somewhat ironically, ultraorthodox elements called for the banning of Stephen Spielberg's *Schindler's List* on the grounds that it contained nudity.)

This cross-cultural collision seems likely to intensify with ultraorthodox gains in the 1996 elections. In addition, religious opposition to birth control, and the double

---

Boys, Girls & Guns

Israel is still technically at war with more than a few of its fellow Middle Eastern countries. This is in addition to being enmeshed in battling Palestinian terrorist groups and struggling to contain the sporadically violent extremist factions within its own society. Consequently, at times half the population of Jerusalem seems to be toting guns. The bus station, in particular, is usually filled with olive green uniforms either arriving home on leave or heading off back to base. Having on occasion to ask, 'Excuse me, could you move your gun so I can sit down there', is an accepted part of bus travel.

What takes more getting used to is the prepubescent appearance of some of the soldiers. Unlike most standing armies, the Israeli Defence Force (IDF) is a citizen's army made up of draftees – men and women both – plucked from civilian life at age 18, fresh from college. With the conscripts barely out of adolescence, it's an army where fatigues are supplemented by Raybans, and M16 rifles double as crucial fashion accessories. Nor is it always necessary to wear a uniform to carry a gun. Any soldier who loses their weapon (though rarely are women assigned to the weapon-carrying infantry units) is liable to seven years imprisonment, so off-duty, jeans and T-shirt clad soldiers sometimes haul their rifles around if there's no secure place to leave them. I once spotted two young men attempting to groove on a Jerusalem dance floor with machine guns slung across their backs – although I suspect this had a lot more to do with narcissism than security.

The initial spell of compulsory service in the IDF stretches for three years in the case of men and two years for women. Once this has been completed every male is assigned to a reserve unit to which they are recalled for about 30 days service each year until the age of 35. Single women are also liable to reserve service up until the age of 34, but in practice they're exempted once they're about 25 years old. Presumably, once a person hits their mid-30s they're assumed to have finally grown out of teenage things like guns. ■

figure families it commonly results in, means that the religious element is expected to be in the majority in Jerusalem within the decade. It's a state of affairs that genuinely frightens the city's secular population, who fear the descent into a darkened, religiously-oppressive state along the lines of Islamic Iran. Anti-haredim protests are common.

As one Jerusalemite interviewed by *National Geographic* put it, 'If we ever get peace around here we'll have a civil war that'll make us wish we had the Arabs back as enemies'.

RELIGION

Sacred to Judaism, Christianity and Islam, no other city in the world is burdened with as much religious significance as Jerusalem.

Judaism

According to high Jewish doctrine, Jews are in the world to be witnesses to the claim that there is one God with whom humans can have contact: God has chosen them to act as messengers whose task it is to pass on these details to the rest of the world. What God has said is written in the Torah (the first five books of the biblical Old Testament). The Torah contains God's will as revealed to the Jews through their leader, Moses, over 3000 years ago. It contains 613 commandments, interpretations of which cover fundamental issues such as

GADI FARFOUR   MARY OLIVER

The distinctive dress of ultraorthodox Jews is worn to show humility avoiding idolatry, murder and sexual abuse, and apparent trivialities such as never eating cheeseburgers and not driving a car or making toast on Saturday. Judaism is an extremely complex faith, and the Torah is only the foundation of Jewish sacred literature. There are also the prophetic, historical and poetical books that constitute the rest of the Old Testament. The prophetic books rank second only to the Torah in Judaism, with Isaiah being the most important.

Another major written part of the Jewish faith is the Talmud, which includes the Mishnah. This great collection of writings was completed during the early centuries of the Christian era. About 2000 authors contributed towards the 63 books of the Talmud, covering rabbinical interpretations of the scriptures and commentaries. Virtually every aspect of life is touched upon and it is this work that many spend a lifetime studying. In days gone by, some scholars in Eastern Europe were said to know it all by heart.

Dress Ultraorthodox Judaism involves some pretty distinctive dress. For men the required garb is a heavy, long, black coat, a black hat (on Shabbat often replaced by a grand fur hat), a tieless white shirt, and more hair on the face than on the head. The hair is also teased into hanging side curls, known as *payot*. Women's clothing is not as ritualised, and it seems to be generally enough to appear dowdy and unappealing with as little flesh showing as possible. The hair is often hidden away under a *snood* (hair net).

This dour apparel, which is worn year-round with no concessions made even on the hottest days, serves two main purposes: humility, to remind the haredim that they are less than God and to rid themselves of feelings such as vanity; and mourning, for the Temple which will be rebuilt for the return of the Messiah. Not all orthodox Jews wear these clothes but they still strictly follow the Jewish Law.

When praying, many orthodox males don the *tallit* (prayer shawl). On each of the four corners of the tallit are *tzitzit* – symbolic tassels as directed by the Torah. While the regular tallit is specifically for prayer, the Torah's instruction is to wear a garment with tzitzit all day, therefore traditional Jews wear the *tallit katan* (small prayer shawl) all day, and the larger tallit just for prayers.

The most common sign of a religious Jew is the *yarmulke* or *kippa* (skullcap). There is no universally recognised size for yarmulkes and you will see various styles, colours and materials used. Many interpret the

Shabbat

The most important meal of the week in most Jewish homes is the Friday night dinner at the start of Shabbat, the Jewish holy day. In Judaism, the 'day' begins when the sun sets, so Friday afternoon is spent cleaning the house before setting the dinner table with the best linen and crockery. Traditionally, religious fathers and sons go to the synagogue while the women prepare the meal. On his return the father blesses the children and recites from the Old Testament.

Shabbat is supposedly a joyful day and a time to appreciate life and God, therefore no work of any kind may be carried out on Shabbat. The orthodox maintain a particularly meticulous code which forbids writing, handling of money, and the operation of machinery of any kind – even switching on a light is taboo. ■

covering of the head as a sign of modesty before God and an acknowledgement of his supremacy.

Childhood By Jewish law, a boy should be circumcised on the eighth day after birth. The more traditional, though not necessarily religious, Jews treat it as an important ceremony with family and friends gathered to witness the occasion.

When he reaches the age of 13, a Jewish boy becomes *bar mitzvah*, meaning that he is now subject to Jewish law and therefore, for religious purposes, an adult. On the Shabbat after his 13th birthday he reads from the Torah in the synagogue for the first time. This involves about a year's preparation and it's often an emotional and noisy occasion with older relatives making their presence felt. Witnessing a bar mitzvah at the Western Wall can be one of the highlights of a visit to Jerusalem. Nowadays there is also a *bat mitzvah* ceremony for Jewish girls.

Synagogues, Rabbis & Prayers Unlike Christian churches, the synagogue isn't just a prayer hall. It is also a place for the study of religious texts, and a venue for meetings of the community council and the rabbinical court. At one time, some synagogues would have had an attached bakery to prepare the special unleavened bread *(matza)* that's baked once a year for *Pesah* (Passover), and maybe a bath-house *(mikveh)* for ritual washing.

It's possibly as a result of such utilitarianism that synagogue architecture is so unprepossessing. There are

Yarmulkes come in all sizes and colours

no domes or minarets, flying buttresses or spires; in fact, from the outside it's often quite difficult to identify a synagogue. You have to look for small indicators such as *menorahs* (the seven branched candelabra), the Star of David, or a *mezuzah*, a small box beside the doorway containing an extract from the Torah on parchment. Mezuzah are also commonly attached to the entrances of homes and public buildings. It's a common custom for Jews to kiss their fingers after touching the mezuzah as they enter and leave.

The focal point of the interior of a synagogue, normally set in the eastern wall, is a cupboard containing one or more copies of the Torah. These are written in Hebrew on parchment, by a scribe with a quill pen, and kept as a scroll on two rollers. The cupboard is known as the Holy Ark *(Aron Hakodesh)* and is covered by a curtain *(parochet)*. A light is kept burning continually in front of the Ark, in remembrance of the continual light in the Temple and as a mark of respect to the holiness of the Scrolls.

In the centre of the synagogue is the reading-desk, normally on a raised platform *(bimah)*. On Shabbat and festivals, readings from the Torah are made from here. The sexes are seated separately, often with a gallery for the women. Basically, the men feel that the women's presence would distract them from their prayer.

Jews should pray three times a day – in the morning, afternoon and evening – with certain additional prayers to be said on Shabbat and holidays.

Heads must be covered at all times in a synagogue but otherwise the apparent lack of decorum during services often surprises first-time visitors. People talk to each other and wander in and out of the synagogue, and children play.

Tefillin You may notice at the Western Wall, and perhaps in some of the bus stations, Jewish men wrapping a leather strap around their arm and wearing a small box strapped to their head. These are *tefillin – tefillin shel yad* is the strap wrapped around the arm and hand and *tefillin shel rosh* is placed around the head. Both parts include a box, enclosed in which is a parchment inscribed with a stipulated portion of the Torah. The shel yad binds the arm, therefore the body; the shel rosh binds the mind. The purpose is to remind Jews that the mind, heart and body are to be used for good and not evil.

Death & the Afterlife Jewish teaching says that at death the body returns to God, so funerals take place within 24 hours to get the deceased there all the quicker. It's also considered a humiliation to leave the dead unburied for any longer than necessary.

There is no cremation in traditional Judaism, because Jews believe in a physical resurrection on the Day of Judgement. Many Jews are bitterly opposed to autopsies for this reason.

Jewish men rip their clothes as a gesture of mourning. This puts the mark of his broken heart on his clothing and can also provide an outlet for the anguish and

EDDIE GERALD

The menorah is a universally recognised symbol of Judaism

emotion that a mourner feels. Today this is usually expressed by a symbolic tearing of a lapel. There is no prayer for the dead as such, but *kaddish*, a prayer that praises God, is recited on the dead person's behalf, preferably by one of their sons.

Visitors to Jewish graves place stones rather than flowers on the grave, because this is a more permanent way of showing that a visit has been made and also involves the mourner in the act of burying the deceased, thus helping to return them to God.

Non-Jews & Conversion Devout Jews believe that the future of their people can only be ensured by the continuity of Jewish families. Therefore the idea of one of their own marrying a non-Jew strikes them with horror – it means the end of a family line. Even if the non-Jew is willing to convert, the orthodox view is that wanting to marry a Jew is not sufficient reason for becoming Jewish. In fact, Jews are not at all keen on the idea of outsiders joining their faith, and as a deterrent conversion to Judaism is usually a rigorous and slow process.

The good news is that, according to a rabbinical teaching, non-Jews can be 'saved' by following a few clearly stipulated guidelines. Idolatry, blasphemy, murder, theft and incest are no-goes, as is eating meat that has been cut from a living animal. 'Acting justly' is a little more tricky as it's wide open to interpretation. However, providing non-Jews comply with the above 'Seven Laws to the Sons of Noah', they can at least steer clear of damnation in a Judaic-oriented cosmos.

Islam

The Arabic word Islam means voluntary surrender to the will of Allah (God) and obedience to his commands. A Muslim is a person who accepts and practices the Islamic way of life.

Muslims recognise the existence of Judaism and Christianity, but within Islam Moses and Jesus are only two in a line of prophets that also includes Adam, Noah, Abraham, Ishmael, Isaac, Lot, Jacob and Joseph. The last of the prophets was Mohammed, born in Mecca in 571 AD, who began receiving revelations from Allah when he was aged 40. He began to preach in his home town, attracting a few followers and a lot of persecution, before moving to Medina in 622 (year zero in the Muslim calendar), where he succeeded in establishing the first Islamic state.

Through the Angel Gabriel (Jibrail), Mohammed received the word of Allah enshrined in the Qur'an, the sacred book of the Muslims. It consists of 114 *suras* (chapters) and 6236 verses providing teachings and guidance on all areas of life and the afterlife.

To a Muslim, Christians and Jews share the same religion but they haven't subscribed to the update.

The Muslim Way of Life Simplicity and modesty are encouraged. Muslims are required to cover their bodies properly and decently. Men must be covered from navel to knees, and must not wear pure silk or gold. Women must cover the whole body except the face and hands. A woman's outfit must not arouse a man's base feelings, so skintight, transparent or revealing styles are out.

Non-Muslims should be aware of these dress codes and, out of respect, adhere to them when in predominantly Muslim areas.

Islam strictly forbids the free mixing of the sexes after puberty, a rule that applies to all socialising, not just premarital sex (hence the often unwelcome interest many Muslim males show in western women – their own women are off-limits). Marriages are generally arranged by parents with the couple's consent. According to Muslims, there is no sexual discrimination in Islam. Muslims believe that the husband and wife are equal partners in the family, playing their role in respective fields. Divorce is permitted but is regarded as the most abominable of legal acts. Although extramarital sex is forbidden, Islam permits polygamy – although polygamy is illegal under Israeli law this law doesn't apply to Muslims in the Palestinian Territories, most of whom are monogamous anyway.

Islam is not as complex as Judaism when it comes to food and drink, but Muslims are only allowed to eat animals that are slaughtered in the Qur'anically prescribed manner, and never pigs nor carnivorous animals.

Alcohol is also prohibited.

Mosques The word 'mosque' comes from the Arabic word *mesjid*, meaning a place of adoration. Most mosques have domes and minarets, making them easy to recognise. Inside, facing the holy city of Mecca, is the *mihrab* (or prayer niche), normally an arched alcove about 1.5m high. The *minbar*, a freestanding pulpit, is usually nearby, and it's from here that the *imam* (preacher) gives the Friday sermon. Also at the front of

EDDIE GERALD LEANNE LOGAN

Simplicity and modesty are an important part of the Islamic Arab's way of life

the mosque is the *khatib*, a low, railed wooden platform where a reader sits to recite the Qur'an to the worshippers.

There are no professional priests attached to a mosque. The imam who gives the weekly sermon normally has a regular full-time job. Once every mosque would have had a *muezzin* to cry the call to prayer five times a day from atop the minaret; these days he's largely been replaced by taped recordings.

Not all mosques welcome non-Muslims. Sometimes a sign saying 'For Prayers Only' is posted prominently by the entrance. If you're unsure then ask. You must always remove your shoes before entering any mosque.

ISRAELI MINISTRY OF TOURISM

The Keffiyah – one of Jerusalem's 'must buys'

Christianity

The relative standing of Christian denominations else-where in the world counts for little in Jerusalem. While in an international sense the Vatican-based Roman Catholic Church may be the richest and highest profile branch of Christianity, being a relative newcomer to the Holy Land (established only during the Crusades) it has very little authority in Jerusalem. The Protestants have even less.

The most powerful church is the Greek Orthodox, which has jurisdiction over more than half of Jerusalem's Church of the Holy Sepulchre and a bigger portion of Bethlehem's Church of the Nativity than anybody else. The Greek Orthodox patriarchate has seniority in the Christian hierarchy of Israel, despite the fact that this church represents only a fraction of the world's Christian population and is geographically confined mainly to Greece and the Slavic countries. Similarly, by dint of being one of the first into Palestine, the Armenian Church, with a world congregation of only six million, owns a third of Jerusalem's holy sites. Obscure in the church councils of the world, the Copts and Assyrians are also highly visible in Jerusalem.

There are, of course, age-old disputes over who owns what. In an attempt to settle the issue, in 1757 the Turkish authorities drew up the rights of possession for nine of the most important shrines. Known as the Status Quo, this ruling is still applicable today. However, it has done nothing to end the intense rivalry in the Holy City between the various Christian factions, and these occasionally erupt in fisticuffs in the aisles of the sacred sites – see the Rites & Wrongs box in the Things to See & Do chapter.

Orthodox Church The Greek Orthodox Church is the oldest ecclesiastical body in Jerusalem and is probably the closest successor to the original Judaeo-Christian community of St James. A Greek-speaking Christian community emerged here in the mid-2nd century, gaining importance during the rule of Constantine when most of the holy sites were rediscovered.

The Greek Orthodox Church community of today is predominantly Arabic-speaking but led by an almost exclusively Greek-speaking hierarchy. The Orthodox patriarchate of Jerusalem is the only autonomous church in the country, with all the others being dependent to various degrees on a head office abroad. Jerusalem is also the home of two Russian Orthodox missions and a small Romanian Orthodox community and their church.

Armenian Once a small province of the Soviet Union, Armenia is represented by one of the Holy Land's more powerful Christian communities. Much of Mt Zion is the property of the Armenian Church and it also shares the churches of the Holy Sepulchre and the Nativity with the Orthodox and Latin patriarchates. During the Mandate, the Armenians were a prosperous community of some 5000 people, with their own churches, schools and culture, but due to emigration they number only about 2500 today.

Syrian Orthodox & Copts The Syrians have had a bishop in Jerusalem since 1140, the Copts since 1236. Also called the Jacobites, the Syrian Orthodox Church is headed by an archbishop whose residence is the monastery of St Mark. The Copts, who are from Egypt, have a monastery upstairs at the back of the Church of the Holy Sepulchre. Both of these groups celebrate Christmas at the Armenian altars in the Church of the Nativity, but otherwise they use their own small chapels in the Church of the Holy Sepulchre.

Ethiopian From the Middle Ages until the 16th century, the Ethiopians owned chapels and altars in various holy places. Today they are confined to a ramshackle monastery on the roof of the Church of the Holy Sepulchre.

Catholic The Latin patriarchate of Jerusalem was established by the Crusaders in 1099, ceased to exist in 1291, and was re-established in 1847. Most Catholic religious groups were established here over the past 130 years, except the Franciscans, who for more than 500 years were the sole body in charge of Catholic interests in Palestine and the Middle East.

Protestant Anglican and Prussian Lutherans arrived in Jerusalem 160 years ago. Their aim was missionary work among Jews and Muslims, but the Greek Orthodox Church proved the source of most converts. Today, the Evangelical Episcopal Church is mostly Arab-speaking, and the Anglican Archbishop in Jerusalem presides over a synod made up of Egyptian, Libyan, Sudanese, Iranian and Jordanian bishops.

The Anglicans have no rights in the Church of the Holy Sepulchre, but an arrangement with the Greek Orthodox Church allows them to occasionally celebrate mass in the nearby Chapel of St Abraham. The Anglican cathedral is St George's in East Jerusalem.

The German Lutherans established schools, hospices and hospitals in Palestine, including the Hospice of the Order of St John in Jerusalem and the Augusta Victoria Hospice (now a hospital) on Mt Scopus. There are some non-German Lutheran institutions in Israel, including the Swedish Theological Institute and the Finnish Missionary School in Jerusalem, the Swedish school and hospital in Bethlehem, and the Scandinavian Seamen's churches in Haifa and Ashdod. There are also several minor Protestant groups representing reformed Christianity, including Presbyterians, Baptists, Pentecostalists, Quakers and Adventists.

Christian Zionism & the International Christian Embassy In 1980, when the Israeli Government claimed Jerusalem as the capital of the Jewish state, 13 countries closed their embassies in the city in protest and transferred them to Tel Aviv. Reacting to what they saw as unfair treatment of the Israelis, a group of Christians already living in Israel set up the International Christian Embassy in Jerusalem (ICEJ).

The ICEJ does not claim to represent all Christians, rather it represents a nation of Christian Zionists who interpret the Bible as supporting the Jewish people and the modern state of Israel. In fact, one suspects that the pro-Jewish stand of the ICEJ has its foundations in a fear of Islam. For instance, the ICEJ believe that Israel's borders should rightly include the area which is now Jordan. Christian Zionists also consider Islam's claim of Jerusalem as its third holiest site to be highly questionable.

LANGUAGE

Israel's national language is Hebrew. It is the most spoken language, followed by Arabic. English is also widely spoken and you'll almost always be able to find someone who understands it. Most of the important road and street signs are in all three languages. With the accommodation of worldwide Jewry in Jerusalem, many other languages are commonly understood too – French, German and Yiddish are the main ones, but also Spanish and Russian.

The Hebrew Alphabet

Written from right to left, Hebrew has a basic 22 characters – but from there it starts to get very complicated. Like English, not all these characters have fixed phonetic values and their sound can vary from word to word. You just have to *know* that, for instance, Yair is pronounced 'Ya-ear' and doesn't rhyme with 'hare' or 'fire'.

Other letters change their sound value by the addition of diacritical marks but these diacritical marks are quite often left out. Like Arabic, the same sound can also be represented by what seem like different characters but are in fact the same character but in different forms, depending on where it falls in a word. Also there is a second 'handwritten' alphabet often used for fancy ad copy, store front signs and poster text, in which many of the characters are dissimilar to their 'standard' forms.

It is worth noting that transliteration from Hebrew script into English is at best an approximate science. The presence of sounds unknown in English and the fact that the script is 'defective' (most vowels are not written) combine to make it nearly impossible to settle on one method of transliteration. A wide variety of spellings is therefore possible for words when they appear in Latin script and that goes for place names and people's names as well. We take comfort in the knowledge that the Israelis themselves are no better at this inexact science than we are: one street we found in Haifa is labelled 'Hayim' at one end and 'Chaim' at the other, both transliterations of the same Hebrew name.

Hebrew

Basics

Hello.	*sha-LOM*
Goodbye.	*sha-LOM*
Good morning.	*BO-ker tov*
Good evening.	*erev tov*
Goodnight.	*lie-la tov*
See you later.	*le-HIT-rah-OTT*
Thank you.	*to-DAH*
Please.	*be-va-ka-SHA*
You're welcome.	*al low da-VAAR*
Yes.	*ken*
No.	*loh*
Excuse me.	*slee-KHA*
Wait.	*REG-gah*
What?	*mah?*
When?	*mah-tye?*
Where is ...?	*AYE-fo ...?*
right (correct)	*na-CHON*
hotel	*ma-LON*
room	*khe-der*
toilet	*she-ru-TEEM*

I don't speak Hebrew.
AH-NEElo m'dah-BEHR ee-VREET
Do you speak English?
ah-TAH m'dah-BEHR ang-LEET?

Getting Around

airport	*sde t'oo-FAH*
bus	*auto-boos*
railway	*rah-KEH-vet*
station	*ta-cha-na*
taxi	*monit*

Which bus goes to ...?
AYE-zeh auto-boos no-SE-ah le ...?
Stop here.
ah-TSOR kahn

Post Office & Shopping

post office	*dough-ar*
letter	*mich-tav*
stamps	*boolim*
envelopes	*ma-ata-FOT*
postcard	*gloo-yah*
telegram	*miv-rack*
airmail	*dough-ar ah-veer*
shop	*kha-NOOT*
bank	*bank*
pharmacy	*bait mer-kah-KHAT*
money	*KES-sef*
expensive	*ya-KAR*
cheap	*zol*

How much is it?
KA-mah zeh ule?

Food

breakfast	*ah-roo-CHAT BO-ker*
lunch	*ah-roo-KHAT-tsa-ha-RYE-im*
dinner	*ah-roo-KHAT erev*
restaurant	*MISS-ah-DAH*
menu	*taf-REET*
food	*OKHEL*
bread	*LEKH-hem*
butter	*khem-AH*
cheese	*g'VEE-nah*
egg	*bay-TSA*
ice cream	*glee-DAH*
fruit	*pay-ROT*
milk	*kha-LAV*
vegetables	*YEH-rah-KOHT*

water	*my-im*
wine	*yain*

Days & Time

Sunday	*ree-SHON*
Monday	*shey-NEE*
Tuesday	*shlee-SHEE*
Wednesday	*reh-vee-EE*
Thursday	*cha-mee SHEE*
Friday	*shee-SHEE*
Saturday	*sha-BAT*

What is the time?	*MA ha-sha-AH?*
Seven o'clock.	*ha-sha-AH SHEV-vah*
minute	*da-KAH*
hour	*sha-AH*
day	*yom*
week	*sha-voo-ah*
month	*KHO-desh*
year	*sha-NAH*

Numbers

1	*eh-HAD*
2	*SHTA-yim*
3	*sha-LOSH*
4	*AR-bah*
5	*cha-MAYSH*
6	*shaysh*
7	*SHEV-vah*
8	*sh-MO-neh*
9	*TAY-shah*
10	*ESS-er*
11	*eh-HAD-ess-RAY*
12	*shtaym-ess-RAY*
20	*ess-REEM*
21	*ess-REEM v'ah-KHAD*
30	*shlo-SHEEM*
31	*shlo-SHEEM v'ah-KHAD*
50	*cha-MEESHLEEM*
100	*MAY-ah*
200	*mah-tah-YEEM*
300	*shlosh may-OAT*
500	*cha-MAYSH may-OAT*
1000	*alef*
3000	*shlosh-ET alef-EEM*
5000	*cha-maysh-ET alef-EEM*

Arabic

Learning the characters for the Arab numerals is useful,
especially if you intend shopping in the markets of the Old
City or in East Jerusalem. Note that Arabic numerals are
read left to right, unlike the language, which is read right
to left.

Basics

Hello.	*a-halan/mahr-haba*
Goodbye.	*salaam aleicham/ma-ah-salameh*
Good morning.	*sabah-al-kheir*
Good evening.	*masa'al-kheir*
Please.	*min fadlach*
Thank you.	*shoo-khran*
You're welcome.	*afwan*
Yes.	*ay-wah*
No.	*la*
Where?	*feen?*
Pardon?	*sa-mech-nee?*
hotel	*oteyl*
room	*odah*
toilet	*beyt al-may*

I don't understand.
    mish faahim
Do you speak English?
    tech-kee Ingleesi?
How much is this?
    ah-desh hadah?

Getting Around

airport	*mataar*
bus stop	*mawif al-baas*
railway station	*mahattat train*
right	*yemine*
left	*she-mal*
straight	*doo-ree*

Which bus goes to ...?
    ayya baas yaruh 'ala ...?
Is it far?
    ba'id?
Stop here.
    wa'if huna

Post Office & Shopping

post office	*al-bostah*
letter	*maktuub*
stamps	*tabi'*

envelope	*mughallaf*
airmail	*al-barid al-hawwi*
pharmacy	*farmashiyyeh*
shop	*dukkaan*
expensive	*ghaali*
cheap	*rakhis*

Food

breakfast	*futuur*
lunch	*ghada*
dinner	*'asha*
restaurant	*mat'am*
menu	*menu*
food	*akil*
water	*may*
tea	*schai*
coffee	*kah-wah*

Days & Time

Sunday	*el-ahad*
Monday	*itnein*
Tuesday	*talaata*
Wednesday	*el-arbi'a*
Thursday	*khamis*
Friday	*jumu'a*
Saturday	*sabit*

What is the time?	*gaddesh saa'ah?*
minute	*da'iah*
hour	*saa'ah*
day	*yawm*
week	*jum'a/usbuu'*
month	*shahr*
year	*saneh*

Numbers

0	*sifr*
1	*wa-hid*
2	*tinen*
3	*talatay*
4	*arbaha*
5	*chamseh*
6	*sitteh*
7	*sabah*
8	*tamanyeh*
9	*taisah*
10	*ahsharah*
100	*miyyah*
500	*khamsmiyyah*
1000	*alf*
5000	*khamasta alaf*

Facts for the Visitor

WHEN TO GO

There are few seasonal factors that will drastically affect the enjoyment of your visit. Jerusalem's climate (see Facts about Jerusalem) is not so extreme that there's any specific time to make a point of avoiding, but to miss the worst of the summer heat it's probably best to skip July and August – although it does still cool off considerably in the evenings at this time.

It's also worth being aware of the various Jewish festivals. The major festivals constitute the Israeli high season with a corresponding hike in hotel rates of up to 25%. In addition, all Jewish shops and business completely close down (you'll have difficulty finding anything to eat), and public transport grinds to a halt. The ones to avoid are Rosh HaShanah, Yom Kippur, Sukkot and Pessah (see Public Holidays later in this chapter). They are, however, usually mercifully brief. Jerusalem Easters are extremely colourful, especially the Orthodox which comes a week after the western Christian celebrations, but accommodation may be hard to come by as the city fills up with pilgrims – prebooking is recommended.

ORIENTATION

As cities go, Jerusalem is actually quite small, but finding your way around is made confusing by diffuse distribution and hide-and-seek topography. The first thing to know is that the city is broken into three distinct areas: the Old City, East Jerusalem and the New City (also referred to as West Jerusalem).

Old City

For many visitors this is Jerusalem. Encircled by fortified walls, the Old City is one tightly bound sq km of 20,000 people and 3000 years of history. The Western Wall is in here, as is the Dome of the Rock and the Church of the Holy Sepulchre, built over the site of the biblical Golgotha. Navigation is difficult, as the narrow, gully-like alleys twist, turn and buck, leaving the uninitiated visitor without any sense of direction. Of the seven gates that give entrance to the Old City, the most important are likely to be Jaffa Gate, which is the main access from the New City, and Damascus Gate, which faces East Jerusalem.

New City

This is the predominantly Jewish commercial and administrative district, embracing a diversity of life-styles from the 19th century orthodoxy of the Mea She'arim neighbourhood to the Baywatch-type babes round the pool at the Paradise Hotel. The New City is roughly centred on the triangle formed by King George V St, Jaffa Rd and pedestrianised Ben Yehuda St. The latter two converge at Zion Square, a cramped plaza, which serves as a popular gathering point. Most of the middle and top-end hotels and eating places are around here, along with the most popular cafes and bars. Mahane Yehuda, the New City's cheap market, is just to the west of the central area, while further out are the Knesset building, the Israel Museum and the Holocaust memorial of Yad Vashem.

East Jerusalem

This is the Palestinian Arab part of Jerusalem, lying to the east of HaShalom Rd (the former 'Green Line' that divided Jerusalem between 1948 and 1967). It is a district made up of small businesses, shops, travel agencies, moneychangers, hotels and restaurants, mainly centred on the two main streets of Nablus Rd (Derekh Shechem to the Jews) and Salah ad-Din St. These form a triangle with congested Sultan Suleyman St, which runs in the shadow of the Old City's north wall.

MAPS

A very worthwhile investment is *Carta's Map of Jerusalem* (24 NIS). Alternatively, a company called Map produces a pocket-size 50 page *Jerusalem Street Atlas* (60 NIS). This is far more comprehensive than the Carta map but, for those new to the city, doesn't really give a good impression of how it all fits together. There's also an excellent 1:2500 map, *Jerusalem – The Old City*, produced by the Survey of Israel (15 NIS). More a memento than an on-the-hoof aid, Steimatzky, the bookseller, does a very attractive panoramic 3D map of the Old City (9 NIS). All of these maps are locally produced and should be available from any branch of Steimatzky or from the Society for the Protection of Nature in Israel (SPNI) shop – see the Shopping chapter for addresses.

A free but very poor city map is also handed out at the Jaffa Rd tourist information office.

TOURIST OFFICES

Local Tourist Offices

The main city tourist information office (☎ 625 8844) is at 17 Jaffa Rd, just north-west of the Old City walls (see map 9). Small, with less than obliging staff, it is open Sunday to Thursday from 8.30 am to 4.30 pm, and Friday from 8.30 am to noon, closed Saturday. There's also a second, slightly more friendly tourist information office at Jaffa Gate in the Old City, open the same hours.

In the New City, at 24 King George V St, a niche in the ground floor of the Ministry of Tourism building contains a computerised information stand which is accessible 24 hours a day.

Possibly also of use, the Christian Information Centre (☎ 627 2692; fax 628 6417) on Omar ibn al-Khattab Square, opposite the entrance to the Citadel (see map 14), is very good on everything pertaining to the city's Christian sites and also has a good selection of Jerusalem books. Practising Catholics can apply here for tickets for the Christmas Eve Midnight Mass in Bethlehem. The centre is open Monday to Saturday from 8.30 am to 1 pm, closed Sunday.

The Jewish Student Information Centre (☎ 628 2643; fax 628 8338; e-mail jseidel@jer1.co.il) is at 5 Beit El St in the Jewish Quarter of the Old City (adjacent to the Hurva and Rambam synagogues – see map 14). It has a lounge with refreshments, a library and evening activities, and it provides assistance with accommodation, Shabbat dinners and free tours, as well as general information for the Jewish visitor.

Society for the Protection of Nature in Israel

The Society for the Protection of Nature in Israel (SPNI) is an organisation devoted to environmental preservation. Much of the work is facilitated through 26 field study centres dotted throughout Israel, but the head office is in Jerusalem (☎ 624 4605, 625 2357) at 13 Heleni HaMalka St (see map 9), housed in what was originally a pilgrims' hospice built by the Russian Church. From here they offer tours in and around Jerusalem and also have the country's best shop for maps and hiking-related books and pamphlets. The office is open Sunday to Wednesday from 9 am to 4.45 pm, Thursday from 9 am to 5.45 pm, and Friday from 9 am to 12.30 pm.

Tourist Offices Abroad

Australia
  395 New South Head Rd, Double Bay, Sydney
  (☎ (02) 9326 1700; fax 9326 1676)
Canada
  180 Bloor St West, Suit 700, Toronto
  (☎ (800) 669 2369; fax (416) 964 2420)
Denmark
  Vesterbrogade 6D, Copenhagen (☎ (33) 119 711;
  fax 914 801)
France
  22 rue des Capucines, Paris (☎ (1) 42 61 01 97;
  fax 49 27 09 46)
Germany
  Bettina str 62, Frankfurt-am-Maine (☎ (069) 752 086;
  fax 746 249)
  Stollberg str 6, Munich (☎ (089) 290 4039; fax 228 9569)
  Friedrichstrasse 95, Berlin (☎ (030) 204 2010; fax 204 2013)
Netherlands
  Stadhouderskade 2, Amsterdam (☎ (020) 612 8850;
  fax 689 4288)
UK
  18 Great Marlborough St, London (☎ (0171) 434 3651;
  fax 437 0527)
USA
  800 Second Ave, New York (☎ (212) 499 5650; fax 499 5645)
  5 South Wabash Ave, Chicago (☎ (800) 782 4306;
  fax (312) 782 1243)
  5151 Belt Line Rd, Suite 1280, Dallas (☎ (800) 472 6364;
  fax (214) 392 3521)
  6380 Wilshire Blvd 1718, Los Angeles (☎ (213) 658 7462;
  fax 658 6543)

DOCUMENTS

With all but a few exceptions, a tourist visa is not required to visit Israel; all you need is a passport, valid for at least six months from your date of entry. The exceptions include holders of passports from most African and Central American countries, India, Singapore and some of the ex-Soviet republics.

As a tourist you are normally allowed a three month visit, although visitors entering through the land borders with Egypt and Jordan are often initially only granted a month's stay. On arrival, Israeli immigration officials will give you a duplicate entry permit to fill in. The second copy will be returned to you and you need

AUSTRALIA-ISRAEL CHAMBER OF COMMERCE

Lively Ben Yehuda Street in the cosmopolitan New City

to keep this until you leave the country. Do not lose this small piece of paper or you'll face a long delay in the already lengthy departure procedure.

If you look 'undesirable', or are suspected of looking for illegal employment, immigration officials may question the purpose of your visit and ask to see evidence of a return flight/ferry ticket and financial support. Travellers singled out and then found to have insufficient money to cover their proposed stay have, in the past, been prevented from entering the country and put on the next flight home. More commonly, if unimpressed, immigration may only allow you a shorter stay, of say one month.

Visas & Visa Extensions

If you want to extend your stay beyond the initial three months, you need to apply for a visa. You can do this at the Ministry of the Interior office (☎ (02) 622 8211, 629 0231) at 1 Shlomzion St, in the central area of the New City. The process of applying for an extension visa involves an early start to beat the long queues. The office opens at 8 am and by the time the doors open the queue is usually depressingly long. Once you've gained an audience, convincing the civil servants that you should be allowed to stay can be difficult; one crucial requirement is that you must have proof that you can support yourself without needing to work illegally. If the petition is accepted your stay will be extended for typically three months, although sometimes it can be for one month only and sometimes for six. The process costs 90 NIS, and one passport-sized photo is required. There is no fee for citizens of Belgium, Luxembourg or the Netherlands.

The maximum period a foreigner is allowed to stay in Israel varies according to which official you ask. It can be one month if they don't like the look of you or several years if they do. Usually, one year is the most you can stay without pulling strings.

Expired Visas The 55 shekel question is, what happens if you try to leave Israel after overstaying the initial three months without having obtained an extension? At Ben-Gurion airport, if the overstay is less than a month you may be let off, but then again you may be charged the cost of the visa renewal (90 NIS) *and* have a fine slapped on top; if the overstay is more than a month then you're definitely going to have to dig deep into your pockets. It has also happened that people wildly over the mark have had their passports stamped to bar them from returning to Israel for a period of five years. Expired visa holders attempting to depart from Ovda airport or any land borders will almost certainly be turned away and told to visit the Ministry of the Interior.

Travel Insurance

A collision with the Israeli medical system can cause severe injuries to your finances, and doctors and hospitals in Jerusalem often expect immediate cash payment for health services. It's wise to come protected by a good travel insurance policy. When looking for a policy, coverage against lost baggage, cancelled flights and minor medical bills may be nice to have, but what you're really looking for is coverage against a true catastrophe.

Many travel agents are now keen to sell insurance as part of the flight package and they should be able to advise on the options. Check the fine print as some policies exclude coverage for 'dangerous' occupations

---

The Israeli Stamp Stigma

Israel is the venue for that popular Middle Eastern game, the Passport Shuffle. This involves getting in and out of the country without having your passport stamped with any incriminating evidence to tell that you were ever there. This game was devised because those countries which refuse to recognise Israel (including Lebanon, Syria and the Gulf States) refuse to allow anyone across their borders whose passport is marred by evidence of a visit to the Jewish state. Israeli immigration officials will, if asked, stamp only your entry permit and not your passport. This is fine if you are flying both into and out of Israel, but if crossing by land into either Egypt or Jordan the Arab immigration officers are generally not so obliging, and their entry stamps will be a dead giveaway. ■

---

like rock climbing, motorcycling or diving. If you are likely to engage in anything like that, you don't want a policy which leaves you out in the cold. If you do require medical attention be sure to save all your documentation and invoices and put in a claim to your insurance company as soon as possible.

Hostel & Student Cards

If you have them, bring along your Hostelling International (HI) card and International Student Identity Card (ISIC), both of which can be useful. HI membership will save you money at their affiliated hostels – although they still tend to be way more expensive than the privately owned competition – while an ISIC card entitles the holder to a 10% discount on Egged bus fares over 10 NIS, 20% off fares on Israel State Railways and substantial discounts at most museums and archaeological sites. Even if signs make no mention of student discounts produce your card and ask. Student cards issued by your individual university or college are often not recognised.

EMBASSIES

Israeli Embassies Abroad

These are some of the Israeli embassies and consulates abroad:

Australia
  6 Turrana Ave, Yarralumla, Canberra, ACT 2600
  (☎ (06) 273 1309)

Consulate: 37 York St, Sydney, NSW 2000
(☎ (02) 9264 7933)

Canada
50 O'Conner St, Suite 1005, Ottawa, Ontario KIP 6L2
(☎ (613) 567 6450)
Consulate: 115 Blvd Rene Levesque Ouest, Suite 2620,
Montreal, Quebec H3B 4S5 (☎ (514) 393 9372)

France
3 rue Rabelais, 75008 Paris (☎ (1) 40 76 55 00)
Consulate: 454 rue Paradis, Marseille 13008
(☎ (9) 17 73 990)

Germany
Simrockallee 2, Bonn 53173 (☎ (0228) 934 6500)
Consulate: Schinkelstrasse 10, Berlin 14193
(☎ (30) 893 2203)

Ireland
Berkeley Court Hotel, Suite 630, Landsdowne Rd,
Ballsbridge, Dublin 4 (☎ (01) 668 0303)

Netherlands
47 Buitenhoff, The Hague 2513 AH (☎ (70) 376 0500)

New Zealand
DB Tower, The Terrace 111, PO Box 2171, Wellington
(☎ (04) 472 2362)

UK
2 Palace Green, London W8 4QB (☎ (0171) 957 9547)

USA
3514 International Drive NW, Washington DC 20008
(☎ (202) 364 5500)
Consulate: 800 Second Ave, New York NY10017
(☎ (212) 499 5300)
There are nine Israeli consulates in the USA; phone one of
the above two for contact details.

Foreign Consulates in Jerusalem

Although the Israelis lay claim to Jerusalem as their
capital, this is not recognised by most of the international
community. Instead, most foreign embassies are in Tel
Aviv, with just a handful of consulates in Jerusalem. All
consulates are closed on Saturday and Sunday.

Denmark
5 B'nei Brit St, West Jerusalem (☎ 625 8083)

France
6 Paul Emile Botta St, West Jerusalem (☎ 625 9481)
(see map 10)
Sheikh Jarrah, East Jerusalem (☎ 628 2387)

UK
19 Nashashibi St, Sheikh Jarrah, East Jerusalem
(☎ 582 8281) (see map 10)

USA
18 Agron St, West Jerusalem (☎ 625 3288) (see map 9)
27 Nablus Rd, East Jerusalem (☎ 628 2231) (see map 11)

EDDIE GERALD

Sculpture on top of the Generalli Insurance Building

CUSTOMS

You can bring duty-free into Israel up to one litre of spirits and two litres of wine for every person over 17 years of age, as well as up to 250g of tobacco or 250 cigarettes. Animals, plants, firearms and fresh meat may not be brought into the country. Additionally, video equipment, personal computers and diving apparatus must be declared at customs and a deposit paid to be collected on departure (to prevent you bringing any of this stuff in and flogging it while here).

MONEY

Travellers' Cheques

Travellers' cheques are widely accepted and you'll have no trouble getting them cashed – bearers of Eurocheques can even exchange them at post offices. Beware though; commission charges can be as high as 20 NIS *per cheque* regardless of the amount, so shop around. The best bet is to go to one of the no-commission currency exchange bureaus (see below) or, if you are carrying their cheques, to the American Express Travel service office (☎ 623 1710; fax 623 1520) at 40 Jaffa Rd, close by Zion Square (see map 9). They will replace lost or stolen travellers' cheques, receive mail etc. The office is open Sunday to Thursday from 9 am to 5 pm, but closed on Friday and Saturday. The local agent for Thomas Cook is Awadieh Tours (☎ 628 2365; fax 628 2366) at 23 Salah ad-Din St in

East Jerusalem (see map 11); however, they do not cash cheques.

ATMs

Many bank foyers are equipped with cash-dispensing ATMs accepting all of the major international credit cards. If you don't have your PIN but are carrying a Visa card, Bank Leumi (Zion Square – see map 14) will give you a cash advance, subject to a credit status check. If you lose your plastic, call the Tel Aviv office of your credit card. The numbers are: American Express (☎ (03) 524 2211); Diners Club (☎ (03) 572 3572); Visa (☎ (03) 572 3572); and Eurocard (☎ (03) 576 4444).

Credit Cards

Israelis live on credit and owe their freewheeling life-styles to Visa, American Express, Diners Club and the like. To this end nearly every establishment takes credit cards because if it didn't it wouldn't have any business. We've witnessed breakfasting Jerusalemites cover the cost of their cappuccino and croissant with a piece of plastic.

International Transfers

For anyone unfortunate enough to run out of money, the Israeli post operates a Western Union international money transfer service. For details, go to any post office or call ☎ (177) 022 2131, toll-free.

Currency

The national currency is the new Israeli shekel (NIS). The Hebraically correct plural is *shekelim* but even Israelis when speaking English tend to Anglicise and use 'shekels'. The 'old shekel' was dropped in 1985 as part of a rescue plan to reduce inflation. The new shekel is divided into 100 agorot. There are coins of 10 and 50 agorot and 1 and 5 NIS, and notes of 5, 10, 20, 50, 100 and 200 NIS.

Most Israelis talk in terms of US dollars, not shekels, a habit acquired in the days when the national currency was constantly being devalued. Up-market hotels still quote their prices in dollars as do the HI hostels, most car hire companies and many airlines. At such places, payment in dollars is accepted and, for the customer, it's preferable because payments made in foreign currency are free of the 17% value added tax (VAT). For this reason in this book we give all mid and top-end accommodation rates in dollars, not shekels.

After the dollar one foreign currency is as good as any other and moneychangers and banks will take whatever you've got.

Currency Exchange

Australia	AUS$1	=	2.55 NIS
Canada	CAN$1	=	2.43 NIS
Egypt	E£1	=	0.95 NIS
France	FFr1	=	0.64 NIS
Germany	DM1	=	2.16 NIS
Jordan	JD1	=	4.56 NIS
UK	£1	=	5.34 NIS
US	US$1	=	3.23 NIS

Exchange Rates

If you want the best deal when changing money, go to the legal moneychangers in the Old City and East Jerusalem. The two just inside Damascus Gate seem to give a better price than those anywhere else. The moneychanger just inside the Petra Hostel near Jaffa Gate seems to be open when the others are closed. Other moneychangers can be found on David St, the Old City's main bazaar street going east from Jaffa Gate, and on Salah ad-Din St in East Jerusalem.

In the New City go to Change Point at 33 Jaffa Rd or 2 Ben Yehuda St, neither of which charge any commission. The Jaffa Rd branch is open daily from 9 am to 9 pm, but closed on Saturday. The one on Ben Yehuda St is open from 9.30 am to 7.45 pm, except on Friday, when it closes at 2 pm, and on Saturday, when it is closed all day. Most banks are on Jaffa Rd around Zion Square, and most are open Sunday to Tuesday and Thursday from 8.30 am to 12.30 pm and 4 to 5.30 pm, and Wednesday and Friday from 8.30 am to noon, closed Saturday.

Costs

You can bring an unlimited amount of foreign and local currency into Israel – which is lucky, because you're going to need it by the barrowload. The cost of living in Jerusalem is high, though of course it depends on your requirements. You can sleep cheap in a budget travellers' hostel for less than 20 NIS (US$7) per night and subsist on a diet of reasonably satisfying street food for just a couple of dollars a day. Alternatively, you can run up impressive bills on the gold card at some very swanky hotels and their suitably high-priced dining halls.

Accommodation aside, a reasonable daily budget allowing for a lunch time snack, an evening meal, and sundry sightseeing fees would perhaps be 100 NIS, or a little upward of US$30.

Tipping

Not so long ago, apparently, no-one tipped in Jerusalem. Now your bill arrives appended with a large handwritten 'Service is not included', delivered by a waiter with a steely smile that reads, '15%. No less'. You may frequently feel the money is undeserved but that's not the point – serving staff salaries in Israel are customarily low and the system relies on tips from the customers to even the balance. Therefore, when pricing a menu always allow for that extra percentage on top.

Note that taxi drivers in Jerusalem do not expect to be tipped; they're usually content just to overcharge.

Bargaining

There are few bargains to be had, though of course in the Old City bazaars you can try your luck haggling. This is not always the fun it is made out to be. It can be time-consuming, frustrating and, in general, an unwelcome hassle. The golden rules are: don't start bargaining with a shopkeeper unless you are really interested in buying; have a good idea of the item's value both locally and back home; and don't be intimidated – easier said than done. Do not use large notes or travellers' cheques, as getting change can be a problem.

Basically, the bargaining game is played like this: the shopkeeper usually attracts your attention and gives you a price anywhere between twice to 10 times above the realistic going rate. If you are genuinely interested you pull a face showing disgust or amusement at this quote and state your offer in a 'take it or leave it' manner. This should, of course, be substantially below the amount you are actually willing to pay. Stick to your guns and do not be bullied or cajoled into paying too much. Turning away from a bargaining session can often cut a price in half.

Traditionally, Arab shopkeepers sell their goods cheaper early in the day, as it is believed that a quick first sale means good business later. However, this line is often used to persuade customers to pay more, thinking that they are getting a bargain.

Taxes & Refunds

Israel slaps a value added tax (VAT) on a wide range of goods, but visitors are entitled to a refund on most items purchased with foreign currency in shops that are registered with the Ministry of Tourism (there'll be a sign in the window or at the till). The procedure for reclaiming your 17% seems to have been designed with the specific aim of deterring the faint-hearted.

The net figure on one invoice must be at least US$50, with the exception of electrical appliances, cameras, films, photographic accessories and computers. The purchases need to be wrapped in a sealed plastic bag, of which at least one side must be transparent with the original invoice displayed inside so that it can be read without opening the bag. The bag needs to remain sealed for the duration of your time in Israel.

When leaving from Ben-Gurion airport, go to the Bank Leumi counter in the departure lounge and present your sealed bag. The bank will stamp the invoice, identify the goods and refund in US dollars the VAT paid (less a commission). At other departure points, customs officials do the honours but the refund will be mailed to your home address.

POST & COMMUNICATIONS

Post

The main post office (☎ 624 4745) and poste restante is at 23 Jaffa Rd (see map 9). The main section is open Sunday to Thursday from 7 am to 7 pm, and Friday from 7 am to noon, but closed Saturday. After hours you can send letters, telegrams and telexes from the information desk.

There are several post office branches. The one in Omar ibn al-Khattab Square inside Jaffa Gate in the Old City (see map 14) is open Sunday to Thursday from 7.30 am to 2.30 pm, and Friday from 8 am to noon. There's another in the Jewish Quarter, just off the Cardo by the Broad Wall (see map 14), which is open Sunday, Monday, Wednesday and Thursday from 8 am to 12.30 pm and 4 to 6 pm, Tuesday from 8 am to 1.30 pm, and Friday from 8 am to noon. It is closed Saturday.

East Jerusalem's main post office is on the corner of Salah ad-Din and Sultan Suleyman Sts (see map 11). It's open Sunday and Thursday from 8.30 am to 2.30 pm and 4 to 6.30 pm, Monday, Wednesday and Friday from 8.30 am to 12.30 pm, and Tuesday from 8.30 am to 2.30 pm, closed Saturday.

Postal Rates Letters posted in Jerusalem take seven to 10 days to reach North America and Australia, and a little less to Europe. Incoming mail is fairly quick, taking about three or four days from Europe and around a week from places further afield. At the time of writing, a normal airmail letter to Europe cost 1.50 NIS, to the USA 1.80 NIS and to Australia 2.20 NIS.

Telephone

Jerusalem is included in Israel's state-of-the-art card-operated public telephone system, and international calls can be made from any street call box. Telecards can be bought from lottery kiosks, newsagents or bookshops and come in denominations of 10 units (12 NIS), 20 units (24 NIS) and 50 units (48 NIS). The international access code is 00 followed by the country code and the phone number.

Standard rates apply between 8 am and 10 pm; from 10 pm to 1 am and all day Saturday and Sunday calls are 25% cheaper, while all week between 1 am and 8 am calls are 50% cheaper. A 10 unit phonecard will get you just a couple of minutes, if that, to the USA at peak rates.

You can also make discount international calls from the offices of Solan Telecom at 2 Luntz St (see map 9), a small pedestrianised street running between Jaffa Rd and Ben Yehuda St. It's open 24 hours a day, seven days a week.

The international country code for Israel is 972, and the telephone area code for Jerusalem is 02. Other useful numbers are: information ☎ 144; police ☎ 100; first aid/ambulance ☎ 101 or ☎ 911; fire service ☎ 102.

Mobile Phones Mobile phones can be rented by the day from Quick-Phone (☎ 538 8848) at 27 Strauss St, Shako Land (☎ toll-free 177 022 2554) at 18 King David St or Video City (☎ 623 4539) at 43 Jaffa Rd. Rates start at about US$2 per day.

Fax, Telegram & Telex

To send a fax or telex, go to the main post office. Faxes cost 17 NIS for the first sheet and 9 NIS for any subsequent ones. Faxes can also be sent from Solan Telecom on Luntz St for 12 NIS per sheet, irrespective of the destination, and they'll receive faxes for you for a small fee.

The main post office also operates a 24 hour telegraph service, although you might have to wake up the person on duty. Alternatively, Solan will send telegrams at 25

NIS for the first seven words, address included, and 1.70 NIS for each word thereafter.

E-mail

Customers can send and receive e-mail at the Strudel Internet cafe/wine bar (☎ 623 2101; fax 622 1445; e-mail strudel@inter.net.il) at 11 Mounbaz St in the Russian Compound (see map 9). It has three computer stations linked through Netscape to the Web and computer time is charged at 5 NIS for 15 minutes. Printouts cost 1 NIS per sheet for black & white and 2 NIS for colour.

Another reputably reliable e-mail server in Jerusalem is NetMedia (☎ 679 5860).

Online Services

Israel is very much a computer-literate society and one that has been quick to seize upon the possibilities offered by the Internet. Point-and-click surfers can drop by Jerusalem's Strudel cafe, book domestic air tickets or even 'ask the rabbi'. There is heaps of practical information on the Net and World Wide Web that may be of use to anyone planning a visit to Jerusalem or even living there. The following are just a few suggestions of places to start:

http://www.lonelyplanet.com
This is the Lonely Planet site home page – follow the links to the Travellers' Reports for the latest postings on Israel and Jerusalem.

http://gauss.technion.ac.il/nyh/israel/
Bills itself as the Complete Guide (almost) to the World Wide Web in Israel and boasts over 950 links broken down into categories such as arts, reference and so on.

http://www.city.net/countries/israel
More links specifically geared to the visitor, including categories such as travel and tourism, maps, museums and galleries and lodgings.

http://www.jpost.co.il/
The Internet version of the English-language daily, the *Jerusalem Post*, it includes daily news, columns, features and reviews – and there's no subscription fee.

http://www1.huji.ac.il/jeru/jerusalem.html
A virtual tour through the Old City of Jerusalem with links to information on other parts of the country.

http://imj.org.il
The home page of the Israel Museum in Jerusalem.

strudel@inter.net.il
The home page of the Strudel internet cafe in Jerusalem.

EDDIE GERALD

Policemen in Zion Square, New City

BOOKS

Few places can have inspired more wordage than Jerusalem. During the time we were researching this guidebook, no less than four hefty volumes about the Holy City were published in the UK alone. Our list covers just a few of the more interesting titles. All of the books should be available in paperback (except where noted) from most good English-language bookshops – including those belonging to the Steimatzky chain in Jerusalem (see the Shopping chapter for addresses).

Most books are published in different editions by different publishers in different countries. As a result, a book might be a hardcover rarity in one country while it's readily available in paperback in another. Fortunately, bookshops and libraries search by title or author, so your local bookshop or library is best placed to advise you on the availability of the following recommendations.

Lonely Planet

If you want to see more of the area around Jerusalem, Lonely Planet also publishes *Israel & the Palestinian Territories* and an accompanying *Israel & the Palestinian Territories travel atlas*, as well as the comprehensive, regional *Middle East on a shoestring*.

Guide Books & Reference

Anyone whose visit to Jerusalem is primarily motivated by the city's biblical and ancient history should take a look at *The Holy Land* by Jerome Murphy-O'Conner;

erudite and concise, with some deft touches of humour, this is simply the best archaeological guide there is. For anyone with a specific interest in the subject, *Jerusalem Architecture* (hardback only) by David Kroyanker is a beautifully produced, lavishly illustrated survey of building in the city from the time of King David right up to the 1990s.

Widening the field, the *Blue Guide to Jerusalem* is a supremely scholarly general reference to the art architecture, culture and history of the Holy City.

Travelogues

More autobiography than travelogue, *This Year in Jerusalem* by acclaimed novelist Mordechai Richlieu is a warm-hearted account of a Jewish childhood in Canada, throughout which the Holy City loomed large on the horizon. Richlieu's Jerusalem is in stark contrast to that described in *Roots Schmoots* by Howard Jacobson, a secular Jewish-English intellectual and author who visited the city as part of his investigation into what it means to be a modern-day Jew – he did not seem to like what he found.

Also of Jewish background, author Stephen Brooks fairly well succeeded in casting off any ancestral baggage when he embarked upon his exploration of Israel, recounted in *Winner Takes All*. While Jerusalem only takes up a small part of his book, as an introduction to Israeli society at large it is a highly recommended read.

An even more dispassionate account of the city and surroundings is given in *Riding to Jerusalem*, penned in the 1930s by the intrepid dame of travel writing, Freya Stark. Stark's mode of entry into the city was by donkey; some 60 years later this was marginally improved on by another distinguished woman traveller, Bettina Selby, who made her approach by bicycle – a trip recounted in *Like Water in a Dry Place*.

First published in 1969, *Jerusalem* by Colin Thubron is one of the earliest books by the now feted travel writer. Unfortunately it's also one of his least successful, being extremely self indulgent and made leaden with pomposity.

History

If you are going to read one book during your visit, make it *Jerusalem: City of Mirrors* by Amos Elon. An essayist and historian by trade, and longtime resident of the city, Elon has a great knack for bringing out the relevant in the ancient, darting back and forward through history to illustrate his themes. Best of all, he is adept at lightening otherwise heavy topics with great anecdotes and a deflating wit.

A more straightforward historical narrative is employed in Martin Gilbert's companion studies, *Jerusalem: Rebirth of a City* (dealing with the 19th century), and *Jerusalem in the 20th Century* (hardback only), which while authoritative are also very readable. The second volume is especially good for anyone struggling to understand the events that have led up to the current political impasse. *Jerusalem: The Endless Crusade* by Andrew Sinclair is a one volume textbook retelling some 3000 years of history – while the book is well researched it tends to be greatly undermined by the author's lack of personal involvement in his subject.

General

To be enjoyed rather than believed at face value, *O Jerusalem* by Dominique Lapierre & Larry Collins is a novelisation of the events of the 1948 War. Moving forward several years, a partitioned Jerusalem forms the backdrop of *The Mandelbaum Gate*, Muriel Spark's mannered novel of uptight expatriates. *Winter in Jerusalem* by Blanche d'Alpuget brings the city up to date, playing up the colour and romance of the place to provide a vivid backdrop to a young woman's quest for identity.

If you're hoping to buy a carpet while you're in Jerusalem, have a look at *Oriental Carpets: A buyer's guide*, which includes information on what to look for in a good carpet, as well as full colour photographs of each style of carpet.

For literature by Jerusalem authors, see Arts in the Facts about Jerusalem chapter.

CD ROM

The international-release CD ROM entitled *Jerusalem* is produced by Tyrell Multimedia and published by Simon & Schuster Interactive. It's a visual exploration of 3000 years of the city's history through animation, film clips and fancy graphics. There's also a similar Israeli-produced disk, *Jerusalem 3000*, which purports to do the same thing.

All issues of *The Jerusalem Post* (see below) from October 1988 onward are available on two CD ROMs, kept current with six-monthly updates. As of early 1996 the cost was US$129 (or US$75 for January 1992 to June 1996 only); address enquiries and orders to Jerusalem Post on CD ROM, PO Box 81, Jerusalem 91000 (☎ 531 5603; fax 531 5622; e-mail ninak@jpost.co.il).

NEWSPAPERS & MAGAZINES

The Jerusalem Post is the country's only English-language daily (although there's no Saturday edition). Some find its right wing leanings a little disagreeable, but buy it on Friday for the extensive 'what's on' supplement. You can also visit the *Post* at http://www.jpost.co.il on the Web.

The alternative to the *Post* is the poorly funded, weekly *Biladi – the Jerusalem Times*, which reports purely on Palestinian issues. You'll normally only find the *Times* sold in East Jerusalem and on David St in the Old City.

Look out in the hostels and bars for the freebie *Traveller*, a lively monthly aimed squarely at backpackers, with useful features such as a round-up of the city bar scene and ideas on cheap eating. *Your Jerusalem* is another monthly freebie (pick it up at the Jaffa Rd tourist office), aimed at residents of the city; it's useful for its 'what's happening' listings, restaurant reviews and a good 'events for children' section.

Despite being perceived as largely hostile to Israel, western newspapers are easily found in Jerusalem and they're usually only a day old – try Steimatzky.

RADIO & TV

National Radio 1 (1458AM in Jerusalem) has English-language news bulletins at 7 am and 1 and 8 pm, as well as a current affairs magazine at 5 pm daily. The BBC World Service can be picked up on 639 and 1323kHz and 227MW, while Voice of America is on 1260kHz.

Jerusalem viewers receive Israel's two state TV stations, both of which carry masses of English-language programmes (English-language news on Channel 1 is at 6.15 pm during the week, 4.30 pm Friday and 5 pm Saturday). These are supplemented by Arabic-language Jordan TV and Middle East TV, the latter a Christian station administered by North Americans. Most non-orthodox Israelis also have cable, with its 32 channels including CNN, Sky, BBC World, Discovery and MTV.

For seven day TV and radio listings pick up the Friday edition of *The Jerusalem Post*.

PHOTOGRAPHY

Whatever you run out of or whatever needs replacing, you'll be able to find it in Jerusalem, but there's little doubt that it would have been way cheaper back home.

EDDIE GERALD

LEANNE LOGAN

Keeping up with the news can be a serious
business in Jerusalem

Photography presents no special problems, although
if you take it seriously then you might want to bring
along a polarising filter to counter sun glare. Other than
military installations there's little that can't be photo-

graphed – even IDF soldiers are happy to preen and pose for a visitor's camera. The exceptions are the orthodox Jews, who really dislike having their photograph taken. Arab women often react angrily too if they're snapped unawares, so ask first.

For good photography, the best time of the year to visit is between November and April, when the sky is clear of high-temperature haze and the afternoon sun warms rather than bleaches.

There are a couple of quick processing places on Jaffa Rd (most conveniently, Kodak Express at No 36), but for more specialised needs such as slides or black & white prints, try Schwartz (☎ 625 5046) at 11 Hillel St, Photoshop (☎ 538 4451) at 74 HaNevi'im St, in the courtyard, or Photo Zoom (☎ /fax 628 8750) at 27 Salah ad-Din St in East Jerusalem.

TIME

Jerusalem is two hours ahead of GMT/UTC, eight hours behind Australian Eastern Standard Time and seven hours ahead of American Eastern Standard Time. So when it's noon in Jerusalem it's 5 am in New York, 10 am in London and Paris, and 8 pm in Melbourne.

ELECTRICITY

Israel uses 220V, 50 cycles, alternating current. Wall plugs are the round, two prong type. Bring an adapter if required; it's cheaper than buying one in Jerusalem.

LAUNDRY

With only two machines but plenty of charm, coffee and good home cooking while you wait, Tzipor Hanefesh (☎ 624 9890) is a friendly three storey cafe/laundromat. One machine load costs 7 NIS and a 45 minute drying cycle costs the same. It's at 10 Rivlin St, in the trendy central area of Nahalat Shiv'a (see map 9). There's another good laundromat close by at 12 Shamai St, one block south of Ben Yehuda St. It's open Saturday to Thursday from 9 am to 10.30 pm, and Friday from 8.30 am to 3.30 pm. Star Laundry (☎ 566 9434) at 25 Jabotinsky St in Rehavia collects and delivers free of charge; it's open Sunday to Thursday 8.30 am to 7 pm, Friday 8.30 am to 2 pm, closed Saturday.

WEIGHTS & MEASURES

Israel uses the metric system.

METRIC CONVERSION

Temperature
To convert °C to °F multiply by 1.8 and add 32.
To convert °F to °C subtract 32 and multiply by 0.55.

Length, Distance & Area

	multiply by
inches to centimetres	2.54
centimetres to inches	0.39
feet to metres	0.30
metres to feet	3.28
yards to metres	0.91
metres to yards	1.09
miles to kilometres	1.61
kilometres to miles	0.62
acres to hectares	0.40
hectares to acres	2.47
square miles to square kilometres	2.59
square kilometres to square miles	0.39

Weight

	multiply by
ounces to grams	28.35
grams to ounces	0.035
pounds to kilograms	0.45
kilograms to pounds	2.20
British tons to kilograms	1016
US tons to kilograms	907

A British ton is 2240 lbs, a US ton is 2000 lbs.

Volume

	multiply by
imperial gallons to litres	4.55
litres to imperial gallons	0.22
US gallons to litres	3.79
litres to US gallons	0.26

Five imperial gallons equal just over six US gallons.
A litre is slightly more than a US quart, slightly less than a British one.

HEALTH

Jerusalem presents no major health hazards for the visitor. Probably the biggest health worries you can expect are over-exposure to the sun and possibly an upset stomach caused by the change in diet. No vaccinations are required, however we recommend you vaccinate yourself against hepatitis A. Polio, typhoid, rabies and hepatitis B all occur, and you should consider protection, particularly if you will be travelling to rural areas.

Medical Attention

In emergencies call ☎ 101 (Hebrew speaking) or ☎ 911 (English speaking) or contact the Magen David Adom (☎ 523 133), the 'Red Star of David', which is the Israeli equivalent of the Red Cross. There's also a special medical help line for tourists: ☎ (177) 022 9110. Every day *The Jerusalem Post* carries a list of the city's late-opening pharmacies.

In the Old City, the Orthodox Society (☎ 627 1958), on Greek Orthodox Patriarchate St in the Christian Quarter, operates a low-cost clinic that, we're told, welcomes travellers. It also does dental surgery. The clinic is open Monday to Saturday from 8 am to 3 pm, closed Sunday.

A more expensive alternative is the Jerusalem Medical Centre (☎ 561 0297) on Diskin St in the Kiryat Wolfson district of the New City.

WOMEN TRAVELLERS

In certain areas of Jerusalem, sexual harassment is a constant problem for women travellers. The majority of problems will arise with Arab males but Israeli men are not known for their respectful conduct towards women either. The harassment is rarely physical but even persistent verbal abuse can stop you enjoying your stay.

As far as Arab areas go, it is vital that you dress with great modesty. A headscarf isn't necessary but otherwise think 'nun'. In places like East Jerusalem and the Old City everything from the throat down to the upper arms and calves needs to be covered. No tight-fitting clothes either – a long skirt and blouse or baggy T-shirt fits the bill and is also relatively cool.

However, even nuns – the genuine wimple-wearing articles – are not always exempt from the attentions of wandering hands. How you deal with unwanted attention is a matter of choice. In late 1995, *The Jerusalem Post* reported on three women tourists who resisted the physical advances of some Arab men with a little black-belt karate. The men were left needing hospital treatment. Not every woman has that kind of deterrent at her disposal, and often the best you can do is to politely but firmly turn down the whispered invitations and ignore any come-ons.

In one or two places the best advice, unfortunately, has to be for women not to walk alone; the Mount of

Olives, in particular, has a bad reputation and Lonely
Planet has also received letters from women who've had
unpleasant encounters while walking on the ramparts
of the Old City walls of Jerusalem.

The city's rape crisis centre can be contacted on
☎ 514 455.

GAY & LESBIAN TRAVELLERS

Homosexuality is not illegal in Israel but it's anathema
to Jerusalem's large religious population and as a result
the city's gay and lesbian community is obliged to keep
a low profile.

The Society for the Protection of Personal Rights
(SPPR), which represents gays and lesbians in Israel, has
successfully lobbied in recent years for legislative
changes, and the Knesset now has a committee which
deals with gay rights. All progress in this area may,
however, have come to a halt following the rise to prom-
inence of ultraorthodox and right wing elements in the
1996 parliamentary elections.

There are very few bars and clubs around (Tel Aviv is
a better bet), and all we turned up was the Q Bar (see the
Entertainment chapter). The Tmol Shilshom cafe/book-
shop in Nahalat Shiv'a (see map 9) is also gay-run, but
other than a shelf of second-hand gay fiction that doesn't
amount to much.

For further information about what's going on, call
the gay switchboard (☎ (03) 629 2797) Sunday, Tuesday,
Wednesday and Thursday from 7.30 to 11.30 pm, and
Mondays 7 to 11 pm. The SPPR (☎ (03) 620 4327; fax
525 2341), PO Box 37604, Tel Aviv 61375, also operates a
gay hotline (☎ (03) 629 3681) and publishes a newsletter in
English, *Israel Update* – send a self-addressed envelope for
a copy.

DISABLED TRAVELLERS

Many hotels and most public institutions in Jerusalem
provide ramps, specially equipped toilets and other con-
veniences for the disabled. In particular, the HI-affiliated
Beit Shmuel has rooms specially adapted for wheelchair
access. If you have any particular concerns, try contacting Milbat – The Advisory Centre for the Disabled
(☎ (03) 530 3739) at the Sheba Medical Centre in Tel Aviv
for information and advice.

The Yad Sarah Organisation (☎ 644 4444) at 43
HaNevi'im St also lends wheelchairs, crutches and other
aids free of charge – a small deposit is required. It's open

AUSTRALIA-ISRAEL CHAMBER OF COMMERCE

Riding the lions at the Windmill Gardens, Mamilla

to visitors Sunday to Thursday from 9 am to 7 pm, Friday from 9 am to noon.

The Museum of the History of Jerusalem at the Citadel has a signposted route around the museum designed especially for disabled people.

JERUSALEM FOR CHILDREN

Jerusalem is not particularly child friendly. The congested roads of the New City mean children have to be kept on a tight leash; similarly so the packed alleyways of the Old City, where your offspring are in constant danger of being washed away by the relentless human undertow. There are, however, quite a few open, green spaces free of the press of bodies and vehicles where the kids can run free – Liberty Gardens has the added attraction of its train carriage puppet theatre (☎ 561 8514 for schedule details) and plenty of climbing frames, clamberable sculptures and football courts.

Other good youngster-friendly places are the Biblical Zoo (especially at feeding time – ☎ 643 0111 for details), which has a special children's zoo and creative play area, and the Bloomfield Science Museum, stuffed with plenty of hands-on exhibits. The Israel Museum (☎ 670 8935) has a full line-up of children's events each month, including song and play for pre-schoolers, and cartoon screenings (all in English). Older children might also enjoy the Citadel, a castle with lots of turrets, towers and battlements.

There's also a company which specialises in creating custom tours of the city for families with children. They are called Kids' Jerusalem Adventures (☎ /fax 536 3449; e-mail kidsjlmadv@netmedia.co.il).

For further ideas look out for the gushingly named *Israel Loves Kids, Kids Love Israel* by Barbara Sofer – it should be available from branches of Steimatzky. For more general information see Lonely Planet's *Travel With Children* by Maureen Wheeler.

LIBRARIES

Books on Jerusalem as well as other general nonfiction and fiction titles and English-language newspapers and magazines are available to the public at two British Council libraries: 4 Abu Obeida St (☎ 628 2545) in East Jerusalem (turn right just past the Tombs of the Kings – see map 11) and 3 Shimshon St (☎ 673 6733) in the south of the New City. Both are open Monday to Thursday from 10 am to 1 pm and 4 to 7 pm, and Friday from 10 am to 1 pm, closed Saturday and Sunday. There's another good library at the Hebrew Union College at 13 HaMelekh David St in the New City (see map 9). It's open Sunday to Thursday from 8 am to 5 pm.

CULTURAL CENTRES

In addition to the two British Councils (see the Libraries section above) there is also an American Cultural Center (☎ 625 5755) at 19 Keren HaYesod, which is open Sunday to Thursday 10 am to 4 pm, Friday 9 am to noon, an Alliance Francaise (☎ 625 1204, 625 7167) on Agron St, opposite the Supersol supermarket, both in the New City (see map 10), and a French Cultural Centre (☎ 628 2451) at 21 Salah ad-Din St in East Jerusalem (see map 11).

USEFUL ORGANISATIONS

Located at 6 Koresh St, PO Box 31417, Jerusalem, the Alternative Information Centre (☎ 624 1159; fax 625 3131) is a joint Israeli-Palestinian project that provides information on developments in Palestinian society and the Israeli response. Specifically geared to assisting visiting journalists, the AIC will also help individual travellers interested in learning more about local politics. It publishes two periodicals, the weekly *The Other Front* and the monthly *News From Within*.

The Palestinian Human Rights Information Centre
(☎ 628 7076/7; fax 628 7070) is at 12 Masa'udi St, Top
Floor, PO Box 20479, East Jerusalem. Part of the Arab
Studies Society, the PHRIC publishes the monthly
Human Rights Update, which summarises human rights
violations committed by the Israeli army and Jewish
settlers in the Occupied Territories, along with research
reports on human rights issues. It also provides guidance to travellers.

In operation for over 20 years, the Volunteer Tourist
Service has assisted hundreds of thousands of tourists
visiting Israel. Completely voluntary, the organisation
helps visitors with problems, answers queries, and
traces lost relatives and friends. It can also arrange a visit
to an Israeli home, matching up the visitor's profession
or hobby with that of the host. Volunteers can be found
at Ben-Gurion airport between noon and 8 pm or in the
lobbies of major hotels from 6 to 8.30 pm except Friday
and Jewish holidays.

DANGERS & ANNOYANCES

While security and safety in a large sense are not matters
which should concern the average visitor, theft is just as
much of a problem in Jerusalem as it is anywhere else.
The standard precautionary measures should be taken.
Always keep valuables with you or locked in a safe –
never leave them in your room or in a car or bus (unhappily there are more than a few fellow travellers who
make their money go further by helping themselves to
other people's). Use a money belt, a pouch under your
clothes, a leather wallet attached to your belt, or extra
internal pockets in your clothing. Keep a record of your
passport, credit card and travellers' cheque numbers.

Crowded tourist spots and markets are an obvious
hunting ground for pickpockets, so take extra care.

BUSINESS HOURS

The most important thing to know is that on Shabbat,
the Jewish sabbath, most Israeli-run shops, offices and
places of entertainment close down. Shabbat starts at
sundown Friday and ends at sundown Saturday. During
this time you'll find it tough to get anything to eat, you
can't easily change money and your movements are
restricted because most buses aren't running. The
country kicks back into action on Saturday evening,
when the cafes, bars and restaurants always experience
a great post-Shabbat rush.

Predominantly Muslim areas like East Jerusalem and the Muslim Quarter of the Old City remain open on Saturday but close early on Friday. And Christian-owned businesses (concentrated in the relevant quarter of Jerusalem's Old City) close on Sunday.

Standard Israeli shopping hours are Monday to Thursday from 8 am to 1 pm and 4 to 7 pm or later, and Friday from 8 am to 2 pm, with some places opening after sundown on Saturday, too.

PUBLIC HOLIDAYS

One patient researcher some years ago sat down to compile a list and discovered that between the various religions and their different denominations the people of Israel celebrate more festivals each year than there are days. Our list below describes just some of the more notable holidays in the annual calendar.

Jewish

Be well prepared for any Jewish religious holidays that are celebrated during your visit. The Jewish holidays are effectively like long bouts of Shabbat and if you're caught off-guard you can be rendered immobile for a

EDDIE GERALD

Jewish festivities can be inspiring spiritual events

EDDIE GERALD

The Hall of Rememberance at Yad Vashem is a sobering monument to the Holocaust

couple of days at a time, maybe without food, maybe without money. The main ones to beware of are Rosh HaShanah, Yom Kippur, Sukkot and Pesah.

Rosh HaShanah

Rosh HaShanah is one of the two days of the Jewish calendar known as Days of Judgement or Days of Awe (the other is Yom Kippur). As with all Jewish holidays, prayer services begin the eve of the holiday, in this case continuing for two days.

Characteristic foods eaten on Rosh HaShanah include pomegranates, apples dipped in honey or other honeyed foods to augur a sweet year, and tongue or fish heads to mark the 'head of the year', a direct translation of 'Rosh HaShanah'.

Yom Kippur

Known as the Day of Atonement, Yom Kippur ends the 10 days of penitence which begin on New Year's Day. For the observant, Yom Kippur means 25 hours of complete abstinence from food, drink, sex, cosmetics (including soap and toothpaste) and animal products. The time is spent in prayer and contemplation and all sins are confessed. As the only Jewish holiday equivalent to Shabbat in sanctity, Yom Kippur is the quietest day of the year in most of Jerusalem.

Sukkot & Simhat Torah

On the Festival of Sukkot most Jews, religious or not, erect home-made *sukkot* (shelters) in commemoration of the 40 years which the ancient Israelites spent in the wilderness after the exodus. The sukkot, hammered together from plyboard but with a roof only of loose branches through which the sky can be seen, sit out on the balconies of apartments, in gardens and even in hotels and restaurants. For the seven day duration of the festival all meals are taken in the sukkot and the ultraorthodox even go as far as sleeping in these makeshift huts.

Hanukah

Also known as the Festival of Lights, Hanukah celebrates the triumphant Maccabean revolt. Its symbol is the *menorah* (seven branched candelabra), and one of its candles is lit each night for a week. A special Hanukah lamp should also be displayed by each house, usually hung in the window – in Mea She'arim these are often hung outside the building, making it an enchanting district to wander through during the time of the festival.

Tu B'Shevat

The Mishnah name this day as the New Year for Trees and it's customary to eat fruit and nuts, in particular the carob fruit. Since independence, the day has been observed as a time for tree-planting.

Purim

Purim, the Feast of Lots, celebrates the Jews' refusal to compromise their religious principles by bowing before secular authority (see the Book of Esther 3-10). Despite such a serious, if highly relevant, theme, the holiday has a carnival atmosphere, and fancy dress is the order of the day. The streets are filled with proud parents and their Batmen, Madonnas and Power Rangers. In the evening it's the turn of the dames, fairies and gangsters.

A nation of non-drinkers, Purim is an annual opportunity for the Israelis to atone: according to tradition they are supposed to get so drunk that they can't distinguish between the words 'bless Mordechai' and 'curse Haman'. The most popular Purim foods are Haman's Ears (Oznei Haman) – fried, three-cornered pastries filled with apricots or other fruits and covered in poppy seeds.

Pesah

Pesah, the Feast of Passover, celebrates the exodus of the Jews, led by Moses, from Egypt. The festival lasts a full week, during which time most Jewish stores (including foodstores and markets) are closed (or open for limited hours only). Instead of making ordinary leavened bread, bakeries produce *matza*, a flat tasteless variety which is made in discs of up to a metre in diameter. There's no public transport on either the first or last day of the festival.

Holocaust Day (Yom HaSho'ah)

Periodically throughout the day sirens wail to signal two minutes of silence in remembrance of the six million victims of the Holocaust – it's an incredibly moving and eerie experience as everyone on the streets stops and puts their bags down, and all traffic comes to a halt, engines are extinguished and nothing moves.

Mimouna

This festival takes place the day after the last day of Pesah, and has been celebrated by the North African Jewish communities for generations. Mimouna's exact origins are unknown but one theory is that it's an Arabisation of the Hebrew word *emunah*, meaning faith or belief, in the coming of the Messiah and the redemption of the Jews. North African Jews organise street parties and open-house celebrations. Foreigners – Jews and non-Jews alike – are warmly invited to join in. Check the Jaffa Rd tourist information office for the local arrangements.

Independence Day (Yom Ha'Atzmaut)

On 14 May 1948 Israel became an independent state and since then the day has been celebrated by Jews worldwide (note that the date changes with the lunar calendar). Expect parades, aerial flypasts, concerts, picnics and fireworks.

Lag B'Omer

Ending 33 days of mourning, Lag B'Omer is a rite of spring, a celebration of the day when a plague was lifted in Jewish history. The modern-day celebrations include parades, parties and bonfires.

Muslim

Muslim holidays in Jerusalem are not as disruptive as the Jewish ones. Even during Ramadan, when Muslims fast during daylight hours, the heavy tourist presence in the Old City means that it is expedient for most Muslim-run cafes, restaurants and food stalls to remain open.

Birth of the Prophet

This is Mohammed's birthday, celebrated with much consumption of sticky and sickly sweets and confectionery.

Lailatul Miraj

This remembers the night Mohammed ascended to heaven from the Temple Mount in Jerusalem.

Ramadan

For non-Muslim visitors, the major effect of this month-long dawn-to-sunset fast is that the less commercial Muslim Arab areas are very quiet, with many businesses open for only limited hours.

Eid al-Fitr

This is the great feast to mark the end of Ramadan. Muslims express their joy at the end of their fast by offering a congregational prayer, preferably in an open field. They should express their gratitude to Allah for enabling them to observe the fast, thus preparing them for life as a Muslim. Special dishes are prepared and it is customary to visit relatives and friends, to go out for a day trip and to give presents to children. Everyone eats a great deal.

Eid al-Adha

This is the most important feast of the Muslim calendar. It commemorates the occasion when Allah asked Abraham to sacrifice his son, Ishmael. A lamb was

Holy Fire
At a few minutes after 1 pm every Greek Easter Sunday the Church of the Holy Sepulchre is witness to the miracle of the Holy Fire. Observed by a press of thousands of worshippers, the Greek Orthodox Patriarch enters the tomb and the doors are sealed behind him. After a pause, the lights go out, a peal of bells ring and the Patriarch reappears brandishing a torch blazing with the Holy Fire. The flame is immediately spread from one candle to the next to illuminate the whole church.

Those wishing to see the show should get there very early – the devout begin arriving the day before and spend the previous night sleeping on the cold stone floors around the tomb. ■

sacrificed instead of the boy after Abraham had shown his readiness to obey Allah. Today Muslims offer a congregational prayer on the day, followed by a sacrifice – mainly of sheep, but also goats or cows. The meat of the sacrificed animal is given to needy people and to older relatives. Clothes and money are sometimes given, too.

Christian

Many visitors with a Christian background will find festivals in Jerusalem are celebrated very differently from the way they are used to. This is largely due to the domination of the Orthodox Church, and also to the fact that Christianity is very much in third place in the religious stakes here. Christmas Day, for example (ignoring the fact that it is celebrated on three separate occasions by the various denominations), is just another day for most people.

Christmas Day

Apart from 25 December, Christmas is celebrated on 7 January by the Orthodox and on 19 January by the Armenians. The event to attend is the midnight mass on Christmas Eve (24 December), held at Bethlehem's Church of the Nativity. During the day a procession departs from Jerusalem for the church but, due to the popularity of the service, not everyone gets in. Pew space inside the church is reserved for ticket-holding observant Catholics only (the tickets, which are free, must be applied for in advance at the Terra Sancta office in the Christian Information Centre at Jaffa Gate). The rest of the crowd, along with an international mass choir, congregates outside the church in Manger Square where a large video screen relays the service being conducted inside. It can be

Public Holidays 1997
Jewish holidays follow a lunar calendar and so fall on a
different date each year according to the western Gregor-
ian calendar. For instance, in 1996 Rosh HaShanah,
which marks the beginning of the Jewish new year, fell on
26 September, while in 1997, it is on 2 October. However,
it will always fall around this time, unlike the Muslim
holidays which, following the Islamic calendar, move
forward 11 days each year. Therefore, Ramadan, which
starts on or around 10 January in 1997, will begin again
around 31 December later that same year.

Consult an Israeli tourist information office for public
holidays in 1998 and 1999.

January
    Orthodox Christmas (7)
    Ramadan (10)
    Armenian Christmas (19)
    Tu B'Shevat (19)
February
    Eid al-Fitr (10)
    Black Hebrew Day of Appreciation & Love
March
    Purim (23)
    Good Friday (28)
    Easter Sunday (30)
April
    Orthodox and Armenian Good Friday (4)
    Orthodox and Armenian Easter Sunday (6)
    Eid al-Adha (18)
    Pesah (22-28)
    Armenian Holocaust Day (24)
    Mimouna (29)
May
    Holocaust Day (4)
    Muslim New Year (9)
    Independence Day (12)
    Lag B'Omer
June
    Liberation of Jerusalem Day (4)
    Shavuot (11)
July
    Prophet's Birthday (18)
October
    Rosh HaShanah (2-3)
    Yom Kippur (11)
    Sukkot/Simhat Torah (16-23)
November
    Lailatul Miraj (27)
December
    Hanukah (24-31)
    Western Christmas (25)

an extremely cold night, so wrap up well if you're going. Buses back to Jerusalem run irregularly all night.

Easter

Celebrated first by the Roman Catholics and the Protestants and then about two weeks later by the Orthodox Church, Easter means absolute chaos in Jerusalem's Old City. The Via Dolorosa and the narrow streets around the Church of the Holy Sepulchre become clogged with pilgrims staking out their spots for the various services and processions. Note that at this time pilgrims fill many of the cheap hostels in Jerusalem's Old City and completely block-book everything in Bethlehem.

Armenian Holocaust Day

Every year on 24 April the Armenians commemorate their overlooked tragedy with a parade and service in the Old City.

SPECIAL EVENTS

Throughout the year, Jerusalem is a major venue for special events, in particular national celebrations of Jewish festivals and the annual Israel Festival. Usually held sometime during May or June, this is a three week programme of cultural events featuring music, theatre and dance which makes good use of some of the city's unique venues such as the Citadel, Sultan's Pool and the Mt Scopus amphitheatre.

February

Jerusalem Musical Encounters

March

International Festival of Poets
International Judaica Fair

May, June

Israel Festival

July

International Film Festival

August

International Puppet Theatre Festival

September

Early Music Workshop

October

Jerusalem Marathon

For further information, contact the events department of the Ministry of Tourism (☎ 625 8152; fax 625 9837).

WORK

It's not difficult to find casual work in Jerusalem, it's just difficult to make it pay. In many cases employers are just out to exploit a plentiful supply of cheap, sometimes desperate, foreign labour.

As in any other city, the catering industry soaks up the largest number of illegal workers. It's unlikely, however, that you'll be waiting on tables (and thus benefiting from the heavy tipping) – instead you'll be washing dishes or cleaning, and getting around 10 to 15 NIS per hour.

There's a lot of labour-intensive work around, particularly in construction, an area that the South African travellers seem to have monopolised. Most hostels also employ people to work at the reception or bar – the pay is nothing great but you get your bed for free and maybe enough money to cover food and beer.

Women might find more appeal in au pair work. There are a couple of reputable agencies that match applicants with families on a short-term basis and pay US$500 to US$700 a month, with accommodation and meals on top. The *Traveller* newspaper carries ads for the au pair agencies.

For other work check out the notice boards and ask around at hostels (Palm, Al-Arab and Tabasco in Jerusalem) and bars.

EMERGENCY

In emergencies dial ☎ 100. Arab police seem to be responsible for basic duties in East Jerusalem and the Old City and their station is on Omar ibn al-Khattab Square, beside the Citadel (see map 14). However, they are most likely to refer you to the central police station in the Russian Compound in the New City (see map 9). The city's lost and found office is also here. It's open Sunday, Tuesday and Thursday from 7.30 am to 4 pm, Monday and Wednesday from 7.30 am to 2 pm, and Friday from 9.30 am to 12.30 pm, closed Saturday. See the Health section for medical services.

Getting There & Away

AIR

Jerusalem is served by Ben-Gurion airport, Israel's only major international air terminal. For details of getting to and from the airport, which is about 50 km west of the city centre, see the Getting Around chapter.

For airport information call ☎ (03) 971 0000; for recorded English-language flight information call ☎ (03) 971 2484.

From Abroad

Airfares to Israel vary considerably according to season. July to September, and Jewish holidays in particular, mean much higher prices. Note that it is often difficult to get a flight out of Israel in a hurry, so think carefully before travelling there on a one-way ticket.

The USA & Canada New York offers the widest choice of carriers, but you can also fly from Los Angeles, Chicago, Miami, Atlanta and Toronto. Many North American travellers prefer to fly nonstop with El Al for security reasons. El Al also flies via London, Manchester or Paris. TWA flies nonstop and via Paris for less than El Al, and Delta started flying to Ben-Gurion airport in 1991. All of these airlines have discounted fares from time to time. The Belgian carrier Sabena, which offers an overnight stay in Brussels, is often good value. Cheap fares cost around US$700 return to Ben-Gurion airport from New York.

Another choice is to fly via Eastern Europe. The journey time is longer than a direct flight, and the Eastern European airlines' reputation for awful service and delays is pretty much deserved, but the low fares offered by Tarom (Rumanian Airlines), Hungarian and Czechoslovak Airlines can be tempting options.

The *New York Times*, the *LA Times*, the *Chicago Tribune* and the *San Francisco Examiner* all produce weekly travel sections in which you'll find any number of travel agents' ads. Council Travel and STA have offices in major cities nationwide. The magazine *Travel Unlimited* (PO Box 1058, Allston, Mass 02134) publishes details of the cheapest air fares and courier possibilities from the USA to destinations all over the world.

In Canada, Travel CUTS has offices in all major cities. The *Toronto Globe & Mail* and the *Vancouver Sun* carry travel agents' ads. The magazine *Great Expeditions* (PO Box 8000-411, Abbotsford BC V2S 6H1) is useful.

Australia & New Zealand There are no direct flights between Australia or New Zealand and Ben-Gurion. However, a number of carriers fly via Asia or Europe. One-way tickets range from about A$1100 to A$1400 in low season, and cost A$100 to A$300 more in high season. Return tickets cost between A$1650 and A$2250 in low season and A$1900 to A$2750 in high season. Some of the cheaper airlines are Olympic via Athens, Alitalia via Rome, Egypt Air/Air Sinai via Cairo, and Korean Airlines via Seoul. Thai and Ansett fly to Bangkok and Hong Kong and their flights link with El Al flights.

At the top end of the price range is British Airways, South African and KLM. Another option is to buy a round-the-world ticket with, say Qantas or British Airways, or a cheaper one with Alitalia combined with United Airlines. Fares are about A$2000 low season and A$2400 in high season.

STA and Flight Centres International are major dealers in cheap air fares. Check the travel agents' ads in the Yellow Pages and ring around.

The UK A number of charter flights to Ben-Gurion from the UK continue to offer the best deals at around £220 for a 12 month open return. This can come down to as little as £180 for a one to four week return. A one-way charter ticket averages about £140. In 1996 the cheapest scheduled flights were with Olympic at £229 open return. To secure a cheap fare for summer and Christmas-time flights, however, you must book well in advance.

It is worth shopping around London and Manchester's cheap flight specialists. STA, with branches throughout the UK, is regularly amongst the cheapest, as are Trailfinders and the various Earls Court Rd cheap ticket specialists. It may also be worth contacting Israel Travel Service (☎ (0161) 839 1111; fax 839 0000) in Manchester, a private and extremely helpful outfit with extensive experience.

Check out the ads in the *Times* and the Sunday newspaper travel supplements, and in London look in the free magazines such as *TNT* which are distributed outside many central tube stations.

Continental Europe Most European countries also have charter flights to Ben-Gurion with considerable savings on scheduled fares: the cheapest are Germany, France, Belgium, the Netherlands and Scandinavia. Prices are slightly higher than the UK.

The inexpensive option of flying via Eastern Europe is also available to northern European countries (see The USA & Canada above).

Asia Hong Kong is the discount plane ticket capital of the region. Its bucket shops are at least as unreliable as those of other cities. Ask the advice of other travellers before buying a ticket.

STA, which is reliable, has branches in Hong Kong, Tokyo, Singapore, Bangkok and Kuala Lumpur.

Egypt There are El Al and Air Sinai flights available between Ben-Gurion and Egypt (Cairo and the Red Sea port of Hurghada), which will save you having an Egypt-Israel border stamp in your passport. The flights cost about US$155 one way, US$220 return.

Within Israel

Arkia, the national domestic carrier, flies from the airport at Atarot, north of the city, direct to Eilat and Rosh Pina, with further connections to Haifa and Tel Aviv. There are no flights on Saturday. Arkia's office in the city centre (☎ 625 5888) is in room 121 in the Klal building at 97 Jaffa Rd (see map 9).

Airline Offices

Other airline offices, all in the New City unless otherwise stated, are:

Air France
    3 Shlomzion HaMalka (☎ 625 2495)
    As-Zahra St, East Jerusalem (☎ 628 2535)
Alitalia
    23 Hillel St (☎ 625 8653)
    20 Salah ad-Din St (☎ 628 3515)
British Airways
    33 Jaffa Rd (☎ 625 6111)
Delta Airlines
    15 Shamai St (☎ 624 8199)

Painful Departures

The advice to air travellers departing Ben-Gurion is to turn up at the airport a good three hours before the scheduled flight time. The reason for this is that everyone boarding a plane out of one of Israel's airports (and that includes domestic flights) is subject to a rigorous cross-examination as part of security procedures. Middle-aged American couples with names like Weintraub can waltz through this in minutes and can probably leave turning up at the departure hall until only 1½ hours before the flight. Everyone else, especially the independent traveller with a backpack, ought to bring a long engrossing novel.

The idea of the questioning, carried out before check-in, is to establish whether you pose a security threat – ie is there any likelihood that in amongst your three weeks worth of unwashed smalls there is something of an even more explosive nature. Factors that will arouse the suspicions of your inquisitors are things like a visit to the Gaza Strip or the West Bank and whether you've made any Palestinian acquaintances. If this is the case, chances are that your baggage will receive a thorough and time-consuming search.

This was something I wished to avoid the last time I passed through Ben-Gurion airport, so in answer to where had I been during my stay in Israel I mentioned only Tel Aviv, Jerusalem, the Dead Sea and Eilat – the main tourist sites. 'Jericho?', the soldier enquired. 'No,' I lied, Jericho being part of the West Bank, 'I didn't have time this trip'. She motioned for me to open my bag anyway and rummaged around casually while asking further questions. I thought I was doing OK – the sly 'How did you like Jericho?' she tossed in failed to catch me out – but then I could only slump in defeat at the damning evidence I had completely forgotten about until revealed by her search: my inflatable Yasser Arafat. ∎

El Al
   12 Hillel St (☎ 625 6934)
Iberian Airlines
   8 Shamai St (☎ 623 2919)
KLM
   33 Jaffa Rd (☎ 625 1361)
Lufthansa
   16A King George V St (☎ 624 4941)
Olympic
   33 Jaffa Rd (☎ 623 4538)
Sabena
   23 HaMelekh David St (☎ 623 4971)
SAS
   14 As-Zahra St, East Jerusalem (☎ 628 3235)
Swissair
   31 HaNevi'im St (☎ 623 1373)

Tower Air
14 Hillel St (☎ 625 5137)
TWA
34 Ben Yehuda St (☎ 624 1576)

Departing Israel by Air

The tax for foreigners flying out of Ben-Gurion is around US$12 but this is accounted for in the cost of your ticket (small cheese compared to Israeli citizens who are stung for about US$50 to US$75 each time they leave their country).

BUS

Jerusalem can be reached by bus from Egypt or Jordan, both of which have open land borders with Israel; Lebanon and Syria do not.

To/From Egypt

Forbidden until the signing of the 1979 peace accord, travel between Israel and Egypt is now a thriving part of the tourist scene. There are two border crossing points, Rafah and Taba. Buses between Cairo and Jerusalem travel direct via the Rafah crossing (Rafiah to the Israelis); Taba is the crossing if you want to travel via Sinai – take a normal Egged bus to Eilat and change there.

Two tour companies in Jerusalem do the Rafah route:

Egged Tours
44A and 224 (by the bus station) Jaffa Rd (☎ 530 4883), by the bus station.
Buses depart Thursday and Sunday at 6.30 am.
Mazada Tours
9 Koresh St (☎ 623 5777), behind the Jaffa Rd tourist office (see map 9).
Buses depart Monday to Friday at 7.30 am. There are also overnight services on Tuesday and Thursday, departing at 7 pm.

The journey takes roughly 10 hours and a ticket costs about 90 NIS (US$30) one way or 135 NIS (US$45) return. Add to that an Israeli departure tax of 90 NIS (US$30) (payable usually to the bus company) and an Egyptian entry tax of LE7 (US$2.50). You can change money at the border.

To/From Jordan

Unlike Egypt, which maintains a 'you keep to your side of the fence and I'll keep to mine' peace with Israel, Jordan and the Jewish state have become best buddies, exchanging coach loads of visitors on a daily basis. The Allenby/Hussein Bridge, which until very recently served as the only meeting point of the two neighbours, has been supplemented by two other crossings – Jordan River, up in the Galilee region, and Arava, just a couple of km east of the centre of Eilat. But as it is only 30 km from Jerusalem (and 40 km from Amman), the Allenby/King Hussein Bridge crossing remains the most convenient for Jerusalem.

At the time of writing there are no official bus services between the two capitals, and the best way of reaching the border is to take a 30 NIS service taxi from opposite Damascus Gate in Jerusalem. Ask for 'Al-Malek Hussein', not Allenby Bridge which is the Israeli name and may not be understood. The journey takes about 45 minutes. Note that anyone turning up here without a valid visa will be sent back (the nearest Jordanian embassy is in Tel Aviv. Alternatively, the Jordan River and Arava border posts will issue visas).

Crossing can take anything up to three hours depending on the traffic – try to avoid being there between 11 am and 3 pm, the busiest period. The Israeli exit tax is 83.50 NIS (and rising all the time). Once you're through all the immigration procedures and out the other side, look for the white service taxis which charge JD2 per person to Amman; the yellow cars are 'special' taxis which charge JD10 to JD12 for the same ride.

The bridge is open Sunday to Thursday from 8 am to 10.30 pm, and Friday and Saturday from 8 am to 1 pm. These times change frequently so it's advisable to check with the tourist information office in Jerusalem.

Internal

Israel's bus network is dominated by Egged, the second largest bus company in the world after Greyhound. Although the interurban buses are always busy, those heading for the Dead Sea and in particular Eilat are the only ones for which you need to reserve seats in advance. Buses for the Dead Sea are always busy and seem to operate independently of official timetables. The simple rule is to make a start as early as possible.

Unless otherwise stated, buses run daily between about 5.30 am and 11 pm, with the last buses on Fridays being around 3 pm and the first buses on Shabbat leaving about 6 pm. The central bus station is on Jaffa Rd, on the west side of town (see map 1). Call ☎ 530 4555 for intercity bus information.

The left-luggage office is at 195 Jaffa Rd, out of the station and directly opposite. It's open Sunday to Thursday from 7 am to 7 pm, and Friday from 7 am to 1 pm, closed Saturday. The charge is 5 NIS per item per day.

Beersheba (90 minutes; 22.50 NIS) every 30 minutes until 8.30 pm

Eilat (4½ hours; 43 NIS) 7 and 10 am, 2 and 5 pm; book a day in advance

Ein Gedi (90 minutes; 18 NIS) 8.40 am and 4, 7.45 and 9.40 pm; you can also take the Eilat or Masada buses

Haifa (two hours; 27.50 NIS) every 45 minutes, last bus 7.15 pm

Masada via Ein Gedi (1¾ hours; 21 NIS) 8.45, 10.30 and 11 am, noon and 1 pm; you can also take one of the Eilat buses

Safed (three hours; 40 NIS) only one or two a day; take a Tiberias bus and change

Tel Aviv (one hour; 13.70 NIS) every 10 to 15 minutes; bus No 405 goes to the central bus station, bus No 480 goes to the Arlosoroff terminal

Tiberias (2½ hours; 28 NIS) every hour until 7 pm

TRAIN

There are no international trains to or from Jerusalem, only internal lines. Jerusalem's railway station (☎ 673 3764) is in David Remez St, at the southern end of HaMelekh David St (see map 10). This is the end of the little used line running from Haifa via Tel Aviv. There are only two trains a day, departing at 8.30 am and 3 pm (3 pm only during the winter), and the fare to/from Tel Aviv is about 12 NIS, while to Haifa it's 18 NIS. The journey to Tel Aviv takes over two hours, but the scenery is said to be beautiful. Several buses run between the railway station and the New City. To reach the Old City it is perhaps just as easy to walk as it is to take a bus.

CAR & MOTORCYCLE

Egypt and Jordan both have open land borders with Israel; Lebanon and Syria do not. Private cars may cross the borders but not taxis or hire cars. Drivers and riders of motorbikes will need the vehicle's registration papers, and liability insurance. For Israel an international drivers' permit is not necessary – your domestic licence will do.

Sherut (Service Taxi)

Sheruts make an affordable alternative to the buses, and on Shabbat they are the only way of getting around all but the Palestinian areas. In the New City, regular services include the following main destinations:

Tel Aviv
    HaBirah (☎ 623 2320), 1 Harav Kook St, opposite Zion Square.
    Kesher-Aviv (☎ 625 7366), 12 Shamai St, south of and parallel to Ben Yehuda St.
    Cost: 11 NIS per person; Friday and Saturday 20 NIS.
Haifa & Eilat
    Yael Daroma (☎ 622 6985), Shamai St, next door to Kesher-Aviv; reservations a day in advance are normally necessary.

Service taxis to all West Bank destinations as well as those to the Gaza Strip depart from a service taxi rank across from Damascus Gate in East Jerusalem (see map 12). They operate daily from about 5 am until about 5 pm, after which time the service becomes less dependable, with fewer passengers to fill the vehicles.

HITCHING

Hitching is never entirely safe in any country in the world, and Israel is no different. There have been incidents in which hitchhikers in Israel have been abducted and killed and not all, it's thought, for political reasons. Travellers who decide to hitch should understand that they are taking a small but potentially serious risk. At least hitch in pairs and let someone know where you are planning to go. And, above all, women should never hitchhike without male company.

You will notice, however, a large number of soldiers soliciting lifts by the roadside. This is because it's traditional, and actively encouraged, for Israelis to give lifts to soldiers – so bear in mind that if you are hitchhiking you will be last in line for a lift if there are any IDF uniforms to be seen. Note that even female soldiers are forbidden to hitchhike because of the potential danger. Also, take note that sticking out your thumb is not the locally accepted way to hitch a lift. Here it means something more basic and impolite, although most locals recognise the foreigner's intentions. The local way to hitch is to point down at the road with your index finger.

TRAVEL AGENTS

The student travel agency ISSTA (☎ 625 7257) is at 31 HaNevi'im St and is open Sunday, Monday, Tuesday and Thursday from 9 am to 6 pm, and Wednesday and Friday from 9 am to 1 pm, closed Saturday. Mona Tours (☎ 625 3002) at 4 Hillel St also specialises in discount flights for students and youth travellers and claims to offer the cheapest air fares in Israel.

Tel Aviv's The Travel Centre (☎ (03) 528 0955; fax 528 7307) also specialises in discount fares to Europe. They will send tickets to Jerusalem at no extra charge.

WARNING

The information in this chapter is particularly vulnerable to change: prices for international travel are volatile, routes are introduced and cancelled, schedules change, special deals come and go, and rules and visa requirements are amended. Airlines and governments seem to take a perverse pleasure in making price structures and regulations as complicated as possible. You should check directly with the airline or a travel agent to make sure you understand how a fare (and ticket you may buy) works. In addition, the travel industry is highly competitive and there are many lurks and perks.

The upshot of this is that you should get opinions, quotes and advice from as many airlines and travel agents as possible before you part with your hard-earned cash. The details given in this chapter should be regarded as pointers and are not a substitute for your own careful, up-to-date research.

Getting Around

THE AIRPORT

United Tours bus No 111 shuttles between Ben-Gurion (turn left out of the arrivals terminal) and Jerusalem's central bus station (45 minutes; 20 NIS), with departures about once an hour. En route it picks up/drops off at the following New City hotels: Jerusalem Renaissance, Park Plaza, Holiday Inn, Sheraton Plaza, Jerusalem Tower (the closest stop to central Jerusalem and the Old City), King David and the YMCA, Moriah, Laromme and the Mt Zion Hotel (also the stop for St Andrew's Scottish Hospice).

Egged bus No 947 also runs direct between the airport and central bus station every half-hour.

Neither of these services is very convenient for the Old City or East Jerusalem, especially if you're carrying heavy luggage and need to look for a place to stay. A better option in that case would be to take a sherut (minibus, also known as 'service taxis'). Though slightly more expensive (30 NIS or US$10), the sheruts will take you to any requested destination in the city. They run 24 hours a day, departing whenever they're full.

To get to the airport call Nesher sheruts (☎ 623 1231, 625 7227) of 21 King George V St, on the corner of Ben Yehuda St (see map 9). They pick up from anywhere in the city, seven days a week, 24 hours a day, and the cost is still 30 NIS. Reserve one day ahead.

If you want to get a 'special' taxi (that is, a non-shared one), it will cost you about 95 NIS from the airport to the city centre. This fare goes up approximately 30% between 9 pm and 5.30 am. The prices are displayed on a board at the airport, so you shouldn't have to haggle.

BUS

Egged

Most urban buses in Jerusalem are operated by the Egged company. Within city limits there's one flat fare which stays the same whether you ride just one stop or 10. At the time of writing this fare is 3.70 NIS (no transfers). You buy your ticket from the bus driver.

Despite the frequency of most services they do fill up, especially in the rush hours which occur roughly Monday to Thursday between 7 and 8 am and 4 and

6 pm, and most of Saturday evening. Operating times vary with the route, but most buses run from about 5.30 am to about midnight.

Remember, beware of Shabbat: on Friday, and the eve of Jewish holidays, buses only run until 3 or 4 pm, and on Saturday services don't resume until sunset.

Currently, these are the major routes:

Bus No 1 goes from platform D of the central bus station to Mea She'arim, Jaffa Gate, Mt Zion and then to the Old City's Jewish Quarter.

Bus No 7 goes from the bus station down Keren HaYesod, through Talpiot and out to Ramat Rachel.

Bus No 9 goes from Jaffa Rd to the Knesset, the Israel Museum and the Givat Ram campus of the Hebrew University and then into Rehavia via Ramban St and down Keren Ha Yesod.

Bus No 13 goes from Kiryat HaYovel via Jaffa Rd to Jaffa Gate.

Bus No 17 goes to Ein Kerem

Bus No 18 runs the length of Jaffa Rd, connecting the New City centre with the bus station.

Bus No 20 goes from Yad Vashem via Jaffa Rd to Jaffa Gate.

Bus No 23 goes from Yad Vashem via Jaffa Rd to Damascus Gate.

Bus No 27 goes from Hadassah Medical Centre to Mt Herzl and Yad Vashem, along Jaffa Rd past the central bus station, left along HaNevi'im and via Strauss and Yezehekel Sts to the Nablus Rd bus station near Damascus Gate.

Bus No 28 goes from Jaffa Rd to Mt Scopus and French Hill.

For city bus information call ☎ 530 4555.

Multifare Discount Pass Bus drivers or the ticket offices at the central bus station sell a monthly discount pass called a *hofshi hodshi*, which allows for unlimited travel within the city during that calendar month. The pass costs 148 NIS and is on sale only at the beginning of each month.

Arab Buses

These serve East Jerusalem and outlying towns and villages such as Bethany and Bethlehem. While Jewish buses tend to be air-conditioned, clean, fast and modern, the Arab buses are virtual antiques, and not well kept ones at that. If you have the choice use a sherut instead – they're only slightly more expensive but are much faster. The Arab bus stations are on Nablus Rd and Suleyman St (see map 11).

CAR

Traffic in Jerusalem is horrendous, and unless you expect to be regularly criss-crossing town then a car is more trouble than it's worth. In addition, Israelis exhibit near suicidal tendencies once behind the wheel and over 18,000 have been killed in road accidents countrywide since 1948 – more than have died in all the wars with their Arab neighbours.

Road Orthodoxy
When death and disablement prove insufficient incentives to get drivers to slow down, the ultraorthodox road safety campaigners play on even greater fears. Signs in the Mea She'arim district display the macabre message, 'Drive Carefully: the Pathologist Awaits' – a reference to autopsies that they claim have been carried out indiscriminately in Jerusalem's hospitals in violation of Jewish religious law. ■

Road Rules

In Israel you drive on the right-hand side of the road. Seat belts should be worn at all times by front seat occupants. The speed limit is 50 km/h (31 mp/h) in built up areas and 90 km/h (56 mp/h) elsewhere unless stated, but this is typically ignored. There seems to be a lack of regulatory road signs, but virtually all major cities, towns and places of interest are signposted in English.

Parking

With a rapid increase in private car ownership, parking is a major problem in Jerusalem. Street parking is strictly regulated. To avoid a ticket or having your car towed, be sure to follow the rules.

Generally, there is no free street parking in most city or town centres; parking cards need to be purchased from the post office or street kiosks. Each parking card has five hours' worth of street parking, and costs about 35 NIS. With a parking card affixed to the car's front window, you can park where the kerb is marked by blue and white stripes. You cannot legally park anywhere else.

Between 7 am and 5 pm, you can only park on a marked kerb for one hour. Between 5 and 10 pm you can

EDDIE GERALD

Decorative signs placed by the Jerusalem Municipality on
points of interest in the New City

park for longer, with a set of displayed parking cards
indicating the number of hours parked. Overnight
parking on the blue and white stripes is unregulated. If
you need to park for a longer period during the day, use
a public car park.

Car Rental

Local car hire firms generally offer lower rates than the
international companies like Avis, Budget and Hertz.
Eldan, in particular, stands out, with good rates and
offices nationwide. If you are planning to drive throughout the country, it can be a good idea to use a company
that has a few offices in case you need a replacement car.
Note that you are not allowed to take hired vehicles into
Sinai or over the border into Jordan.

Prices do vary dramatically and shopping around is
recommended. Based on three days' rental, look at
around US$55 to US$75 per day for a Fiat Uno or similar,
with air-con, insurance and unlimited mileage. July and
August rates are substantially higher than the rest of the
year. Be wary of initial quotes – check if insurance and
unlimited mileage are included, and if there is a
minimum rental period.

Most car rental companies require that drivers be over
21 years old and have a clean, valid driver's licence (an
International Driving Permit is not necessary for most
nationalities).

AutoRent – King David Hotel (☎ 624 4222) HaMelekh
    David St
Avis – 22 HaMelekh David St (☎ 624 9001)
Best – 178 Jaffa Rd (☎ 389 226)
Budget – 8 HaMelekh David St (☎ 624 8991)
Eldan – 24 HaMelekh David St (☎ 625 2151)
Eurodollar – 8 HaMelekh David St (☎ 623 5467)
Europcar – 8 HaMelekh David St (☎ 624 8464)
Hertz – 18 HaMelekh David St (☎ 623 1351)
Reliable – 14 HaMelekh David St (☎ 624 8993, 624 8204)
Sa-Gal – 14 HaMelekh David St (☎ 624 1516)
Splendid – 14 HaMelekh David St (☎ 624 2488; fax 242 557)

An often overlooked alternative to the Jewish-owned
companies are the Palestinian operations. In addition to
any political reasons for giving them your business, their
cars are considered 'protected' in East Jerusalem and
other Arab areas, including the West Bank, and should
be spared the hostility and stones that on occasion are
still targeted towards Jewish cars with yellow plates.

Holy City – East Jerusalem, behind the US Consulate
    (☎ 582 0223; fax 582 4329)
Orabi – Jerusalem St, Al-Bireh, near Ramallah (☎ 995 3521;
    fax 995 3521)
Petra – Main St, East Jerusalem(☎ 582 0716; fax 582 2668)

TAXI

Sherut (Service Taxi)

Sheruts, or service taxis, are usually stretch-Mercedes,
seating up to seven passengers, or the little bug-like
Volkswagen vans, which operate on a fixed route for a
fixed price just like a bus. If you are uncertain about the
fare, just ask your fellow passengers. Regular rates are
normally about 20% more than the bus, but are sometimes on a par.

With a sherut you can get out anywhere along the way,
but you pay the same fare regardless. After dropping off
a passenger the sherut then picks up replacement passengers wherever possible.

On some routes, sheruts operate as bus stand-ins on
Shabbat, providing the only transport whilst Egged is
off the road.

'Special' Taxi

Drivers of 'special' (that is, non-shared) taxis have a
terrible reputation with tourists and locals alike for over-
charging and being generally unhelpful and impolite.

The usual 'my meter doesn't work' or 'for you my friend, special price' (more likely to be double than a discount) tricks are popular. Be sure that the meter is used or risk paying too much. Roughly speaking, a trip across town should cost 10 to 15 NIS.

BICYCLE

There's just too much traffic in Jerusalem to make cycling a comfortable way of getting around. For anyone who is in less than perfect physical shape, there are also a good few too many hills. But if you really insist, contact the Jerusalem Cycle Club (☎ 016 062, 561 9416) for information on where to get spares and so on.

ORGANISED TOURS

A good introduction to the city is Egged Tours' Route 99, Circular Line. This service takes you on a comfortable coach to 36 of the major sites, with basic commentary in English (sort of) provided by the driver. A single ticket is 15 NIS, valid for a day's unlimited travel, enabling you to get off and back on wherever you wish; bear in mind, however, the infrequency of the service: it operates Sunday to Thursday with departures at 10 and 11 am, noon and 1, 2 and 4 pm, and on Friday with departures at 10 and 11 am and noon. The coach leaves from Ha'Emek St by Jaffa Gate but you can board at any of the stops and it's a continuous circular route (taking 1½ hours in total), ending up where it started.

Egged also runs a half-day tour of Jerusalem's Old City departing Sunday to Thursday at 9.30 am and costing 60 NIS, and a half-day trip to Yad Vashem and Bethlehem Sunday to Thursday at 2 pm, again costing 60 NIS. For further information visit the Egged Tours offices at 44A Jaffa Rd (☎ 625 3454, 625 4198) or 224 Jaffa Rd (☎ 530 4422) near the central bus station.

Walking Tours

Up-to-date details of the following and other walking tours are available at the tourist information office on Jaffa Rd.

Free Walking Tours The Jaffa Rd tourist information office organises a free Saturday morning walking tour around a different part of the city each week. Meet at 10 am by the entrance to the Russian Compound at 32 Jaffa Rd. Unfortunately these free tours inevitably attract a large crowd so although the guides are well informed you'll often struggle to hear them.

The Sheraton Plaza Hotel (☎ 625 9111), on the corner of King George V and Agron Sts in the New City, offers free walking tours most days of the week, and non-guests are welcome. Meet in the hotel lobby at 9 am.

The Jewish Student Information Centre (see under Tourist Offices in the Facts for the Visitor chapter), which is committed to giving young Jews a fresh awareness of being Jewish, organises free walking tours of Jewish sites in the Old City's Jewish and Muslim quarters. Visit the centre or phone ☎ 628 2643 for current schedules.

Zion Walking Tours Enjoying one of the best reputations for Old and New City tours, Zion (☎ 628 7866; fax 629 0774) has its office on Omar ibn al-Khattab Square, opposite the entrance to the Citadel. Particularly good value is a three hour 'Four Quarters' tour of the Old City departing Sunday to Friday at 9 and 11 am and 2 pm and costing 24 NIS (students 18 NIS) per person. Other tours include the Pre-Temple Period route, the Underground City of Jerusalem and Mea She'arim.

Society for the Protection of Nature in Israel (SPNI) The SPNI organises mainly hikes and treks in the surrounding countryside but each Thursday beginning at 8 am it runs a full day tour of the Old City. It's limited, however, only to the Jewish parts. The cost per person is 132 NIS. For contact details see Tourist Offices in the Facts for the Visitor chapter.

Archaeological Seminars These are narrowly focused Jewish-oriented Old City tours such as Jerusalem in the First Temple Period and Jerusalem in the Second Temple Period. Each lasts three hours and costs 45 NIS. Tours depart from the Archaeological Seminars office (☎ 627 3515; fax 627 2660) at 34 Habad St in the Jewish Quarter.

Things to See & Do

THE OLD CITY

A bazaar of living history, the Old City is a densely packed labyrinth of more than 100 streets, 1000 shops and stalls, and 3000 years of human experience. As you walk along the Via Dolorosa you are treading on the same paving stones that were there at the time of Christ – they were uncovered while new sewers were being dug in the 1970s. Rather than store them in a museum, the municipality had them relaid. It is this perpetuation of the ancient in the 20th century that creates the appeal of the Old City.

The Old City is administered by the Israelis but is predominantly Arab in make-up and appearance. The two do not as a rule mix (although in the past there were times when they cohabited quite peacefully), and instead the Old City is divided into four hazily defined quarters. At the same time, it's focused on three definite centres of gravity. The Christian and Armenian quarters have developed in homage to the Church of the Holy Sepulchre, the site traditionally considered to be that of Jesus' crucifixion. The Muslim Quarter huddles in the shadow of the Haram ash-Sharif/Temple Mount, site of the Dome of the Rock, while the Jewish Quarter is oriented towards the Western Wall, the last vestige of the Second Temple.

Walls & Gates

The walls as they exist today, all 4.3 km of them, are the legacy of Suleyman the Great, who oversaw their construction between 1536 and 1541. The northern wall, including Damascus Gate, was built first and then extended south, at which point it was delayed by a dispute over whether or not Mt Zion and the Franciscans' monastery should stand within or without. To save time and expense the builders decided against looping around the monastery, leaving the Franciscans out in the cold. Popular legend has it that when news reached Suleyman of the miserly cost-cutting exercise he was furious and had the architects beheaded. Another version of the tale had them put to death so that they

Highlights

Any list of highlights is a completely subjective matter, doubly so with Jerusalem, a city which has always managed to inflame passions while dividing opinions with an equal intensity.

- The Old City viewed in early morning light from the Mount of Olives.
- Drinking mint tea at one of the cafes just inside Damascus Gate, watching the cinematic crush passing by.
- The Western Wall lit by moonlight with the Dome of the Rock silhouetted above.
- The tranquility of the Bloomfield Gardens and their view across the Hinom Valley to Mt Zion.
- Evenings amongst the cafe-cruising and bar-hopping crowds of Nahalat Shiv'a.
- The sobering quality of Yad Vashem.
- The early evening colour, smells, and especially sounds of Mahane Yehuda market, as traders try to make their last sales of the day.
- The art collection at the Israel Museum, strong on late 19th/early 20th century works, with a few surprises.

would never build another wall to challenge the magnificence of Jerusalem's.

There were seven gates in Suleyman's walls. To these, in the late 19th century, was added an eighth, still known as the New Gate. All but the Golden Gate on the eastern side of the Haram ash-Sharif/Temple Mount are accessible and, time permitting, you should try to make a point of entering or leaving the Old City by each of them.

Note that each of the gates has at least three names; one by which it's known to the Arabs, one by which it's known to the Jews, and a more internationally recognised Anglicised name. While almost everybody recognises the names Damascus Gate and Jaffa Gate, if you wanted an Arab taxi driver to take you, for example, to Herod's Gate, you would have to ask for Bab as-Zahra.

The following description of the gates begins with the Damascus Gate and continues clockwise around the wall.

Damascus Gate One of the most impressive structures of Islamic architecture in Jerusalem, Damascus Gate is also the busiest and most photogenic of the Old

City gates. The amphitheatre-like plaza out the front was created in the early 1970s. It now serves as a makeshift marketplace and it's a great place to sit and observe the bustle.

The gate itself dates in its present form from the time of Suleyman the Great, although there had been a gate here long before the arrival of the Turks. This was the main entrance to the city as early as the time of Herod Agrippas, who ruled in the 1st century BC. The gate was considerably enlarged during the reign of the Roman Emperor Hadrian. The foundations of Hadrian's 'Great Gate' were uncovered during major renovations in 1967 and are now open to visitors. Facing the outside of the gate, take the steps to your right which lead down to a small plaza; go through the door under the walkway and the old Roman gate is on your right at the foot of the wall. It's actually only one of two small entrances which flanked a much larger central gate – this is clearly illustrated on an adjacent copper wall plaque.

Inside, some of the old Roman gatehouse has been excavated, and its cavernous rooms now house a collection which illustrates the development of the gate area. It's worth a visit. The **Roman Square excavations**, as they're known, are open Saturday to Thursday from 9 am to 5 pm, and Friday from 9 am to 2 pm. Admission is 3.50 NIS. One of the entrances to the ramparts above is also through here.

To the Arabs this gate is known as Bab al-Amud (Gate of the Column), after a column – erected by the Roman Emperor Hadrian – which once stood in a square just inside the gate. This column is shown on the Madaba map, a Byzantine-era mosaic discovered in Jordan, a copy of which is on display in the Roman Square excavations. In Hebrew it's Sha'ar Shechem (Nablus Gate).

Herod's Gate It was just 100m east of this gate that the Crusaders breached the city walls on 15 July 1099. The name was derived from a mistaken belief held by 16th and 17th century pilgrims that one of the nearby buildings was once the palace of Herod the Great.

In Hebrew the gate is Sha'ar HaPerahim and in Arabic, Bab as-Zahra (Flower Gate).

St Stephen's Gate This is the gate which leads to the Mount of Olives and Gethsemane. From their positions on that biblically famed hillside, Israeli paratroopers fought their way through this gate on 7 June 1967 to capture the Old City.

Although Suleyman called it Bab al-Ghor (the Jordan Gate), the name never stuck and it became known as St Stephen's Gate after the first Christian martyr, who was stoned to death at a spot nearby. The Hebrew name, Sha'ar Ha'Arayot (Lions Gate), is a reference to the two pairs of heraldic lions carved either side of the archway.

Golden Gate Uncertainty surrounds this sealed entrance to the Haram ash-Sharif/Temple Mount. The Jewish Mishnah mentions the Temple's eastern gate and there are Herodian elements in the present structure. The gate was probably sealed by the Muslims in the 7th century to stop non-Muslims entering the Haram ash-Sharif/Temple Mount. An alternative version has it that the Arabs walled up the gate to spite those Jews who believe that this is the gate through which the Messiah will enter Jerusalem at the time of the Second Coming (Ezekiel 44:1-3).

Dung Gate In Hebrew this gate is Sha'ar HaAshpot. The popular theory as to how these two unflattering appellations came about is that at one time the area around the gate was the local rubbish dump. Its Arabic name is Bab al-Maghariba (Gate of the Moors) because North African immigrants lived nearby in the 16th century.

Presently the smallest of the city's gates, at one time it was even more diminutive. The Jordanians widened it during their tenure in the city in order to allow cars through. You can still make out traces of the original, narrower Ottoman arch.

Zion Gate This gate had to be punched through to give access to the Franciscan monastery left outside the walls by Suleyman's architects. During the 1948 War, Israeli soldiers holding Mt Zion also tried to burst through here in a desperate attempt to relieve the besieged Jewish Quarter. First they tried to dynamite the wall at a spot 100m east of the gate (it still bears the scar) and when that failed they launched an all-out assault which ended disastrously. A memorial plaque to the fallen is inset within the gate while the bullet-eaten facade gives some indication of how ferocious the fighting must have been.

To the Jews the gate is Sha'ar Ziyyon, while in Arabic it's Bab Haret al-Yahud (Gate of the Jewish Quarter).

Jaffa Gate The actual gate is the small block through which the doglegged pedestrian tunnel passes (the dogleg was to slow down charging enemy forces – you'll

ANDREW HUMPHREYS

The Jaffa Gate: the main point of contact between
Jerusalem's Old and New Cities

find the same thing at Damascus and Zion gates); the
breach in the wall through which the road now passes
was only made in 1898 in order to permit the visiting
Kaiser Wilhelm II and his party to ride with full pomp
into the city.

Just inside the gate, on the left as you enter, are two
graves said to be those of Suleyman's architects,
beheaded for leaving the Franciscan monastery outside
the walls.

The Arabic name for the gate is Bab al-Khalil (Gate of
the Friend), which refers to the holy city Hebron (Al-

GADI FARFOUR

Crowds bustle through the market surrounding the
Damascus Gate

Khalil in Arabic). In Hebrew it is Sha'ar Yafo because this
was the start of the old road to the historical port of Jaffa;
Yafo in Hebrew.

New Gate This is the most modern of all the gates,
opened in 1887 by Sultan Abdul Hamid to allow direct
access from the newly built pilgrim hospices to the holy
sites of the Old City's Christian Quarter. In Hebrew it's
Sha'ar HeHadash, and in Arabic, Bab al-Jadid.

Ramparts Walk

One of the best ways to see the Old City and its surroundings is to walk around the top of the walls.
Sections of the ramparts are as far as 15m above street
level and the views across the Old City rooftops are
superb. This walk will also enable you to make some
kind of sense of the layout of the place.

It's not a good idea to make the walk after rain or
especially after snow, as, despite new paving and guard-

rails, the stone can be slippery underfoot. In addition, women should not walk unaccompanied here at any time, as to do so would be to risk sexual assault and mugging.

It isn't possible to make a complete circuit of the wall because the Haram ash-Sharif/Temple Mount stretch is sealed off for security reasons. Instead the walk is in two sections: Jaffa Gate north to St Stephen's Gate (via New, Damascus and Herod's gates) and Jaffa Gate south to Dung Gate (via Zion Gate).

While you can descend at any of the gates, getting up onto the walls is only possible at two of them. At Jaffa Gate the stairs for the Damascus Gate walk are on the left as you enter the Old City, through an arch in the facade of the Golden Gate jewellery shop; the stairs for the Dung Gate stretch are outside the walls, 100m south of Jaffa Gate. At Damascus Gate the ramparts are reached by going through the Roman Square excavations (see the Damascus Gate section of Walls & Gates above).

The walls are open Saturday to Thursday from 9 am to 4 pm, and Friday and holiday eves from 9 am to 2 pm. The section from the Citadel to Zion Gate is open Sunday to Thursday until 9.30 pm. Tickets cost 8 NIS and are valid for four admissions over two days (three at the weekend), allowing you to do the combined 3.5 km walk gradually. Note that tickets cannot be purchased on Saturday.

Rooftop Promenade

For a different perspective on the Old City, climb the metal stairway on the corner of Habad St and St Mark's Rd (see map 14) or the steep stone stairs in the south-western corner of the Khan as-Sultan (see map 12), both of which lead onto the rooftops around the David St and Al-Wad markets. Come up in the day for a peek through the ventilation ducts at the bustle below, but also make a night-time visit to appreciate the Old City in moonlit silhouette.

The Citadel (Tower of David)

This is one of the country's most impressive restoration projects and a major museum complex, so it's worth paying a visit to the Citadel early in your stay for an excellent grounding in Jerusalem history.

The Citadel started life as the 1st century palace of Herod the Great. A megalomaniacal builder, Herod furnished his palace with three enormous towers, the largest of which was reputedly modelled on the Pharos of Alexandria, one of the seven wonders of the ancient world. The chiselled-block remains of one of the lesser towers still serve as the base of the Citadel's main keep. Following Herod's death the palace was used by the Roman procurators as their Jerusalem residence until it was largely destroyed by Jewish rebels in 66 AD. The Byzantines, who came along some 250 years later, mistook the mound of ruins for Mt Zion and presumed that this was David's palace – hence the name Tower of David. They constructed a new fortress on the site.

As Jerusalem changed hands, so did possession of the Citadel, passing to the invading Muslim armies and then to the Crusaders, who added the moat. It took on much of its present form in 1310 under the Mamluk Sultan Malik an-Nasir, with Suleyman the Great making further additions between 1531 and 1538. Suleyman is responsible for the gate by which the Citadel is now entered, and it was on the steps here that General Allenby accepted the surrender of the city on 9 December 1917, bringing to an end exactly 400 years of rule by the Ottoman Turks.

Fittingly for a site that acts as a microcosm of the city through the ages, the Citadel today also serves as the **Museum of the History of Jerusalem** (☎ 624 7111, or for the 24 hour information service ☎ 629 4411). Its numerous rooms contain some impressive dioramas and artefacts, holograms and videos which tell a version of the city's story. Visitors can follow one of four or five special signposted routes through the museum, including one for the disabled. One of the highlights is a detailed large-scale model of Jerusalem, made in the late 19th century and discovered almost 100 years later, forgotten in a Geneva warehouse. It's displayed in an underground chamber reached from the central courtyard garden.

The entrance to the Citadel is just inside Jaffa Gate. It's open Sunday to Thursday from 10 am to 5 pm, and Friday, Saturday and holiday eves from 10 am to 4 pm. Admission is 18 NIS (students 14 NIS). At 11 am daily there's a free guided tour in English.

Every important historical site in Israel seems to feel the need to put on a sound and light show and the Citadel joins the club with a production of questionable quality. The show is presented in English each Monday and Wednesday at 9.30 pm and in French each Monday at 10.30 pm. Wrap up well if you are going because Jerusalem evenings are often surprisingly cold, even in summer.

Haram ash-Sharif/Temple Mount

Dominating not just the Old City but in some ways the whole country, this vast esplanade has become a spiritual keystone to the Jewish and Muslim faiths and something of an obstacle to peace between the two peoples.

All three monotheistic faiths agree on the most holy nature of this place (ancient Mt Moriah on which Abraham was called to sacrifice his son in a test of his faith – Genesis 22:2-19), but in no way does a shared sense of sanctity translate into any form of kinship. Instead, the Mount (the closest spot on earth to paradise in Muslim lore) is surrounded by barbed wire and sharpshooters and patrolled by watchful flak-jacketed soldiers. Religious Jews still bristle at the presence of the Muslims on the site of Solomon's Temple (I Kings 5-8), destroyed by Nebuchadnezzar (II Kings 25) and replaced by the Second Temple which stood until its destruction by the Romans in 70 AD. Muslims, who have worshipped at their mosque here for 1300 years, rebuff all Jewish demands for access, seeing in them a further erosion of Palestinian rights in the face of Zionism. Periodically there are clashes at the gates, tear gas mists the air and more blood is spilt. The angel may have stayed the hand of Abraham but he's done far less well since.

For the uninvolved visitor, the Haram ash-Sharif (Noble Sanctuary in Arabic; the Jewish term is Har HaBayit, or Temple Mount) is a relaxing contrast to the noise and congestion of the surrounding narrow streets. An artificial platform built by Herod the Great when he enlarged the Second Temple, it's a flat paved area the size of a couple of adjacent football fields. Its edges are fringed with some attractive Mamluk-era buildings and at the south the older Al-Aqsa Mosque, while positioned at the centre is the Dome of the Rock. There are nine gates connecting the enclosure to the surrounding narrow streets, but although you can leave the compound by any of them, non-Muslims are only allowed to enter through two: Bab al-Maghariba (Gate of the Moors), reached from the Western Wall plaza, and Bab as-Silsila (Chain Gate), at the eastern end of Bab as-Silsila St.

Entrance to the Haram itself is free, but to visit the two mosques (highly recommended) and the museum, a ticket must be purchased for 22 NIS (students 12 NIS). Get the ticket from the ticket kiosk just inside the Bab al-Maghariba.

Visiting hours are slightly confusing as they are based around Muslim prayer schedules, which follow the

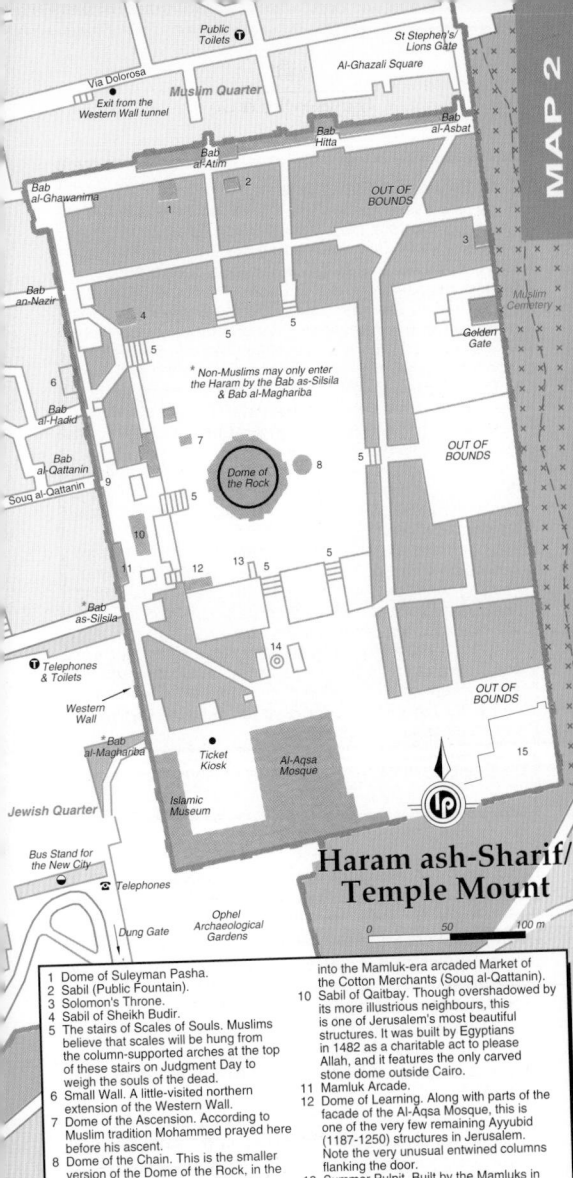

MAP 2

Public Toilets

St Stephen's Lions Gate

Al-Ghazali Square

Via Dolorosa
Exit from the Western Wall tunnel

Muslim Quarter

Bab al-Asbat

Bab al-Atim

Bab Hitta

Bab al-Ghawanima

OUT OF BOUNDS

Bab an-Nazir

Muslim Cemetery

Golden Gate

* Non-Muslims may only enter the Haram by the Bab as-Silsila & Bab al-Maghariba

Bab al-Hadid

Bab al-Qattanin

Souq al-Qattanin

Dome of the Rock

OUT OF BOUNDS

* Bab as-Silsila

Telephones & Toilets

Western Wall

* Bab al-Maghariba

OUT OF BOUNDS

Ticket Kiosk

Al-Aqsa Mosque

Jewish Quarter

Islamic Museum

Bus Stand for the New City

Telephones

Dung Gate

Ophel Archaeological Gardens

Haram ash-Sharif/ Temple Mount

0   50   100 m

1 Dome of Suleyman Pasha.
2 Sabil (Public Fountain).
3 Solomon's Throne.
4 Sabil of Sheikh Budir.
5 The stairs of Scales of Souls. Muslims believe that scales will be hung from the column-supported arches at the top of these stairs on Judgment Day to weigh the souls of the dead.
6 Small Wall. A little-visited northern extension of the Western Wall.
7 Dome of the Ascension. According to Muslim tradition Mohammed prayed here before his ascent.
8 Dome of the Chain. This is the smaller version of the Dome of the Rock, in the exact centre of the Haram. Mystery surrounds the reason for its construction. A popular theory is that it was a trial-run for the real thing; another is that it was the Haram's treasury. Its name comes from the legend that Solomon hung a chain from the dome and those who swore falsely whilst holding it were struck by lightning.
9 Gate of the Cotton Merchants. This is the most imposing of the Haram's gates. Make a point of departing through here

into the Mamluk-era arcaded Market of the Cotton Merchants (Souq al-Qattanin).
10 Sabil of Qaitbay. Though overshadowed by its more illustrious neighbours, this is one of Jerusalem's most beautiful structures. It was built by Egyptians in 1482 as a charitable act to please Allah, and it features the only carved stone dome outside Cairo.
11 Mamluk Arcade.
12 Dome of Learning. Along with parts of the facade of the Al-Aqsa Mosque, this is one of the very few remaining Ayyubid (1187-1250) structures in Jerusalem. Note the very unusual entwined columns flanking the door.
13 Summer Pulpit. Built by the Mamluks in the 14th century and renovated by the Ottomans, this was used to deliver outdoor sermons.
14 Al-Kas Fountain. One of many ablutions fountains on the Haram for the ritual washing before prayers.
15 Solomon's Stables. A cavernous vaulted hall under the Haram, constructed by the Crusaders to accommodate their horses. Unfortunately it's closed except by arrangement. This area is out of bounds.

The Jerusalem Syndrome

It is a recognised medical fact that exposure to Jerusalem can send a person mad. It happens to about 200 foreign visitors a year. Overwhelmed by the impact of the Holy City's historical and religious heritage people suddenly believe themselves to be characters from the Bible, like the Canadian Jew who, claiming to be Samson, decided to prove his ID by smashing through the wall of his room to escape. Or there was the elderly American Christian woman who believed she was the Virgin Mary and went to Bethlehem to look for the baby Jesus, inviting anyone who would listen to his birthday party. This sort of deluded behaviour has become a recognised phenomenon known as the Jerusalem Syndrome.

Although many of these individuals arrived at Ben-Gurion airport with a recorded history of mental aberration, about a quarter of those cases on file had no previous psychiatric record.

In perhaps the most serious case so far, in 1969 an Australian Christian fanatic set fire to Al-Aqsa Mosque, causing considerable damage. He believed that he had to clear the Haram ash-Sharif/Temple Mount of non-Christian buildings to prepare for the Messiah. More recently, in spring 1992 a US Christian went into a violent rage in the Church of the Holy Sepulchre and before the security guards were able to subdue him, he had smashed lamps and icons and torn down the cross marking the traditional site of the crucifixion of Jesus.

The Jerusalem Syndrome is nothing new. In the 1930s, an English Christian woman was certain that Christ's

lunar calendar. Basically, the Haram is open Saturday to Thursday (closed Friday) from 8 am to 3 pm, although those inside by then are allowed to stay until 4 pm. During prayers (approximately from 11.30 am to 12.30 pm in winter and 12.30 to 1.30 pm in summer) the museum shuts and entry to the mosques is for Muslims only. Note also that during the month of Ramadan (see the Public Holidays section in the Facts for the Visitor chapter for dates) the Haram is only open from 7.30 to 10 am. It is completely closed on Muslim holidays such as the Eid.

Visitors must be suitably dressed. Long robes are available for those with bare legs and arms, but you should dress appropriately out of respect. As well as patrols of Israeli Defence Force (IDF) soldiers and Palestinian police to keep the peace there are plain-clothed Muslim guards monitoring decency and couples will be accosted if they so much as hold hands.

Second Coming was imminent and would regularly climb Mt Scopus to welcome him back to earth with a cup of tea.

Christian sufferers of the syndrome tend to break down at such traditional sites as the Mount of Olives, the Via Dolorosa or the Garden Tomb, and identify with such characters as Jesus or the Virgin Mary, although John the Baptist is apparently the most popular choice. In addition to Samson, 'incarnations' of Jewish sufferers have included Moses and King David.

As with everything else in Israel, opinions vary on what causes the syndrome. It's been suggested that these are people who have arrived in Israel hoping to find peace and calm, possibly looking for an escape from some kind of turmoil back home, and when instead they encounter the conflict and tension that underlies life in Jerusalem, their minds snap. Although the ages and backgrounds vary, a significant proportion of those afflicted with the syndrome are unmarried 20 to 30 year old Christians or Jews from North America and Western Europe who grew up in religious homes. Men seem to outnumber women two to one.

Most of the syndrome sufferers wind up at the state psychiatric hospital, Kfar Shaul, on the outskirts of West Jerusalem. Treatment tends to take the form of observation until the patient is deemed well enough to be flown home. In most cases, this takes a week or so. Doctors at Kfar Shaul have found it virtually pointless to try to persuade the deluded that they are not who they claim to be. The hospital cites the example of two patients, both claiming to be the Messiah. Put together, each accused the other of being the impostor. ■

In addition, certain unmarked areas are strictly off-limits and if you stray, even unintentionally, you will be lectured and perhaps even arrested. Stay away from the sides of the Al-Aqsa Mosque, the Solomon's Stables corner and the garden on the eastern side.

The self-appointed guides can also be a complete nuisance. They often approach with an official bearing and ask to see your ticket, then with it in hand they'll lead you over to one or other of the mosques while launching into a historical spiel; if you hadn't planned on taking a guide then stop them fast. Their other trick is to fluster people by saying, 'Quick, quick the mosque is closing, you have to hurry to see it'; of course they attach themselves to explain everything 'quick, quick'. Simply don't hand over your ticket to anyone but the guy at the door, who is also the person to ask about closing times. Note that in addition to removing your footwear to enter the mosques, all bags and cameras

The magnificent Dome of the Rock

must be left outside, too – leave someone on watch, as Lonely Planet has received letters advising of thefts.

For best effect, visit the uninspiring Islamic Museum and understated Al-Aqsa Mosque before you visit the spectacular Dome of the Rock.

Islamic Museum Although there are some interesting objects in here they are so badly displayed and labelled that most visitors have little incentive to linger for more than a few minutes. However, admission is included in the price of your ticket to the mosques, so you might as well take a look. Exhibits include ornate architectural pieces from various mosques, weaponry, textiles, ceramics, Qur'ans, glassware and coins.

Al-Aqsa Mosque While the Dome of the Rock serves more as a masthead than a mosque, Al-Aqsa is a functioning house of worship, accommodating up to 5000 praying supplicants at a time.

Believed by some to be a converted 6th century Byzantine church, Muslims maintain that Al-Aqsa was built from scratch from 705 to 715 AD by the son of Abd al-Malik, patron of the Dome. Clarification of the issue is complicated because nothing much remains from the original structure, which was twice destroyed by earthquakes in its first 60 years. What is sure is that the mosque was largely rebuilt in the 10th century, while the facade was remodelled by the Ayyubids (1187-1250). The present-day structure is a conglomeration of restorations and rebuildings, with columns donated, strangely enough, by Benito Mussolini and the elaborately painted ceilings courtesy of Egypt's King Farouk. The intricately carved *mihrab* (prayer niche indicating the direction of Mecca), however, does date from the time of Saladin, as did an equally magnificent carved wooden pulpit which was lost in a 1969 fire started by a deranged Australian Christian.

Dome of the Rock Enclosing the sacred rock upon which Abraham prepared to sacrifice his son and from which, according to Islamic tradition, the Prophet Mohammed launched himself heavenward to take his place alongside Allah, the Dome was built between 688 and 691, making it one of the oldest surviving Islamic monuments in existence. Its patron was the Umayyad Caliph Abd al-Malik. His motives were shrewd as well as pious – the caliph was concerned that the imposing Christian Church of the Holy Sepulchre was seducing Arab minds.

In asserting the supremacy of Islam, Abd al-Malik had his Byzantine architects take as their model the rotunda of the Holy Sepulchre. But not for the Muslims the dark, gloomy interiors or austere stone facades of the Christian structures; instead their mosque was covered, both inside and out, with a bright confection of mosaics and scrolled verses from the Qur'an, while the crowning dome was covered in solid gold that shone as a beacon for Islam.

A plaque was laid inside honouring Al-Malik and giving the date of construction. Two hundred years later the Abbasid Caliph al-Mamun altered this to claim credit for himself but neglected to amend the original date.

During the reign of Suleyman the Great the original, badly deteriorated, exterior mosaics were removed and replaced. They were renewed again in 1963. The gold dome also disappeared long ago, melted down to pay off some caliph's debts. The present convincing anodised aluminium dome has been financed by Gulf State Arab countries. Essentially, however, what you see today is the building as conceived by Abd al-Malik, very little changed since its completion.

Inside, lying central under the 20m high dome and ringed by a wooden fence, is the rock from which Mohammed began his Night Journey (his footprint is supposedly visible in one corner). Muslim tradition also has it that this is the foundation stone of the world.

Mamluk Buildings Make a point of strolling around the northern section of the Haram to admire the facades on the northern and western sides. Mainly religious schools, these buildings feature some delightfully ornate stonework. See Mamluk Buildings in the Muslim Quarter section for more information.

Western Wall

In stark contrast to the gaudy magnificence of the Muslim's Dome of the Rock, the Western Wall (in Hebrew, HaKotel HaMa'aravi or just HaKotel) is nothing more than a bare stone wall. However, it still manages to be one of the most captivating places in all of Jerusalem.

It is part of the retaining wall built by Herod the Great in 20 BC to contain the landfill on which the Second Temple compound stood. The Romans destroyed the Temple in 70 AD but since, according to rabbinical texts, the *shechina* (divine presence) never deserted the wall it's regarded as the most holy of all Jewish sites. The Wall grew as a place of pilgrimage during the Ottoman period

God's Fax Line
Courtesy of Israel's national phone company, Bezek, the pious can now fax the Almighty. Messages received on fax 561 2222 are collected and once a day, Shabbat excepted, taken by telephone company employees down to the Western Wall to be wedged in between the stones. Bezek says that over 100 messages a day are received – more during Jewish holidays. Nothing is charged for the service. ■

where Jews would come to mourn and lament their ancient loss – hence the term the Wailing Wall. At this time houses pressed right up to the wall, leaving just a narrow alley for prayer. (This scene was evocatively portrayed in 1932 by the Russian Jewish artist Marc Chagall – the painting is now held by the Tel Aviv Museum of Art.)

In 1948 the Jews lost access when the whole of the Old City was taken by the Jordanians. Nineteen years later when Israeli paratroopers stormed in during the Six Day War they fought their way directly to the Wall. Their first action on securing the Old City was to bulldoze the neighbouring Arab quarter to create the plaza that exists today.

The area immediately in front of the Wall now operates as a great open-air synagogue. It's divided into two areas, a small southern section for women and a more active, larger northern section for men. Here the black-garbed Hasidim rock backwards and forwards on their heels, bobbing their heads in prayer, occasionally breaking off to press themselves against the Wall and kiss the stones. To celebrate the arrival of Shabbat there is always a large crowd at sunset on Friday and students from the nearby Yeshiva HaKotel shuffle down to dance and sing. The Wall is also a popular site for bar mitzvahs, held on Shabbat or on Monday and Thursday mornings.

The fascination extends beyond the Jewish world. Madonna visited, as did Michael Jackson one Saturday in 1993. His visit in particular raised the ire of the ortho-dox because of the accompanying entourage of camera-clicking press corps (photography is forbidden on the Shabbat). Nevertheless, non-Jewish visitors who dress modestly and, in the case of men, don the compli-mentary *yarmulke* are permitted to approach the Wall.

Notice the different styles of stonework. The huge lower layers are the Herodian stones, identifiable by their carved edges, while the strata above that, which are chiselled slightly differently, date from the time of the

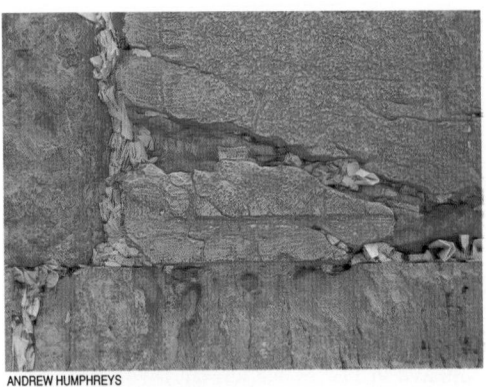

ANDREW HUMPHREYS

Prayers wedged between the bricks of the Western Wall

construction of the Al-Aqsa Mosque. Also visible at close quarters are the wads of paper, from Post-It notes to half-exercise books, stuffed into the cracks: it's a belief that prayers inserted into the Wall have a better than average chance of being answered.

The Wall is accessible 24 hours a day, and admission is free. We very much recommend that you see the place bathed in moonlight.

Wilson's Arch Situated to the north of the men's prayer section, this arch (now inside a room) carries Bab as-Silsila St above to the Haram ash-Sharif/Temple Mount across the former Tyropoeon (Cheesemaker's) Valley. It was once used by priests on their way to the Temple. Look down the two illuminated shafts to get an idea of the wall's original height. Possibly Hasmonean (150 to 40 BC) but at least Herodian, the room's function is unknown. Women can reach this room via an archway west of the men's area, near the telephones. Theoretically, the arch room is open Sunday, Tuesday and Wednesday from 8.30 am to 3 pm, Monday and Thursday from 12.30 to 3 pm, and Friday from 8.30 am to noon, closed Saturday.

Jewish Quarter

Roughly defined as the area south of Bab as-Silsila St and east of Habad St, the Jewish Quarter is an area you'll recognise immediately by its scrubbed stone, the neat, precise edges, and the air of no-one being home.

GREG ALFORD

The graceful arch of Hurva Synagogue

Flattened during the fighting in 1948, the Jewish Quarter has been almost entirely reconstructed since its recapture by the Israelis in 1967. Though modern, the architecture of the quarter is traditional in style, designed to maintain the character of the Old City, though lacking a little in spirit.

There are few historic monuments above ground level but the digging that went on during construction unearthed a number of interesting archaeological finds, some of which date back to the time of the First Temple (around 1000 to 586 BC). Everything is well signposted, and while there's nothing unmissable, the area around the Quarter Cafe is very pleasant and there are great views of the Haram ash-Sharif/Temple Mount and Western Wall from the stairs beside the Church of St Maria.

The Cardo Cutting a broad north-south swath, this is the reconstructed main street of Roman and Byzantine Jerusalem, the Cardo Maximus. At one time it would have run the whole breadth of the city, up to what's now Damascus Gate, but in its present form it stops just south of David St, the tourist souq. It serves as the main entry into the Jewish Quarter from the Muslim and Christian areas.

As depicted on the 6th century **Madaba map** of the Old City (which you can see at the Roman Square excavations), the Cardo would have been a wide colonnaded avenue flanked by roofed arcades. A part of it to the south has been restored to something like its original appearance while the rest has been reconstructed as an arcade of expensive gift stores and galleries of Judaica. There are wells to allow visitors to see down to the levels beneath the street where there are strata of wall from the era of the First and Second Temples.

Upstairs, above one of the Cardo galleries, is a permanent exhibition called **One Last Day**. This is a set of photographs taken by John Phillips, on assignment for *Life* magazine, on the day the Jewish Quarter fell to the Jordanians in 1948. The exhibition can be viewed Sunday to Thursday from 9 am to 5 pm, and Friday from 9 am to 1 pm, closed Saturday. Admission is 4 NIS.

Broad Wall Just east of the Cardo and north of Hurva Square, looking like a derelict lot between blank-faced apartment blocks, is a stretch of crumbling masonry known as the Broad Wall. This is actually an exposed portion of the remains of a fortified stone wall dating from the time of King Hezekiah (circa 701 BC).

Israelite Tower & Rachel Ben-Zvi Centre Buried beneath a modern apartment block on Shone HaLakhot St and reached by a short flight of steps, the Israelite Tower is a gate tower from the time of the Babylonian siege and destruction of the First Temple (roughly 580 BC). The site is open Sunday to Thursday from 9 am to 5 pm, and Friday from 9 am to 2 pm. Admission is 4 NIS, which also covers entry to the Burnt House and the Wohl Archaeological Museum (see below).

Across from the Israelite Tower, the Rachel Ben-Zvi Centre (☎ 628 3448), also on Shone HaLakhot St, exhibits a scale model of Jerusalem in the First Temple period, which illustrates archaeological findings from the period of King David and his followers. Other exhibits include an audiovisual history of the city from 1000 to 586 BC.

The centre is open to visitors Sunday to Thursday from 9 am to 4 pm, and on Friday by appointment only. Admission is 8 NIS (students 6 NIS).

Hurva Square & Synagogues Hurva Square is the tree-shaded social centre of the Jewish Quarter. It's easily identifiable by a lone single-brick arch, almost all that remains of the **Hurva Synagogue**. The synagogue was originally dedicated by the Ashkenazi community in 1864 but was destroyed by the Jordanians in 1948. On regaining control of the Old City in 1967, the Jews decided to rebuild their place of worship but, despite a succession of plans being submitted by various renowned architects, no agreement on how to proceed could be reached. The re-creation of one of the arches that supported the synagogue dome was as far as the matter got.

Adjoining the Hurva Synagogue is the **Ramban Synagogue**, its name an acronym for Rabbi Moshe Ben Nahman. The synagogue was established here in 1400 in a stable bought from an Arab landlord, but problems started when a mosque (the minaret of which still stands) was built nearby. The upshot was that in 1588 the Jews were banned from worship and the synagogue was converted into a workshop. It was reinstated as a house of worship only in 1967, some 380 years later.

South of Hurva Square, on HaTupim St, are four **Sephardic Synagogues**, two of which date back at least as far as the 16th century. In accordance with a law of the time that stated that synagogues could not be taller than neighbouring buildings, this grouping was sunk deep into the ground – a measure which certainly saved the buildings from destruction during the bombardment of the quarter in 1948. Instead, the synagogues were looted by the Jordanians and then used as sheep pens. They have been restored using the remains of Italian synagogues damaged during WWII and are back in use for morning and evening services. The synagogues are open Sunday to Thursday from 9.30 am to 4 pm, and Friday from 9.30 am to 12.30 pm. There is a small admission fee.

Batei Mahseh Square & Shelter Houses Batei Mahseh was at one time the quarter's largest square, presided over by the **Rothschild building**, a grand old thing built in 1871 with funds provided by Baron Wilhelm von Rothschild of Frankfurt – the family emblem is visible, engraved on the upper part of the facade. The building now houses the offices of the Company for the Reconstruction and Development of the Jewish Quarter.

The Shelter Houses facing the Old City walls on Batei Mahseh St were built by Jews from Germany and Holland for the poor of the quarter. Little or no rent was charged and tenants were chosen by lottery. During the last fortnight of the battle for the quarter in May 1948, hundreds of resident Jews also found shelter in their basements.

St Maria of the Germans Located on the northern side of the steps leading to the Western Wall, this was formerly a complex of a church, a hospital and a hospice, built by German Knights Hospitallers around 1128. When archaeologists first unearthed these remains in the

1970s there were demands from the ultraorthodox Jewish community to have them destroyed because they objected to the existence of a church on a major route to the Western Wall.

Museums Perhaps the Jewish Quarter's most impressive complex is the **Wohl Archaeological Museum** (☎ 628 3448), which details the lavish lifestyle enjoyed in the Jewish neighbourhood of Herod's city. Exhibits include frescoes, stucco reliefs, mosaic floors, ornaments, furniture and household objects. It's open Sunday to Thursday from 9 am to 5 pm, and Friday from 9 am to 1 pm, closed Saturday. Admission is 4 NIS, which also covers entry to the Israelite Tower and the Burnt House.

The **Burnt House** (☎ 628 7211), next to the Quarter Cafe, is the reconstruction of a luxurious house in what was the Upper City of the Second Temple era. There's also an audiovisual show presented in a number of different languages, including English. The Burnt House has the same opening hours as the Wohl Archaeological Museum and one ticket is good for the two.

Following the same idea but jumping way forward in time, the **Old Yishuv Court Museum** (☎ 628 4636) at 6 Or HaChaim St (west of the Cardo) is a reconstructed house in which each room illustrates an aspect of Jewish life in the quarter before the destruction of 1948. It's open Sunday to Thursday from 9 am to 2 pm. Admission is 4 NIS (students 2.50 NIS).

Of more limited interest is the **Siebenberg House** (☎ 628 2341), a private residence with excavations in the basement. Finds include a Hasmonean cistern and parts of what may have been an aqueduct that carried water from Solomon's Pools to the Temple. The Siebenberg House is at 35 Misgav Ladakh St (on the corner of HaGittit St) and is open by appointment only.

Jerusalem – a Multi-Media Presentation at 1 Jewish Quarter Rd, near the car park, is a 35 minute audiovisual history of the city aimed squarely at Jewish visitors. If you're looking for some objectivity look elsewhere. Screening times for the English-language version are 11 am, 2 and 5 pm, from Sunday to Thursday.

Muslim Quarter

This is the most teeming and densely populated area of the Old City with some 26,000 inhabitants – twice as many as the three other quarters combined. Depending on your tastes it's either claustrophobic and a hassle, or completely exhilarating. Enter the melee at permanently congested Damascus Gate, squeezing by a tractor and

TONY WHEELER

St Anne's Church stands on the site traditionally believed to be the home of the Virgin Mary's parents

dodging the young Arab boys riding their vendors' carts down the slope. About 100m in the street forks, and there is a busy felafel stall wedged between the two prongs. Bearing to the left is Al-Wad Rd, lined with vast showrooms of brass items such as coffee pots and trays, in among sweet shops, vegetable stalls and an egg stall. This route leads directly to the Western Wall, along the way crossing the Via Dolorosa. The section of the Via Dolorosa heading uphill to the west (right) is crowded with Christian pilgrims, tour groups and shoppers battling for right of way. Souvenir shops line the route, with ceramics a speciality. Bearing to the right at the fork is Souq Khan as-Zeit St, which is even busier than Al-Wad Rd. It's lined with fruit, vegetable, sweet, hardware and oriental spice and nut shops.

St Anne's Church Constructed in a restrained and elegant Romanesque style, St Anne's is generally agreed to be the finest example of Crusader architecture in

Jerusalem. Its popularity with pilgrims, however, has more to do with the tradition that the building's crypt is the site of the home of Joachim and Anne, the parents of the Virgin Mary. Next to the church are some impressive ruins which surround the biblical Pool of Bethesda.

The Crusaders built the church in 1140, at the same time constructing a small adjacent chapel with a stairway leading down to the pool beside which Jesus is supposed to have healed a sick man (John 5:1-18). When Jerusalem fell to the armies of Saladin, St Anne's became a Muslim theological school – an inscription still to be seen above the church's entrance testifies to this. Successive rulers allowed the church to fall into decay, and by the 18th century it was roof-deep in refuse. In 1856 the Ottoman Turks presented the church to France in gratitude for its support in the Crimean War against Russia, and it was reclaimed from the garbage heap.

Apart from its architectural beauty, the church is noted for its acoustics, and a prominent sign requests that only hymns be used for sound checks.

St Anne's is just off the Via Dolorosa, a short distance west of St Stephen's/Lion's Gate. It is open Monday to Saturday from 8 am to noon and 2 to 6 pm (winter 2 to 5 pm), closed Sunday. Admission is 3 NIS. The entrance is marked 'St Anne – Peres Blanc'; do not use the other door marked 'Religious Birthplace of Mary'.

Ecce Homo Arch & the Convent of the Sisters of Zion
East of Al-Wad Rd an arch punctured by two windows spans the Via Dolorosa. This is the 19th century echo of an arch that was the eastern gate of the city during Roman times. The lower portion of the original Roman arch is preserved in the church belonging to the adjacent Convent of the Sisters of Zion. It's thought that the structure would have been a triumphal arch with a high portal in the middle flanked by two smaller gateways; the remains in the church are of one of the smaller arches (the bit spanning the street outside was designed to imitate the arc of the main central arch). The arch is traditionally, if improbably, the place where Pilate took Jesus out and proclaimed, 'This is the man' ('Ecce homo') – improbably, because the arch wasn't constructed until the time of Hadrian, some 100 years after the Crucifixion.

The convent church is open Monday to Saturday from 8.30 am to 12.30 pm and 2 to 5 pm, closed Sunday. Admission is free.

Next door, and the property of the Greek Orthodox Church, is a basement chapel known as the **Prison of**

Christ, which is supposedly the site of the hewn-rock cellars where Jesus and other criminals of the day were held.

Mamluk Buildings Overshadowed by the splendours of the Haram ash-Sharif/Temple Mount, and clustered outside its northern and western walls, are some excellent examples from the golden age of Islamic architecture. This area was developed during the era of the Mamluks (1250 to 1517), a dynasty of soldier-slaves ruling out of Egypt. They drove the Crusaders out of Palestine and Syria and followed this up with an equally impressive campaign of construction, consolidating Islam's presence in the Levant with masses of mosques, *madrasas* (theological schools), hostels, monasteries and mausoleums. Their buildings are typically characterised by the banding of red and white stone (a technique known as *ablaq*) and by the elaborate carvings and patterning around windows and in the recessed portals.

All of these features are exhibited in the **Palace of the Lady Tunshuq**, built in 1388 and found halfway down Aqabat at-Takiya – 150m east of the Tabasco Hostel & Tearooms. The facade is badly eroded but the uppermost of the three large doorways still has some beautiful inlaid marblework, while a recessed window is decorated with another Mamluk trademark, the stone 'stalactites' known as *muqarnas*. The palace complex now serves as workshops and an orphanage. Opposite is the **Tomb of the Lady Tunshuq** (1398).

Continue downhill to the junction with Al-Wad Rd, passing on your right, just before the corner, the last notable piece of Mamluk architecture built in Jerusalem, the **Ribat Bayram Jawish** (1540), a one-time pilgrims' hospice. Compare this with the buildings on Tariq Bab an-Nazir St, straight across Al-Wad Rd, which are Jerusalem's earliest Mamluk structures, built in the 1260s before the common use of ablaq. This street is named after the gate at the end which leads through into the Haram ash-Sharif/Temple Mount, but non-Muslims may not enter here.

Some 100m south on Al-Wad Rd, opposite the Old City Restaurant, is **Tariq Bab al-Hadid St**; it looks uninviting but wander down, through the archway, and enter a street entirely composed of majestic Mamluk structures. Three of the four facades belong to madrasas dating from 1358 to 1440, while the single-storey building is a *ribat*, or hospice, from 1293. The last archway on the left gives access to the Small Wall (see that section below), while the green gate at the end of the street leads into the Haram; again, non-Muslims may not enter here.

Via Dolorosa

Winding up first through the Muslim Quarter and then the Christian Quarter, the Via Dolorosa, or Way of Sorrows, is the route that Jesus took as he carried his cross to Calvary. The sanctity of the modern-day pilgrims' route, however, is based purely on faith, not fact.

The history of the Via Dolorosa can be traced back to the days when Byzantine pilgrims, on the night of Holy Thursday, would go in procession from Gethsemane to Calvary along roughly the same route as today's Via Dolorosa, although there were no official devotional stops en route. By the 8th century, some stops had become customary but the route had changed considerably and now went from Gethsemane around the outside of the city walls to Caiaphas' house on Mt Zion, then to the Praetorium of Pilate at St Sophia near the Temple and eventually to the Holy Sepulchre.

In the Middle Ages, with Latin Christianity divided into two camps, the Via Dolorosa was twinned – each of the two claimed routes primarily visiting chapels belonging to either one or the other faction. In the 14th century, the Franciscans devised a walk of devotion that included some of the present-day stations but had as its starting point the Holy Sepulchre. This became the standard route for nearly two centuries but it was eventually modified by the desire of European pilgrims to follow the order of events of the gospels, finishing at the site of the Crucifixion rather than beginning there.

Historians, however, point to one devastating flaw in the routing of the Via Dolorosa, which is that it's more likely that Jesus was condemned to death by Pilate on the other side of the city at the Citadel, next to Jaffa Gate. This was Herod's palace and Pilate's place of residence when in Jerusalem. Various Bible references to the trial taking place on a platform and in the open support this theory, as the palace is known to have had such a structure. Hence, a more probable route for Jesus to have taken would be east along David St, north through the Butchers' Market of today, and then west to Golgotha. ∎

TONY WHEELER

Stations of the Cross

Every Friday at 3 pm, the Franciscan Fathers lead a cross-bearing procession taking in the Stations of the Cross which attracts many pilgrims, tourists and souvenir hawkers. See the Via Dolorosa map (Map 3), and the Church of the Holy Sepulchre map (Map 4), on pages 125 and 133 respectively, for the locations of the 14 stations.

1st Station Supposedly the spot where Jesus was tried, the 1st station is actually inside the working Islamic Al-Omariyeh College. The entrance is the door at the top of the ramp on the southern side of the Via Dolorosa, east of the Ecce Homo Arch. Entry is not always permitted so don't be surprised if you are asked to leave. There is nothing of official Christian value to see anyway, although there is a great view of the Haram ash-Sharif/Temple Mount through the barred windows on the upper level.

2nd Station Commemorating the condemnation of Jesus and his receiving the cross, the 2nd station is in the Franciscan Church of the Condemnation. The Chapel of Flagellation to the right is where he is said to have been flogged. Built in 1929, the design on the domed ceiling incorporates the crown of thorns, and the windows of the chapel around the altar show the mob who witnessed the event. The church and chapel are open April to September, daily from 8 am to noon and 2 to 6 pm; and October to March, daily from 8 am to 5 pm. Admission is free.

3rd Station This is the point at which the Via Dolorosa joins up with Al-Wad Rd and it's where Jesus fell for the first time. Adjacent to the entrance of the Armenian Catholic Patriarchate Hospice, the station is marked by a small Polish chapel.

4th Station Beyond the hospice, next to the Armenian Church (the wonderfully named Our Lady of the Spasm), this station marks the spot where Jesus faced his mother in the crowd of onlookers. There is a mosaic of a pair of sandals inlaid in the church courtyard which supposedly marks the spot on which Mary stood as Jesus passed by.

5th Station As Al-Wad Rd continues south towards the Western Wall, the Via Dolorosa breaks off to climb to the west; right on the corner is the spot where the Romans ordered Simon the Cyrene to help Jesus carry the cross. It is marked by signs around a door.

6th Station Further along the street, on the left-hand side and easy to miss, is the place where Veronica wiped Jesus' face with a cloth. The Greek Orthodox Patriarchate in the Christian Quarter displays what is claimed to be the cloth, which shows the imprint of a face.

7th Station This is where Jesus fell a second time and it's marked by signs on the wall on the west of Souq Khan as-Zeit St, the main market street at the top of this section of the Via Dolorosa. In the 1st century, this was the edge of the city and a gate led out to the countryside, a fact which supports the claim that the Church of the Holy Sepulchre is the genuine location of Jesus' crucifixion, burial and resurrection.

8th Station This is another station easy to miss. Cut straight across Souk Khan as-Zeit St from the Via Dolorosa and ascend Aqabat al-Khanqah St. Just past the Greek Orthodox Convent on the left is the stone and Latin cross marking where Jesus told some women to cry for themselves and their children, not for him.

9th Station Come back down to where the Via Dolorosa and Aqabat al-Khanqah St meet and turn right (south, away from Damascus Gate) along Souq Khan as-Zeit St. Head up the stairway on your right and follow the path round to the Coptic Church. The remains of a column in its door mark the spot where Jesus fell the third time.

Retrace your steps to the main street and head for the Church of the Holy Sepulchre; the remaining five stations are inside – see the Church of the Holy Sepulchre map (Map 4).

10th Station As you enter the church, head up the steep stairway immediately to your right. The chapel at the top is divided into two naves. The right one belongs to the Franciscans, the left to the Greek Orthodox. At the entrance to the Franciscan Chapel is the 10th station where Jesus was stripped of his clothes.

11th Station Still in the chapel, this is where Jesus was nailed to the cross.

12th Station The Greek Orthodox Chapel is the site of Jesus' crucifixion.

13th Station Between the 11th and 12th stations is where the body of Jesus was taken down and handed to Mary.

14th Station This is the Holy Sepulchre, the Tomb of Jesus. Walk down the narrow stairs beyond the Greek Orthodox Chapel to the ground floor and you will see that the Holy Sepulchre is to be found in the centre of the rotunda, which would be on your left if you were entering from outside. The actual tomb is inside the Sepulchre. Candles lit by pilgrims who make a donation dominate the small tomb, with the raised marble slab covering the rock on which Jesus' body was laid. Around the back of the Holy Sepulchre is the tiny Coptic Chapel where pilgrims kiss the wall of the tomb, encouraged by a priest who expects a donation. See the Christian Quarter section in this chapter for more information about the Church of the Holy Sepulchre.

ANDREW HUMPHREYS

The Souq al-Qattanin Gate features muqarnas (stone
stalactites) and ablaq (bands of different hued stone),
typical of Mamluk structures

Back on Al-Wad Rd, continuing south the road passes
the Souq al-Qattanin (see that section below) and then,
on the left, Sabil Suleyman (see below). It terminates in
a police checkpoint at the mouth of the tunnel down to
the Western Wall plaza. However, the stairs to the left
lead up to the busy Bab as-Silsila St and the Bab as-Silsila
Gate, one of the two ways into the Haram for non-
Muslims. Just before the gate is the tiny kiosk-like **Tomb
of Turkan Khatun** (1352) with a facade adorned with
uncommonly asymmetrical carved geometric designs.
Earlier this century the tomb served as a stall for a
lemonade seller.

Look out also for the restored **Khan as-Sultan**, a 14th
century *caravanserai* (travellers' inn and stables) at the

top end of Bab as-Silsila St. A discreet entrance just up from the large 'Gali' sign leads into a courtyard surrounded by workshops and from a staircase tucked in the left-hand corner as you enter you can climb up to the Old City rooftops.

Souq al-Qattanin Founded on the remains of a Crusader market, the Mamluks built this tunnel-like arcade in the mid-14th century. Almost 100m long, it has 50 shops on the ground floor with residential quarters above. The name means 'market of the cotton merchants'. Sadly, little trade goes on here now and most of the former stores and workshops are just used for warehousing. The complex also included two *hammams* (public baths), one of which is undergoing restoration and may at some future point open to visitors.

Sabil Suleyman This is one of several *sabils* (drinking fountains) erected by the Ottoman Sultan Suleyman in 1536-37. As well as refreshing the populace, the fountains were used for the ritual ablutions that have to be

---

There Goes the Neighbourhood

On Al-Wad Rd, a little south of the fork with Souq Khan as-Zeit St in the heart of the Muslim Quarter, a broad arch bridges the street and from one of its windows hangs a bed-sheet-size Israeli flag. This is the controversial home of the hawkish Israeli politician and war hero Ariel Sharon. In a widely publicised move, Sharon purchased the property as a statement of his belief that Jews should be able to live anywhere within Israel. His lead inspired the formation of Ateret Kohanim, an organisation dedicated to Judaising the Old City, through purchases of property (often covertly) in predominantly Muslim areas.

The majority of less extremist Jews, it should be noted, regard this settlement as needlessly aggressive and Ateret Kohanim do not enjoy widespread support. Nevertheless, Palestinians have little choice but to live with it, and a round-the-clock detachment of IDF soldiers lounges around the doorway of Beit Sharon to see that they do so quietly. Ironically, Sharon doesn't actually live here, underscoring the fact that his purchase of the property was nothing more than a provocative gesture.

It's also illuminating to note that prior to Sharon's occupation, the Israeli government had forbidden an Arab family to move into the Jewish Quarter of the Old City to reclaim an ancestral plot, citing as a reason that it would disturb the homogeneity of the neighbourhood. ■

performed before a Muslim prays. Suleyman's other existing sabils are beside the Bab as-Silsila gate, at the junction of Bab an-Nazir and Al-Wad Sts, on the Haram ash-Sharif/Temple Mount, and outside the city walls just south of Sultan's Pool.

Small Wall This site, also known as the Hidden Wall, is at the end of the last narrow passageway off Tariq Bab al-Hadid St. It is marked by a small sign, visible from Al-Wad Rd where Tariq Bab al-Hadid St begins. This section of wall, now part of a Muslim house, is the same Western Wall that thousands of Jews flock to a few hundred metres to the south. The Arabs living here don't seem to mind the traffic of visitors and have provided an outside light on their 1st floor to enable Jews to read their prayers.

Zalatimo's A sweet shop famed for its pancakes and sticky confectionery, this place is also well-known because its back room opens onto the remains of the original entrance to the Church of the Holy Sepulchre.

Christian Quarter

This quarter houses churches, monasteries and other religious institutions belonging to more than 20 different Christian sects, all subject to the pull of the Holy Sepulchre.

As you enter from Jaffa Gate, the first two streets to the left – Latin Patriarchate Rd and Greek Catholic Patriarchate Rd – indicate the tone of the neighbourhood, named as they are after the offices there. The roads lead to St Francis St, and in this quiet area around New Gate the local Christian hierarchy resides in comfort.

Elsewhere in the Quarter, comfort and quiet give way to the chaos and crush of the tourist bazaars. Descending from Omar ibn al-Khattab Square into the heart of the Old City, **David St** is the main tourist trap, where visitors to the Holy City are victim to a barrage of persistent sales patter offering all manner of kitschy objects that no-one could conceivably ever have any use for. Branching north off David St, **Christian Quarter Rd** deals in a better class of souvenir with an emphasis on religious icons. South-east of the Church of the Holy Sepulchre, the **Muristan Market** is usually less crowded than the other markets and specialises in leather goods, clothes and carpets.

Towards the bottom end David St switches over to food – a row of cavernous vaults on the left with fruit and vegetable stalls inside date from the time of the

Crusades. The street ends by crashing into a trio of narrow alleyways which, if followed to the left, converge into Souq Khan as-Zeit St, one of the main thoroughfares of the Muslim Quarter. The squeamish should avoid the first of these narrow alleys, Souq al-Lahamin, the **Butchers' Market**. Followed to the right, Souq Khan as-Zeit becomes the Cardo and leads into the Jewish Quarter.

Church of the Holy Sepulchre Despite being the central shrine of Christianity, this church is much less distinctive than something like the Dome of the Rock or the Western Wall, and it happens that many people wander in and out without any idea of what they've just visited. Then again, many who do arrive in full knowledge of what the church represents often leave sorely disappointed. Hemmed in by a bunch of other buildings, from outside the church has no visual impact while inside it is dark, cramped and noisy. In his book *Winner Takes All*, author Stephen Brook describes the interior as looking like 'a cross between a building site and a used furniture depot'.

If the church is lacking a little in the appearance of exaltedness, at least its claim to stand over Golgotha, the site of the crucifixion, burial and resurrection of Christ, is fairly well respected.

At the start of the 1st century this was a disused quarry outside what was then the line of the city walls. According to John 19:17 and 41-2, Jesus' crucifixion occurred at a place outside the city walls and with a grave nearby. Archaeologists discovered tombs dating from the correct period, so the site is at least compatible with the story in the gospels. Until at least 66 AD Jerusalem's community held celebrations of public worship at the tomb, at a time when it was Jewish practice to pray at the tombs of holy persons. Hadrian filled in the area in 135 AD to build a temple dedicated to Aphrodite, but the Christian tradition persisted and Constantine and his mother, Queen Helena, chose the site to construct a church honouring Jesus' resurrection. To make room for the new development, substantial buildings had to be demolished; a move of a mere 100m either way would have saved a lot of time and expense but the community insisted that this had to be the church's location – a story that lends credence to the site's claims to authenticity. Work on Constantine's church commenced in 326 AD and it was dedicated nine years later.

When his armies took the city in 638 AD, Caliph Omar was invited to pray in the church but he refused,

A   12th century Crusader facade and entrance.

B   Crusader entrance to Calvary, closed in 1187 to become the Chapel of the Franks.

C   Calvary – reached by the steep stairs on the immediate right inside the entrance.

D   The Chapel of Adam. The bodies of Baldwin I and Godfrey de Bouillon, the Crusader kings, lay on the two benches near the door until they were moved in 1810.

E   The Stone of Unction commemorates Jesus' anointment before his burial. It is not the actual stone on which his body was laid out as it was only put in place in 1810.

F   While all others have been restored, these two columns have been left in the same damaged condition as they were after the 1808 fire. Look carefully and you'll see that they are actually two halves of one column – it used to support the drum of the dome but was removed and sawn in two in the 11th century to carry the newly constructed upper gallery.

G   The tomb monument, memorably described as a 'hideous kiosk'. The 1808 fire destroyed a previous 11th century structure which replaced the rock tomb that the mad Caliph Hakim had removed in 1009. There is usually a queue to get inside.

H   Coptic Chapel at the rear of the Holy Sepulchre.

I   This is part of the 4th century apse and wall, now part of the Syrian chapel.

GREG ELMS

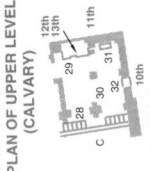

PLAN OF UPPER LEVEL (CALVARY)

STATIONS OF THE CROSS

10th Jesus is stripped of his garments
11th Jesus is nailed to the cross
12th Jesus dies on the cross
13th The body of Jesus is taken from the cross
14th Jesus is laid in the Holy Sepulchre

For stations 1 to 9 see Map 3

MAP 4

Souq Ed Dabbagha

To Muristan Road

St Helena

Christian Quarter Road

Church of the Holy Sepulchre

Not to Scale

See Insert for Upper Level

1 Franciscan Convent
2 Church of the Apparition
3 Franciscan Sacristy
4 Mary Magdalene Chapel
5 Seven Arches of the Virgin
6 Byzantine Arcade
7 Crusader Arcade
8 Prison of Christ
9 St Longinus Chapel
10 Division of the Raiment Chapel
11 St Dimas Altar
12 Chapel of the Discovery of the Cross
13 Church of St Helena
14 Chapel of the Mocking
15 Greek Choir
16 St Nicodemus Chapel of the Syrians
17 Three Maries Altar
18 Tombs of Crusader Kings Baldwin I & Godfrey de Bouillon
19 Armenian Chapel
20 40 Martyrs' Chapel
21 St John's Chapel
22 St James Chapel (Greek Orthodox)
23 Chapel of the Franks
24 Chapel of St Michael & All Saints
25 St John's Chapel (Armenian)
26 St Abraham's Monastery
27 Cisterns of St Helena
28 Golgotha
29 Greek Orthodox Chapel
30 Chapel of Calvary
31 Medici Altar
32 Franciscan Chapel

generously noting that if he did his fellow Muslims would have turned it into a mosque. Instead, in 1009 the church was destroyed by the mad Caliph Hakim. Unable to afford the major repairs necessary, Jerusalem's Christian community had to wait until 1042, when the Byzantine Imperial Treasury provided a subsidy. It wasn't enough to pay for a complete reconstruction of the original church, so a large part of the building was abandoned, but an upper gallery was introduced into the rotunda and an apse added to its eastern side as a sort of compensation. This was the church that the Crusaders entered in 1099 as the new rulers of Jerusalem. They made significant alterations and reconsecrated the building in 1149, on the 50th anniversary of their capture of the city.

The church as it exists today remains to a large extent a Crusader structure, although major repairs and additions were made necessary after a fire swept through the building in 1808. After much wrangling (and a sizeable bribe), the authorities gave the Greek Orthodox the job of carrying out the reconstruction, and it's they who are responsible for the much reviled structure over the tomb of Christ – described by one modern Fransiscan author as looking 'like a gaudy newspaper kiosk in Salonika'.

The Church of the Holy Sepulchre is open daily from 4.30 am to 8 pm (7 pm in winter) to anyone suitably

---

Rites and Wrongs

While the Greek Orthodox, the Armenians, the Copts and the Roman Catholics, along with the Christian Ethiopians and Syrians, are united in a shared set of central beliefs, the equitable shared possession of the Church of the Holy Sepulchre has proved completely beyond them. Territorial claims are zealously guarded and something as seemingly insignificant as the moving of a rug by a few centimetres has in the past resulted in blood being spilt. In the 19th century clergymen at the church would display to visitors the scars and wounds sustained in the frequent interdenominational punch-ups.

When an earthquake in 1927 caused extensive damage and seriously weakened the already crumbling structure the intense rivalry meant that it took over 30 years before the various factions could be brought to cooperate on an agreed programme of repairs.

To circumvent at least one potential area of dispute, the keys to the church have been in the possession of a local Muslim family since the Ottoman period and it's their job to unlock the doors each morning and secure them again at night. ■

dressed – the guards are very strict and may refuse entry to anyone not in compliance.

Christ Church Located just across from the Citadel in the Jaffa Gate area, this was the Holy Land's first Protestant church, consecrated in 1849. It was built by the London Society for Promoting Christianity Amongst the Jews (known today as CMJ: the Church's Ministry Among the Jews). The society's founders were inspired by the belief that the Jews would be restored to what was then Turkish Palestine, and that many would acknowledge Jesus Christ as the Messiah before he returned.

In order to present Christianity as something not totally alien to Judaism, Christ Church was built in the Protestant style with several similarities to a synagogue. Jewish symbols, such as Hebrew script and the Star of David, figure prominently at the altar and in the stained glass windows.

Greek Orthodox Patriarchate Museum On Greek Orthodox Patriarchate Rd this museum (☎ 628 4006) presents some of the treasures of the Patriarchate and goes a little way towards presenting the history of this locally dominant church.

It's open Tuesday to Friday from 9 am to 1 pm and 3 to 5 pm, and Saturday from 9 am to 1 pm, closed Sunday and Monday. Admission is 5 NIS. Follow Greek Catholic Patriarchate Rd north from Jaffa Gate, turn right into Greek Orthodox Patriarchate Rd and it's on the left.

St Alexander's Church On a corner just east of the Holy Sepulchre, this is the home of the Russian mission in exile. The attraction for visitors is a much-altered triumphal arch that once stood in Hadrian's forum, built here in 135. Through the arch and to the left at the top of the steps you can see a section of the pavement which was once part of the platform of Hadrian's temple to Aphrodite.

St Alexander's Church is only open at 7 am on Thursday when prayers are said for Czar Alexander III. The excavations are open Monday to Thursday from 9 am to 1 pm and 3 to 5 pm; ring the bell. There's a small admission fee.

Ethiopian Monastery Follow the route to the 9th Station of the Cross: up the steps off Souq Khan as-Zeit St, at the point at which the street to the Church of the Holy Sepulchre turns to the right, there is a small grey door directly ahead that opens onto a roof of that church.

The cluster of huts here has been the Ethiopian Monastery (known as Deir as-Sultan) since the Copts forced them out of their former building in one of the many disputes between the various Christian groups.

The monks live among the ruins of a Medieval cloister erected by the Crusaders where Constantine's basilica had been previously. The cupola in the middle of this roof section admits light to St Helena's crypt below. Access to the Church of the Holy Sepulchre is possible via two nearby points. One is through the Ethiopian Chapel (most of these monks do not speak much English but are very friendly, so ask for directions) and the other way is to go left out of the Ethiopian monastery and through the Copts' entrance.

Lutheran Church of the Redeemer Dominating the Old City skyline with its tall white tower, the present church was built in 1898 on the site of the 11th century church of St Mary la Latine. The closed northern entrance porch is Medieval and decorated with the signs of the zodiac and the symbols of the months. The tower is popular for its excellent views over the Old City. It's open Monday to Saturday from 9 am to 1 pm and 1.30 to 5 pm, closed Sunday. Admission is 2 NIS.

Church of St John the Baptist Jerusalem's oldest church, St John the Baptist stands in a hidden section of the Muristan area and is usually overlooked, having been buried by the gradual rise of surrounding street levels. However, the entrance from Christian Quarter Rd is clearly signposted. This leads you into the courtyard of a more recent Greek Orthodox monastery where a monk will usually be present to open the church for you. Originally built in the mid-5th century, it was restored after the Persians destroyed it in 614 AD. In the 11th century the merchants of Amalfi built a new church, which became the cradle of the Knights Hospitallers, using the walls of the earlier building. The present facade with the two small bell towers is a more recent addition, along with a few other alterations made to ensure the building's stability.

Armenian Quarter

Although they number only a few million worldwide, the Armenians have their own quarter within the Old City. Theirs was the first nation to officially embrace Christianity when their king converted in 303 AD, and they established themselves in Jerusalem sometime in the following century. The kingdom of Armenia disap-

PETER JOUSIFFE

Ornate doorway within the beautiful St James' Cathedral,
Armenian Quarter

peared at the end of the 4th century and Jerusalem was
adopted as their spiritual capital. They've had an uninterrupted presence here ever since.

The core of the quarter is actually one big monastic
compound, a reminder of the fact that until relatively
recently the Armenian presence in Jerusalem was traditionally purely religious. This began to change earlier
this century with the arrival of a large secular element
fleeing Turkish persecution. That persecution escalated
in 1915 to an attempted genocide in which over 1.5
million Armenians were killed.

The community today, which numbers about 1500, is still very insular, having its own schools, library, seminary and residential quarters discreetly tucked away behind high walls. The gates to this city within a city are closed early each evening.

There's little to see for the casual visitor, but if you can make it during the limited hours that its doors are open then it is well worth taking a look inside St James' Cathedral. Armenian ceramics are also justly famous and there are a couple of good showrooms off Armenian Orthodoxy Patriarchate Rd.

Armenian Compound About 1200 Armenians now live in what used to be a large pilgrims' hospice. It became a residential area after 1915 when refugees from the Turkish massacres settled here. The empty, wide courtyards are a rare sight in the Old City. The area is generally closed to visitors but you can telephone (☎ 628 2331) or ask at the entrance to St James' Cathedral to make an appointment for a visit.

St James' (Jacques') Cathedral Attending mass here could seriously shake the non-faith of an atheist. With the air loaded with incense, diffusely glowing golden lamps hung from the ceilings and the floors covered in dark, richly patterned carpets, this place has a seductive aura of ritual and mystery lacking in every other Christian site in this most holy of cities.

It was the Georgians in the 11th century who first constructed a church here in honour of St James, on the site where he was beheaded and became the first martyred disciple. The Armenians, in favour with the ruling Crusaders, took possession of the church in the 12th century and the two parties shared restoration duties. The tiles date from much later, the 18th century, and were imported from Turkey.

The church is on Armenian Orthodoxy Patriarchate Rd and is only open for services, which are held Monday to Friday from 6.30 to 7.15 am and 2.45 to 3.30 pm, and Saturday and Sunday from 2.30 to 3 pm. Admission is free.

Mardigian Museum Originally a theological seminary (1843), with an attractive courtyard enclosed by arched colonnades on two levels, the building that houses this museum (☎ 628 2331) is a lot more fascinating than most of the exhibits it presents. It's open Monday to Saturday from 10 am to 5 pm, closed Sunday. Admission is 5 NIS (students 3 NIS).

St Mark's Chapel This is the home of the Syrian Orthodox community in Jerusalem, whose members here number about 200. (There are only about three million worldwide, of whom two million are in Malahar in central India.) The Syrian Orthodox believe the chapel, on Ararat St, occupies the site of the home of St Mark's mother, Mary, where Peter went after he was released from prison by an angel (Acts 12:12). It is claimed that the Virgin Mary was baptised here, and according to Syrian Orthodox tradition this, not the Coenaculum on Mt Zion, is where the Last Supper was eaten. One thing to look out for is the painting on leather of the Virgin and Child attributed to St Luke and, according to the caretaker, painted from life.

The chapel is open Monday to Saturday from 7 am to noon and 2 to 5 pm, closed Sunday. Admission is free but donations are welcome.

Alix de Rothschild Craft Centre This is a small gallery (☎ 628 6076) at 4 Or HaChaim St displaying ceramics, glass, enamel and textiles by Jewish artists and craftspeople. It's open Sunday to Thursday from 10 am to 4 pm and admission is free.

MT ZION

Now meaning the steep slope south from the Old City walls beyond Zion Gate, in the Old Testament period Mt Zion referred to a hill east of what is now known as the City of David. The name change came in the 4th century, based on new interpretations of religious texts. This compact area contains the possible site of the biblical Last Supper and a less probable Tomb of David. Also here is the **grave of Oskar Schindler**, the man with the list; from Zion Gate walk directly ahead, downhill, bearing left at the fork to go past the Chamber of the Holocaust, round the bend and cross the road to the entrance of the Christian cemetery in which he's buried.

The hustlers who offer themselves as guides on Mt Zion are a particularly unpleasant lot, persistent and occasionally quite nasty when their services are declined. They also have a scam going outside David's Tomb in which they ask for a donation in exchange for a cardboard yarmulke; men do need to cover their heads to visit but yarmulkes are handed out gratis inside the tomb and no donations are requested.

King David's Tomb

A Crusader structure erected two millennia after his death, the Tomb of King David provides little spectacle. What's more, the authenticity of the site is highly disputable – the likelihood is that David is buried under the hill of the original Mt Zion, east of the City of David. However, this is one of the most revered of the Jewish holy places, and from 1948 to 67, when the Western Wall was part of the territory held by the Jordanians and off-limits to Jews, the tomb was the stand-in main centre of pilgrimage. It still serves as a popular prayer hall.

To get to the tomb head south from Zion Gate, bear right at the fork and then left. It's open Saturday to Thursday from 8 am to 6 pm, and Friday from 8 am to 2.20pm. Admission is free.

The Coenaculum

Popularly thought to be the site of the Last Supper (*coenaculum* is Latin for dining hall), this is the only Christian site in Israel administered by the local government. Part of the King David's Tomb complex, the Coenaculum (also known as the Cenacle) was a site of Christian veneration during the Byzantine period. In the Middle Ages the Franciscans acquired it, but were later expelled by the Turks. Under the Turks the Coenaculum became a mosque and Christians were barred from entering, just as Jews were kept from King David's Tomb.

Like the Tomb, the Coenaculum hall dates from the time of the Crusaders, and to the right of the entrance there is a pair of faded Crusader coats of arms. The southern wall still bears the niche hollowed by the Muslims as a mihrab when they converted the chapel into a mosque.

The Coenaculum is above King David's Tomb, reached via a discreet stairway behind a door to the left that leads up from the courtyard. Many visitors mistake the first large room for the real thing, but you need to walk across the hall to enter the much smaller chamber beyond which is where Jesus supposedly shared the Last Supper (Matthew 26:26-35, Mark 14:15-25, Luke 22:14-38, John 13-15, 17; Acts 1:12-26 and Acts 2:1-4, I Corinthians 11:23-25).

The Coenaculum Chapel is open daily from 8 am to noon and 3 to 6 pm, but the Last Supper room closes at 4 pm. Admission to both is free. Special services are occasionally held; contact the Christian Information Centre for details.

PETER JOUSIFFE

The simple appearance of the Church of the Dormition
belies its rich interior

Museum of King David

This museum next to King David's Tomb is associated
with the Diaspora Yeshiva, the adjacent Jewish school
for religious study. The main exhibit is some rather
bizarre modern art. The only reason for the museum's
existence appears to be to raise money for the yeshiva –
donations of at least 5 NIS are strongly encouraged. It's
open Sunday to Thursday from 10 am to 5 pm, and
Friday from 10 am to 2 pm, closed Saturday.

Church & Monastery of the Dormition

This beautiful neo-Romanesque church is the traditional
site where the Virgin Mary fell into 'eternal sleep'; its

Latin name is Dormition Sanctae Mariae (Sleep of Mary). The current church and monastery, owned by the German Benedictine order, were designed by a German architect, Heinrich Renard, and consecrated in 1906. The church suffered damage during the battles for the city in 1948 and 1967 when its tower, which overlooked Jordanian army positions on the Old City ramparts below, was used by Israeli soldiers.

The church's interior is a bright contrast to many of its older and duller peers nearby. A golden mosaic of Mary with the baby Jesus is set in the upper part of the apse; below are the Prophets of Israel. The chapels around the hall are dedicated to saints: St Willibald, an English Benedictine who visited the Holy Land in 724; the Three Wise Men; St Joseph, whose chapel is covered with medallions featuring kings of Judah as Jesus' forefathers; and St John the Baptist. The floor is decorated with names of saints and prophets and zodiac symbols.

The crypt features a stone effigy of Mary asleep on her deathbed with Jesus calling his mother to heaven. The chapels around this statue were donated by various countries. In the apse is the Chapel of the Holy Ghost, with the Holy Ghost shown coming down to the Apostles.

The church is open daily from 8 am to noon and 2 to 6 pm. Admission is free. The complex also has a pleasant cafe where cakes and drinks (including beer) are served.

Church of St Peter in Gallicantu

Almost hidden by the trees and the slope of the hill, the Church of St Peter 'at the Crowing of the Cock' is the traditional site of the denial of Jesus by his disciple Peter (Mark 14:66-72 – 'before the cock crow thou shalt deny me thrice').

Built on the foundations of previous Byzantine and Crusader churches, the modern structure is also believed to stand on the site of the house of the high priest Caiaphas, where Jesus was taken after his arrest (Mark 14:53). A cave beneath the church is said to be where Christ was incarcerated. Whatever your beliefs, the view from the balcony of the church across to the City of David, the Arab village of Silwan and the three valleys that shape Jerusalem is reason enough to justify a visit.

The church is open Monday to Saturday from 8 to 11.45 am and 2 to 5 pm (May to September from 2 to 5.30 pm), closed Sunday. Admission is free. The church is reached by turning east (left) as you descend the road leading from Mt Zion down and around to Sultan's Pool.

Roman steps lead down from the church garden to the Gihon Spring in the Kidron Valley.

KIDRON VALLEY

Apart from the wonderful views, the points of interest here are the tombs. These can be reached by following the road north from the entrance to Hezekiah's Tunnel or by taking the downhill path off Jericho Rd about 150m south of the Church of All Nations. The Arab village that clings to the eastern slope of the valley is Silwan. Sites referred to in this section can be found on map 17.

Valley of Jehoshaphat

The most northern part of the Kidron Valley, this is the area between the Haram ash-Sharif/Temple Mount and the Mount of Olives. Jehoshaphat in Hebrew means 'God shall judge', and this narrow furrow of land is where the events of the Day of Judgement are to take place. All of humanity will be assembled together on the Mount of Olives, with the Judgement Seat on the Haram opposite. Two bridges will appear, spanning the valley, one made of iron and the other made of paper. According to God's judgement each person will be directed to cross one or the other. But we know the ending – the Bible gives it away: the iron bridge will collapse and those sent across it die, while the paper bridge holds up with the promise of eternal life.

At the southern end of the Valley of Jehoshaphat are four Jewish tombs (known collectively as the Kidron Valley tombs), some of the most complete monuments from the time of the Second Temple.

Absalom's Pillar Dating from the 1st century, this monument is easily identified by its inverted funnel-shaped roof. Absalom was the son of King David, who suffered an ignominious end when he rebelled against his father (II Samuel 15-18). The roof aside, the monument is wholly carved in one piece from out of the hillside.

Tomb of Jehoshaphat Located behind Absalom's Pillar, this 1st century burial cave is notable for the impressive frieze above its entrance.

Tomb of B'nei Hezir Just to the south of Absalom's Pillar, this is a burial cave hewn out of the rock face. The gaping entrance is framed by a Greek-style pediment supported by two columns. An inscription on the frieze, between the columns, indicates that this is the tomb of the B'nei Hezirs (sons of the Hezirs), a family of Jewish priests (Nehemiah 10:20). St James is popularly believed to have hidden here when Jesus was arrested nearby.

Tomb of Zechariah Like the neighbouring Tomb of B'nei Hezir, that of Zechariah, which features a cube with a pyramid on top, betrays a Greek influence – in this case, in the form of Ionic pilasters decorating the facades. Jewish tradition says the prophet Zechariah (II Chronicles 24:20-21) is buried here, but as usual archaeological evidence suggests otherwise – Zechariah died in the 6th century BC while the tomb dates from the 1st century BC.

City of David

The oldest part of Jerusalem, dating from before the 20th century BC, this is the confirmed site of the city captured and developed by King David. The excavations are the result of work, still in progress, that started in 1850.

Of interest to archaeologists is a signposted path which leads around the excavations. The excavations include the Canaanite citadel of the Jebusite town that David conquered, a fortress built by David, and Jerusalem's Upper City where the wealthy resided and where buildings destroyed in the Babylonian conquest of 586 BC once stood.

The site is open daily from 9 am to 4 pm and admission is free. From the Dung Gate, head east (downhill), take the road to the right (just past the parking lot), then take a left along the path with the sign (just past the grocery store) and follow it down to the bottom of the hill where you turn right. If you don't see a sign, ask for directions, as the slopes are too steep to want to get lost on. Continue downhill to reach Warren's Shaft.

Warren's Shaft

This was built by the Jebusites to ensure their water supply during a siege. It is just inside their city's defence wall and this is possibly where Joab entered the City of David (II Samuel 5:8, I Chronicles 11:6). About 100m down from the entrance to the City of David excavations, a small museum features photos of the excavation work with explanations of the water supply situation as it used to be. A spiral staircase leads to a tunnel extending into the shaft, so bring a flashlight.

The shaft (☎ 628 8141) is open Sunday to Thursday from 9 am to 5 pm, and Friday from 9 am to 1 pm, closed Saturday. Admission is 5 NIS (students 3 NIS).

From Warren's Shaft, you can then proceed down to Hezekiah's Tunnel at the bottom of the hill.

Gihon Spring, Pool of Shiloah & Hezekiah's Tunnel

The Gihon Spring was the main reason why the Jebusites settled on the low Ophel Ridge rather than choosing the adjacent higher ground. Gihon means 'gushing', quite suitable as the spring acts like a siphon, pouring out a large quantity of water for some 30 minutes before almost drying up for between four and 10 hours. There is believed to be enough water to support a population of about 2500. The tunnel was built in about 700 BC by King Hezekiah to bring the water of the Gihon into the city and store it in the pool of Shiloah, or Siloam. Its purpose was to prevent invaders, in particular the Assyrians, from locating the city's water supply and cutting it off (II Chronicles 32). The tunnel's length is 533m (335m as the crow flies).

Although narrow and low in parts, you can wade through the tunnel; the water is normally about half a metre to a metre deep. Due to the siphon effect it does occasionally rise, but only by about 15 to 20 cm.

The entrance steps leading down to the water are Medieval. After about 20m the tunnel turns sharply to the left, where a chest-high wall blocks another channel which leads to Warren's Shaft (this can be visited near the City of David excavations; see above). Towards the tunnel's end the roof rises. This is because the tunnellers worked from either end and one team slightly misjudged the other's level. They had to lower the floor so that the water would flow. A Hebrew inscription was found in the tunnel, and a copy can be seen in the Israel Museum in West Jerusalem. Carved by Hezekiah's engineers, it tells of the tunnel's construction.

You enter the tunnel at the Gihon Spring source on HaShiloah Rd down in the Kidron Valley and just south of the rest house. Turn right as you get to the foot of the hill from Warren's Shaft.

It's open Sunday to Thursday from 9 am to 5 pm, and Friday from 9 am to 3 pm, closed Saturday. Admission is free. The wade takes about 30 minutes; wear shorts and suitable footwear. A torch (flashlight) is also required – although candles are sold at the entrance they won't stay lit in the tunnel because of the draughts.

MOUNT OF OLIVES

Rising above the city on its eastern flank, the Mount of Olives is dominated by the world's oldest and largest **Jewish cemetery** and the many churches commemorating the events that led to Jesus' arrest and his ascension to heaven.

The cemetery dates from biblical times. Its importance is based on the belief that this will be the site of the resurrection of the dead on the Day of Judgement when the Messiah comes (Zechariah 14:1-11). Waiting here to meet him, and no doubt snap up the rights to the event, is former media baron Robert Maxwell, interred in one of the hillside tombs.

Most of the Mount's churches and gardens are open in the morning, closing for at least two hours towards noon and reopening again in the mid-afternoon. However, the real draw – and what makes a visit to the Mount of Olives a 'must' – is the panoramic view it affords of the Old City. Up at the top, in front of the **Seven Arches Hotel** (cause of much controversy as it was built by the Jordanians over part of the ancient Jewish cemetery) is a promenade which triggers compulsive camera clicking in all who visit. Sunset isn't necessarily the best time to visit, as at this time of day the Old City is usually thrown into silhouette; instead come first thing in the morning, when the light is best.

You can walk from East Jerusalem or from St Stephen's Gate in the Old City, or take the bus to avoid what most find a strenuous walk. Arab bus No 75 runs from the station on Sultan Suleyman St.

Augusta Victoria

The Augusta Victoria complex was constructed in the late 19th century, a German entry in the 'bigger, bolder, more imposing' competition to achieve pre-eminence in the Holy City through overbearing architecture. Though nominally a church and attached hospice, this grouping of buildings has been called a vast monument to German imperialism. Fittingly, it became the headquarters of the German-Turkish military command during WWI. Following their defeat, the compound was taken over by the British and put into use as the residence of their high commissioner. These days Augusta Victoria serves as an UNRWA-run hospital for Palestinians.

The Augusta Victoria **Church of the Ascension** has some noteworthy mosaics, paintings and masonry work, while the 65m high tower has great views across to the Old City and the Judean Desert. The church is

---

Warning

In a recent report in the *Jerusalem Post*, a priest who brings visitors to the Mount of Olives noted that during one week alone several people had had their pockets picked, a guide had been beaten up, and a woman had been sexually assaulted. Lonely Planet has also received letters from women readers who suffered unpleasant experiences while walking around here. In light of this, our advice has to be that women definitely should not visit the Mount of Olives alone or even in pairs – go with male accompaniment or as part of a group. ∎

---

open Monday to Saturday from 8 am to 5.30 pm. Admission is free, but it costs 2 NIS to go up the tower (6 NIS if you use the elevator). Arab bus No 75 stops outside.

Russian Chapel of the Ascension

Marked by a needle-point steeple – the tallest structure on the Mount of Olives – this church and monastery is built over the spot from which the Orthodox church claims Jesus made his ascent to heaven. It is closed to the public.

Mosque of the Ascension

Confusingly also sometimes referred to as the Church or Chapel of the Ascension, this is an alternative site for Jesus' journey skyward. The spot is marked by an odd little octagonal structure which dates back to Crusader times – although it stands on the site of an earlier Byzantine church. Saladin authorised two of his followers to acquire the site in 1198 and it has remained in Muslim possession since, functioning as a mosque. Christians are permitted to celebrate here each year on the anniversary of the Ascension, 40 days after Easter.

The stone floor bears an imprint said to be the footstep of Jesus. Perhaps the reason for its unconvincing appearance today is that pilgrims in the Byzantine period were permitted to take bits of it away.

Opening hours vary but the cost of admission is 2 NIS.

Church of the Pater Noster

Beside the cave in which Jesus spoke to his disciples, Queen Helena, mother of Constantine, the Roman Emperor, had this church built. (It is also known as the Church of the Eleona – derived from the Greek word

PETER JOUSIFFE

The Mosque of the Ascension

ANDREW HUMPHREYS

The Church of All Nations at the foot of the Mount of Olives

elaion, meaning 'olives'). Destroyed by the Persians in 614, the site later became known as the place where Jesus taught the Lord's Prayer, a belief which inspired the Crusaders to construct an oratory among the ruins in 1106.

The most interesting things here are the attractive tiled panels where the Lord's Prayer is inscribed in over 60 languages.

As you enter the gate, turn left and then right. The tomb is that of Princess de la Tour d'Auvergne, who purchased the property in 1886 and built the neighbouring Carmelite convent. The actual cave can be reached by going around the cloister to the left, down some stairs and through the first door on the right.

The site is open Monday to Saturday from 8.30 to 11.45 am and 3 to 4.45 pm, closed Sunday. Admission is free.

Tombs of the Prophets

Slightly to the north and below the viewing promenade are some ancient tombs, reputedly those of the prophets Haggai and Malachi, who lived in the 5th century BC.

The site is open Sunday to Friday from 9 am to 3 pm, closed Saturday. Admission is free.

Church of Dominus Flevit

The original church on this site was built by Medieval pilgrims who claimed to have found the rock on the Mount of Olives where Jesus had wept for Jerusalem (Luke 19:41) – hence, Dominus Flevit, meaning 'the Lord wept'.

When the present day, tear-shaped church was being built in 1954 and 1955 (designed by an Italian architect, Antonio Barluzzi), excavations unearthed a 5th century monastery, the mosaic floor of which is on display, and a large cemetery dating back to about 1500 BC. The view of the Dome of the Rock from the window of the altar is particularly attractive.

The church is open daily from 8 am to noon and 2.30 to 5 pm. Admission is free.

Russian Church of Mary Magdalene

Although badly tarnished by the weather, the seven gilded 'onion' domes of this White Russian church are still one of Jerusalem's most attractive and surprising landmarks. It was built by Alexander III in 1886 in memory of his mother, Maria Alexandrovna, and is styled in the manner of Muscovite churches of the 16th and 17th centuries. The church is now a convent and has one of the city's best choirs. It's only open on Tuesday and Thursday from 10 to 11.30 am. Admission is free.

Church of All Nations & Garden of Gethsemane

Designed by the same architect responsible for Dominus Flevit up the hill, the classically styled Church of All Nations is notable for the glistening golden mosaic that adorns its facade (the mosaic depicts Jesus assuming the suffering of the world, hence the church's alternative name, the Basilica of the Agony). Built in 1924 it was financed by a consortium drawn from 12 nations. It's the successor to two earlier churches, the first erected in the 4th century but destroyed by an earthquake in the 740s, the second an oratory built over the ruins by the Crusaders but abandoned in 1345 for reasons unknown.

Around the church is the popularly accepted site of Gethsemane, the garden where Jesus was arrested (Mark 14:32-50). The garden has some of the world's oldest olive trees (in Hebrew *gat shmanim* means 'oil press'), three of which have been scientifically dated as over 2000 years old, making them witnesses to whatever biblical events may have occurred here.

The garden is open daily from 8.30 to 11.30 am and 2.30 to 4 pm. Admission is free. Entrance is not from the main road but from the narrow, steeply inclined alleyway running up behind the church.

Tomb of the Virgin Mary

On her death, sometime in the middle of the 1st century, Mary was supposedly interred here by the disciples. A monument was first constructed in the 5th century but was repeatedly destroyed. Almost hidden in the valley, the present monument is a Crusader edifice from the 12th century, built on Byzantine foundations. It is owned by the Greek Orthodox Church, while the Armenians, Syrians and Copts have shares in the altar.

The tomb is open Monday to Saturday from 6 to 11.45 am and 2.30 to 5 pm, closed Sunday. Admission is free.

On the main road beside the stairs down to the tomb, the small cupola supported by columns is a memorial to Mujir ad-Din, a 15th century Muslim judge and historian.

St Stephen's Church

This Greek Orthodox church is on the southern side of the main Jericho road as it curves away from the Old City walls towards the Mount of Olives. Largely ignored by guides and visitors alike, it was completed in 1968 as a 'modern Byzantine' church. It is near the site where Stephen, the first Christian martyr, was stoned to death. The two pleasant ladies who look after the church are happy to guide visitors around. Ring the bell to see if anyone is in – there are no set hours. Admission is free.

MT SCOPUS

Scopus (from the Greek *skopeo*, meaning 'to look over') lies north on the same ridge that at its south is the Mount of Olives. It overlooks one of the most vulnerable approaches to Jerusalem and its strategic location has played a decisive role in the many battles for the city over the centuries. In 70 AD the Roman legions of Titus camped here, as did the Crusaders in 1099, and the British in 1917. During the 1948 War, Arab forces attacked from here. One of the anomalies of the 1949 cease-fire was that Mt Scopus became an Israeli-held enclave in Jordanian territory. Every two weeks a convoy under UN protection was allowed to cross from Jewish West Jerusalem to the encircled mount to bring in supplies and relieve the Israeli garrison.

In addition to the Hebrew University campus and the military cemetery, other places of note here include **Hadassah Hospital**, designed in the 1930s by German architect Erich Mendelsohn and renowned as one of the world's top medical centres, and the Mormon University. Take Arab bus No 75 to the Augusta Victoria Hospital and walk 20 minutes, or take Egged bus No 4, 4A, 9, 23 or 28 from Jaffa Rd in the New City to the university.

Hebrew University

Founded in 1925 and featuring some distinctive modern architecture, the Mt Scopus campus of the Hebrew University was the world's first secular Hebrew institute of higher learning. Between 1948 and 1967, when Mt Scopus was a Jewish enclave isolated in Jordanian-held territory, the university was relocated to Givat Ram, and it is now split between the two sites. There are free guided tours in English, from Sunday to Thursday at 11 am, lasting from 60 to 90 minutes. These leave from the Bronfman Visitors' Centre in the administration building. The modern **Hecht Synagogue** stands out as the major attraction for visitors, although the best views are from the **amphitheatre**.

Views of the City
Following is a rundown of the best places from which to view Jerusalem – see the relevant sections in this chapter for opening times and admission costs.

Mount of Olives The Mount of Olives affords the classic panorama of Jerusalem with the golden dome rising above the city walls. Come early in the morning when the sun is behind you and the view is at its clearest.

Mt Scopus From here there are marvellous views of the city to the west and, from the amphitheatre, even better views to the east across the Judean Desert to the Dead Sea.

Dormition Monastery This monastery is on Mt Zion just outside the city walls.

Lutheran Church of the Redeemer Right in the middle of the Old City, the church tower offers photographers the best shots of the Haram ash-Sharif/Temple Mount.

Haas Promenade A favourite spot for strolling Jerusalemites, this is an attractive stepped terrace in the south of Jerusalem which faces up the Hinnom Valley to the Old City.

The City Tower In the New City on the corner of Ben Yehuda and King George V Sts, the City Tower is a multistorey shopping mall with a rooftop restaurant, the Jerusalem Delight, that offers 360° views of the city centre rooftops.

YMCA The belfry tower of the YMCA building on Ha-Melekh David St has great views across the Hinnom Valley to Mt Zion and the Old City.

Kanfei Air Tours These aerial tours are pricey but unforgettable – see Activities at the end of this chapter for further details.

Mormon University

The Brigham Young University was opened in 1987 amidst much protestation, particularly by Orthodox Jews who feared the Mormons were intent on missionary activity. In large part due to the support of then mayor Teddy Kollek, a firm advocate of religious and cultural tolerance, the Mormons were finally permitted

AUSTRALIA-ISRAEL CHAMBER OF COMMERCE

Hecht Synagogue at the Hebrew University

to establish their centre. The resulting building is quite beautiful – a stepped structure that ripples down the slope of Mt Scopus in a series of landscaped terraces. Guided tours of the campus are available at 10.30 and 11.30 am and 2.30 and 3.30 pm from Tuesday to Friday. Public concerts are also regularly held in the university's glass-enclosed auditorium, which has stunning views over the Old City.

WWI Cemetery

This is the burial site for those soldiers from the British Commonwealth forces who died in the Palestinian campaign of 1917. Various remembrance services, including ANZAC Day (for Australians and New Zealanders) are held here, attended by the mayor of Jerusalem, other local dignitaries and military personnel.

EAST JERUSALEM

East Jerusalem is the Palestinian Arab sector of the city. It stretches north from the Old City walls up to Sheikh Jarrah, and to the east encompasses the swell of the Mount of Olives and the cluster of villages on its slopes, including Silwan, Abu Dis and Bethany. The heart of the district is centred on converging Salah ad-Din St and Nablus Rd, which is where you'll find most of the shops, eating places and accommodation. Recognisable tourist sites are few, although the Garden Tomb is pleasant and the Rockefeller Museum contains some impressive exhibits. Lively and chaotic during the day, East Jerusalem completely closes down at dusk.

Solomon's Quarries

Midway between Damascus and Herod's gates is this vast cave beneath the north wall of the Old City. Part of a quarry, stone chiselled from here was, in all likelihood, used by Herod in his many construction projects, and maybe even by Solomon in the construction of the First Temple. Far more recently the builders of the YMCA (1933) in the New City received special dispensation to use stone from the quarry in the construction of the communion room in the building's tower.

In Jewish tradition the cave is known as Me'arat Zidkiyahu (Zedekiah's Cave), because legend has it that the last king of Judah, Zedekiah, used it as an escape route to flee the armies of Nebuchadnezzar. The cave extends for over 200m beneath the Old City, and while there's little to see it does offer cool refuge on a hot day.

The cave is open Sunday to Thursday from 9 am to 5 pm, Friday from 9 am to 2 pm, and Saturday from 9 am to 4 pm. Admission is 4.50 NIS (students 2 NIS).

Rockefeller Museum

Set up with a gift of US$2 million donated by the Rockefeller family in 1927 and opened 11 years later, the Palestine Archaeological Museum, as it was then known, was at one time the leading museum of antiquities in the region. However, the museum has received little attention in recent times; while some of the exhibits are impressive, particularly the carved beams from the Al-Aqsa Mosque and the stone ornamentation recovered from Hisham's Palace in Jericho, the presentation is off-puttingly dour and musty compared to other more modern Israeli museums. The central courtyard with its tiled fountain – loosely inspired by the Alhambra in Spain – is still a pleasant place to sit and escape the city's noise and fumes. The pockmarks on the walls are bullet holes from the fighting in 1967.

The Rockefeller (☎ 629 2627) is open Sunday to Thursday from 10 am to 5 pm, and Friday and Saturday from 10 am to 2 pm. There are free guided tours in English on Sunday at 11 am. Admission is 12 NIS (students 8 NIS).

Armenian Mosaic

Unfortunately, at the time of our last visit there was no admission to this site, but anyone interested in seeing what is possibly the most attractive mosaic floor in all the Middle East should enquire at the Mardigian Museum in the Armenian Quarter of the Old City. Laid in the 5th or 6th century, the mosaic depicts a vast grapevine within which are perched some 45 colourful birds and baskets of fruit. The detail is superb and the colours are still incredibly brilliant. The floor belongs to what was the Mortuary Chapel of St Polyeuctus, an Armenian officer in the Roman army who was martyred for his Christianity. An Armenian inscription where the apse should begin reads 'For the memory and salvation of the souls of all Armenians whose names are known to God alone'.

The building housing the mosaic is just around the corner from, and behind, the Ramses Youth Hostel on HaNevi'im St.

Garden Tomb

This is an alternative site for the crucifixion and resurrection of Christ which, while enjoying little support for its claims, is appreciated by many for its tranquillity and charm. As one Catholic priest is reported to have said, 'If the Garden Tomb is not the true site of the Lord's death and resurrection, it should have been'.

Biblical significance was first attached to this location by General Charles Gordon (of Khartoum fame) in 1883. Gordon refused to believe that the Church of the Holy Sepulchre could occupy the site of Golgotha, and on identifying a skull-shaped hill just north of Damascus Gate he began excavations. The suitably ancient tombs he discovered under the mound confirmed his conviction that this was the true site of the crucifixion and burial of Jesus.

Archaeologists have subsequently scotched the theory by dating the tombs to the 5th century BC. Cynics suggest that the continued championing of the Garden Tomb has more to do with the fact that it's the only holy site in Jerusalem that the Protestants have any stake in.

It's open Monday to Saturday from 8.30 am to noon and 2 to 5.30 pm, closed Sunday. Admission is free. On Sunday at 9 am an interdenominational service with singing is held – it lasts about 50 minutes. To get to the tomb from Sultan Suleyman St, head north along Nablus Rd and turn right along Schick St.

St George's Cathedral

Named after the patron saint of England, traditionally believed to have been martyred in Palestine early in the 4th century (see the boxed aside, St George of Lod and England, in this section), this is the cathedral church of the Anglican Episcopal Diocese of Jerusalem and the

St George of Lod and England

Several flights a day connect London with Ben-Gurion airport, located on the outskirts of the small town of Lod, but few of those travelling this route would be aware of the little quirk of history which links these two places. Lod is the burial site of St George, the slayer of the dragon and patron saint of England.

George was a conscript in the Roman army who was executed in 303 AD for tearing up a copy of the Emperor Diocletian's decree that forbade the practice of Christianity. He was buried in Lod (then Lydda) and a Byzantine church was built over his tomb. This church was subsequently dismantled by the Mamluk Sultan Baybars (the stones were used to build a nearby bridge) and replaced with a mosque dedicated to Al-Khadr, the 'Green One', a saintly Islamic folkloric figure who roughly equates to George. How this character came to be patron saint of England is unknown, although the fantastical legends of George that were doing the rounds in the Levant would have been carried back to Europe by the Crusaders. ∎

Middle East. It was consecrated in 1912, but very soon after the Turks closed the church and used the bishop's house as their army headquarters during WWI. When the British took Jerusalem in 1917, the truce was signed here in the bishop's study. The cathedral has two congregations, Arabic and English speaking, and the complex includes a popular guesthouse (see the Places to Stay chapter) and school.

The church compound is a piece of the Mandate frozen in time. The church features many symbols of the British presence in Jerusalem: a font given by Queen Victoria, memorials to British servicemen, a royal coat of arms, an English oak screen and the tower built in memory of King Edward VII. The cathedral is just south of the junction of Salah ad-Din St and Nablus Rd. It has no set hours for visiting and no admission fee is charged.

Tombs of the Kings

The first archaeologist to excavate here decided that this complex must be the tombs of the Kings of Judah because of the majesty of its facade. While the name has stuck, it has since been proved that this is the 1st century tomb of Queen Helena of Adiabene, Mesopotamia, who converted to Judaism in 45 AD and travelled to Jerusalem with her children. It has been described by one scholar as one of the country's 'most interesting ancient

GREG ALFORD

Ammunition Hill, a memorial to the dead of the Six Day War

burial places', but only archaeology buffs are likely to agree.

The tomb is to the north of St George's Cathedral, and it's open to visitors Monday to Saturday from 8 am to 12.30 pm and 2 to 5 pm, closed Sunday. Admission is 5 NIS (students 3 NIS).

Tourjeman Post Museum

Overlooking the former Mandelbaum Gate area – which wasn't a gate at all but the UN-supervised access point between the Jewish New City and Jordanian occupied Jerusalem between 1948 and 1967 – this museum is in an old Turkish house used by the Israelis as a frontier position. With the touchy theme of 'a divided city reunited', it presents a distinctly Zionist picture of the period when the city was physically divided by concrete barriers and barbed wire.

A little tricky to find, the museum (☎ 628 1278) is on HaShalom Rd. From the Damascus Gate area walk north up HaNevi'im St, turn right after the Ramses Hostel onto HaShalom Rd, and it's on your left after a few minutes walk.

The museum is open Sunday to Thursday from 9 am to 5 pm, and Friday from 9 am to 1 pm, closed Saturday. Admission is 5 NIS.

Ammunition Hill

Although not strictly in East Jerusalem, Ammunition Hill is just north of the Palestinian neighbourhood of

Sheikh Jarrah. Another partition-era site, this was Jordan's main fortified outpost on the Jerusalem front and during the Six Day War it was taken by the Israelis in the first major battle for the Old City. Now a public park, the bunker complex has been converted into a museum of the war and a memorial to the many Israeli lives lost in the fighting.

The museum (☎ 582 1932) is open Sunday to Thursday from 9 am to 5 pm, Friday from 9 am to 1 pm, closed Saturday, and admission is 3 NIS. To get to the park walk north along Nablus Rd, straight on through Sheikh Jarrah, and turn left at the sports ground. Alternatively take Egged bus Nos 9, 25 or 28 from the New City and ask for Givat HaTahmoshet (Ammunition Hill).

THE NEW CITY – CENTRAL

The central district of the New City largely took shape during the time of the British Mandate. Although now primarily a place to shop, dine and drink, the sense of history here, albeit recent history, is no less acute than in the Old City.

Notre Dame

Whether it's the predominant use of stone or the result of a paranoid defensiveness that comes from having so many various creeds and sects vying for influence in one place, much of the city's religious architecture has a distinct bastion-like appearance. This reaches its pinnacle in the Notre Dame de France Hospice (begun in 1884, completed in 1904), a hostelry for French pilgrims that takes the form of a vast, imposing fortress that even manages to dominate Suleyman's Old City walls. Reinforcing the muscular imagery, up on the roofline a five metre high statue of Mary stands flanked by two crenellated turrets.

It's fitting that between 1948 and 1967, when Jerusalem was divided, the south wing of the Notre Dame was used as an IDF bunker and frontier post. The heavy battle damage the building suffered was patched up in the 1970s, and now Notre Dame operates as a busy international pilgrim centre with a highly rated guesthouse (see the Places to Stay chapter) and restaurant (see the Places to Eat chapter). It also includes an arts centre promoting traditional local Christian art.

Immediately to the west of the Notre Dame, on the corner site, is the **St Louis Hospital** built by the French between 1879 and 1896, and still in use as an institution for terminally ill patients.

Old & New City Hall

Just to the west of Notre Dame, on Zahal Square, the building with the rounded facade is Jerusalem's former City Hall. It was built during the time of the Mandate and was originally the headquarters of Barclays Bank – you can still see 'BB' wrought into the iron grills on the ground floor windows. Between 1948 and 1967 it served as another frontline bunker on the border between Jewish West Jerusalem and the Arab-held areas – an episode recorded in the bullet-pocked stonework. At the time of writing the building was no longer in use, having been replaced by the adjacent new City Hall complex.

Completed in summer 1993, the City Hall complex is a mix of new and renovated old buildings around a newly created public plaza, Safra Square. Picking up on elements of traditional Jerusalem architecture, such as the ablaq stonework, the complex is quite attractive, especially the date palm court at the Jaffa Rd edge of the plaza. The municipality's Department of Information (☎ 624 1379) based here gives guided tours of the new City Hall every Monday at 9.30 am; meet in Safra Square near the palms, opposite the main post office.

Russian Compound

During the 19th century the masses of Russian pilgrims visiting Jerusalem far outnumbered pilgrims from any other country. Therefore in 1860 the Russian Church acquired this site outside the city walls and within just a few years developed it into a virtually self-contained compound that included a cathedral-church, residences, a hospital, several hospices and quarters for the Russian consulate. Although the Soviet government sold most of the buildings to the Israeli government in 1964 for oranges, the compound today is still dominated by the Kremlin-inspired green cupolas of the **Church of the Holy Trinity**, consecrated in 1872.

The church (closed to the public) occupies the site where the Assyrians camped in about 700 BC, and in 70 AD Roman legions assembled here during the Jewish revolt. In front of the building, under a grille, is the 12m high **Herod's Pillar**, believed to have been intended for the Second Temple. It cracked during chiselling and was abandoned here.

Most of the Russian pilgrims were poor peasants who paid for their journey with their life savings, but the nobility also visited, and for them a large hostel was built with deluxe facilities and furnishings. Known as the **Sergei building**, after its patron Prince Sergei Romanoff,

EDDIE GERALD

EDDIE GERALD

EDDIE GERALD

Top: The fortress-like facade of the Notre Dame
Middle: The Church of the Holy Trinity
Bottom: The New City Hall complex

son of Czar Alexander II, the hostel (on present-day Heleni HaMalka St) is easily distinguishable by its two round crenellated towers. After the 1917 Revolution halted the flow of pilgrims from Russia, the empty hostel was taken over by the British mandatory government. It now houses Israel's Agriculture Ministry. It's also home to the Jerusalem offices of the Society for the Protection of Nature in Israel (see the Tourist Offices section in the Facts for the Visitor chapter).

During the Mandate period, certain other compound buildings were requisitioned by the British, earning the area the nickname of 'Bevingrad' after the British Foreign Secretary Ernest Bevin, a man much reviled by the Jews of Palestine. The building behind the church to the right was the British headquarters, while the adjacent former Russian women's hostel was used as a prison. As such, these were targets for attacks by the Jewish paramilitary underground. The hostel/prison is now the **Hall of Heroism (Museum of the Underground)** (☎ 623 3166), devoted to those same resistance organisations. It is open Sunday to Thursday from 8 am to 4 pm, and Friday from 10 am to 1 pm, closed Saturday. Admission is 8 NIS.

Nahalat Shiv'a

Situated right at the heart of the New City centre, Nahalat Shiv'a is the bar and cafe-filled equivalent of London's Covent Garden. It was one of the first residential areas to be created outside the walls of the Old City, founded in 1869 by a consortium of seven families – hence the name, 'Quarter of the Seven'. However, by the time of the British Mandate its narrow alleys and tight courtyards had become almost deserted and the area was slated for clearance. It survived, but was threatened with destruction once again in the 1950s by a municipality intent on modernisation. Somewhere along the line someone saw the light, and instead of being flattened the neighbourhood received a facelift. Commercial revitalisation followed and the small cluster of picturesque lanes are now the flourishing focus of the New City's nightlife, home to a cache of trendy eateries and open-all-hours cafes bars. See the Places to Eat chapter.

Museum of Italian Jewish Art & Synagogue

In 1952, with no Jews left in Conegliano Veneto near Venice, the interior of that town's 18th century synagogue was dismantled and reassembled here. It now serves the needs of Italian Jews in Jerusalem and is the only synagogue outside Italy where the ancient Italian liturgy is performed.

The architecture and art displayed in the adjacent museum is there for public appreciation. The synagogue/museum (☎ 624 1610) is on the south-west fringe of Nahalat Shiv'a at 27 Hillel St. It's open Sunday to Tuesday and Thursday from 10 am to 1 pm, and Wednesday from 4 to 7 pm. Admission is 10 NIS. Shabbat services are held here.

Zion Square & Ben Yehuda St

Pedestrianised Ben Yehuda St (known in Hebrew as the *midrahov*, from a combination of the words for street and pavement) is the secular heart of Jerusalem. Much of the city's best shopping is on or around here. With the absence of traffic, the broad sloping street is instead congested with the street furniture of countless cafes, making it a favourite place for quick lunches or languorous coffees. Entertainment, of sorts, is provided by buskers who are typically Russian immigrants with accordion-accompanied songs of melancholy or, in summer, young Americans with acoustic guitars and an excruciating preference for Don McLean.

At its lower end, Ben Yehuda is linked to Jaffa Rd by Zion Square. This is a cramped and shabby plaza that nonetheless continues to serve as the focal point of the New City. It is a popular rallying point for demonstrations, a venue for agitated orators to get up on their soap box, and a place to meet and hang out for the city's youth. The square is also home to one of the city's biggest planning foul-ups, a hideous multistorey tower block that is totally out of keeping with the surrounding architecture.

Ticho House (Beit Ticho)

The former home of Dr Abraham Ticho and his artist wife, Anna, this combination of museum, art gallery, shop, library and cafe is now administered by the Israel Museum.

Dr Ticho, a Jew, was a leader in the field of ophthalmology and during the British Mandate was responsible for saving hundreds of Palestinian Arabs from blindness. Included in the exhibits is Dr Ticho's study and some documents and letters of interest, in particular those dealing with his work for the Arabs, as well as his collection of Hanukkah lamps and some examples of Anna Ticho's art.

However, the appeal of the museum is secondary to the popularity of its charming ground floor cafe, which also spills out onto a terrace overlooking a large, tranquil garden.

Ticho House (☎ 624 5068) is just off Harav Kook St. It's open Sunday, Monday, Wednesday and Thursday from 10 am to 5 pm, Tuesday from 10 am to 10 pm, and Friday from 10 am to 2 pm, closed Saturday. There's no admission charge.

The cafe is open Sunday to Thursday from 10 am to midnight, Friday from 10 am to 3 pm, and Saturday from sunset to midnight.

The neighbouring building, along the north side of Ticho St, the little alley leading to Ticho House, is also of some historical significance. Known as **Beit David**, this large block was another of the earliest settlements outside the city walls and would have originally housed a number of Jewish families. The upper storey, which is a later addition, was home to the first Ashkenazi Chief Rabbi of Palestine and is open to the public as the **Rabbi Kook Museum**.

HaNevi'im Street

HaNevi'im, or Street of the Prophets, divides the worldly central New City (map 9) from the isolationist ultraorthodox neighbourhoods that lie just to the north (map 8). During the 19th century it was one of the city's main thoroughfares and the address of choice for many European (and other) consulates, missions and agencies. The street remains the most convenient route for anyone staying in East Jerusalem or around Damascus Gate to reach the Russian Compound or Zion Square area of the New City.

One of the most prominent and striking structures on the street is the **Italian Hospital**, built early this century, but with decoration, red roof tiles and square tower borrowed from 16th century Florence. (The architect was Antonio Barluzzi, who also designed two of the churches on the Mount of Olives.) It wasn't a hospital for long, as during the Mandate it was taken over by the British air force. It now houses the Israeli Ministry of Education & Culture.

Just to the east of the Italian Hospital is the **Ethiopian Consulate**, a memorial to the times when Israel enjoyed a close relationship with the government of Haile Selassie. It has an attractive blue and gold lion mosaic above the door (see Ethiopia St below).

At No 58 HaNevi'im is **Thabor House**, which was built and occupied by a Swiss Protestant missionary

EDDIE GERALD
Colonnade in the new City Hall overlooking the
Old City

turned architect and amateur archaeologist, Conrad
Schick. A self-taught draughtsman, Schick is most
famous for designing the original settlement of Mea
She'arim, the Leper Hospital in Talbiyeh, and this, his
eccentric house. It's fashioned like a mini German castle,
and various ancient artefacts that Schick discovered are
embedded in the facade. The house is now owned by the
Swedish Theological Institute – they will usually allow
curious visitors into the courtyard.

A few doors down from Thabor House at No 64 is the
one-time Jerusalem home of the English pre-Raphaelite
painter **William Holman Hunt** (1827-1910), who arrived
in the city in 1854. During his time here, the evangelical
Holman Hunt painted several of his best known, bibli-
cally-inspired works using local residents as his models.
The house is now a private residence and is closed to the
public. Further west on HaNevi'im St is the **Anglican
School**, built in 1901 as the English Mission Hospital. It
takes the form of seven pavilions built in a semicircle
around a front lawn. HaNevi'im St was a prime site for
missionary activities because of the proximity of the new
Jewish neighbourhoods. These activities infuriated the
local orthodox communities and they boycotted the hospital facilities. It might be sweet revenge then that the
school, which is attended by the children of diplomats
and UN personnel, is soon to close – the building has
been bought by an ultraorthodox organisation.

HaNevi'im St ends – or starts, depending on where
you set out from – with the **Davidka Monument**, at
Davidka Square, where an example of the primitive and

EDDIE GERALD

Ben Yehuda Street, the place to go for endless coffees and
the city's best shopping

unreliable mortar of the same name is displayed. This
weapon was used by the Jews to great effect in 1948 – it
did little physical damage but the story goes that it made
such a loud noise that it scared the living daylights out
of the enemy.

Ethiopia St

Tucked away on narrow, leafy Ethiopia St, the impressive, domed **Ethiopian Church** would be a major feature
in most cities, but in Jerusalem it is often overlooked.
Built between 1896 and 1904, the church's entrance gate
features the carved Lion of Judah, an emblem believed
to have been presented to the Queen of Sheba (Ethiopia)
by Solomon when she visited Jerusalem.

This church is open March to September daily from 7
am to 6 pm (slightly shorter hours in winter) and admission is free.

Opposite the church is **Ben Yehuda House**, where the
great linguist lived and did much of his work on the
revival of the Hebrew language (see the Literature
section in the Facts about Jerusalem chapter). A plaque
marking the house was stolen by ultraorthodox Jews,
who strongly disapprove of the language's everyday
use, feeling it should be reserved for religious use only.

Bezalel School of Art

Near the junction of King George V and Ben Yehuda Sts,
at 10 Shmuel HaNagid St (see map 9), this is Israel's

premier art school, founded in 1906. It is named after the Old Testament artist Bezalel Ben-Ouri (Exodus 31:2-11).

Next door to the main school building, at 12 Shmuel HaNagid St, the **Artists' House** (☎ 223 653) features an art gallery, shop and a bar/restaurant. The gallery is open Monday to Friday from 9 am to 1 pm and 4 to 7 pm, Saturday and Sunday from 10 am to 1 pm and 4 to 7 pm, and admission is free. The bar/restaurant is open daily, usually until after midnight.

Mahane Yehuda Market

About a km west of Zion Square between Jaffa Rd and Agrippas St, this fabulous market is a spectacle in its own right even if you don't want to do any shopping. We've never seen bigger, redder strawberries than we saw here, and an unflinching nature is required to buy the fish which have to be brained into submission before they can be wrapped. Other stalls laden with all manner of fruit, vegetables, pickles, olives and cheeses stand among cheap butcheries, bakeries and wholesale *mahkolets* (grocery shops).

On Agrippas St there are several great places for spicy *meorav Yerushalmi* (barbecued meats), and these are open from the early evening until early morning (see the Places to Eat chapter).

The market is at its gloriously bustling best on Thursday and Friday during the pre-Shabbat scramble.

Gan Ha'Atzmaut

Created by the British during the Mandate period, Gan Ha'Atzmaut (Independence Park) is Jerusalem's largest public park. That said, it has little to recommend it – it is unkempt, surrounded by traffic and offers none of the wonderful views of other grassy areas such as the Bloomfield Gardens. The eastern part of the park is actually a Muslim cemetery, within which is the **Mamilla Pool**, a large and ancient rainwater cistern.

Heichal Shlomo & the Great Synagogue

At the southern end of King George V St, facing the Sheraton Plaza Hotel, this 1960s complex is supposedly styled along the lines of Solomon's Temple – Heichal Shlomo literally means 'Solomon's Mansion' – and is the seat of the Chief Rabbinate of Israel and the Supreme Religious Centre. The emblem of the scales of justice is featured on both sides of the entrance.

The Modesty Squads
Made bold by the empowerment that came with their parliamentary gains in the 1996 elections, the ultra-orthodox communities of Jerusalem have been flexing their muscles. No longer content to signal their objections and prejudices with tersely worded signs and sermons, since summer 1996 so-called 'modesty squads' have taken to assaulting women they believe are dressed immorally. According to a newspaper report, one Israeli employee of the Education Ministry, which is located on the fringes of Mea She'arim, was attacked by haredim 'swinging chains and pipes and throwing stones'. She ran to her car only to find that the mob had slashed her tyres. Another female ministry worker narrowly escaped being brained with iron bars and having her car set on fire.

We have yet to see how the Jerusalem authorities will react to the zealots and for the moment can only urge visitors to the ultraorthodox neighbourhoods to take particular care concerning their dress. ∎

The **Wolfson Museum** (☎ 624 7112) housed inside the massive building features presentations of religious and traditional Jewish life. It's open Sunday to Thursday from 9 am to 1 pm. It is closed on Friday and Saturday. Admission is 5 NIS.

Next door to Heichal Shlomo, and part of the same complex, is the Great Synagogue. The building has been condemned by many as an extravagant waste of money.

MEA SHE'ARIM & THE BUKHARAN QUARTER

Mea She'arim and the Bukharan Quarter, along with neighbouring Ge'ula and other small adjacent neighbourhoods, are the heartland of Jerusalem's ultra-orthodox contingent. The residents (known in Hebrew as *haredim*) mostly dress in 18th century Eastern European styles, with the slight differences in their heavy garb denoting the different sects. They are mainly devoted to religious study and are frequently financed by fellow ultraorthodox communities abroad.

A result of the uncompromising interpretation of Jewish Law here is the attitude of residents towards strangers. Signs proclaim 'Daughters of Israel! The Torah requires you to dress modestly'. The edict applies equally to non-Jewish daughters too, as other notices make plain. Women visitors to the area must not wear shorts or off-the-shoulder tops – loose fitting skirts (long trousers are frowned upon for showing off the figure too much) and long-sleeved blouses are recommended. Male visitors should also refrain from walking through Mea She'arim in shorts. Do not walk arm in arm or even hand in hand with anyone, and kissing in public is a most definite taboo. Most ultraorthodox Jews dislike being photographed – in fact, their interpretation of Jewish Law forbids it.

The more extreme characters have been known to stone those, Jewish and non-Jewish, who break these codes of conduct, however unwittingly. Signalled or verbal objections are more common, though.

Mea She'arim

Possibly the world's most reluctant tourist attraction, this ultraorthodox Jewish district is the only remaining example of the *shtetl* (ghettos) which existed before the Holocaust in Eastern European Jewish communities.

The district's main artery is **Mea She'arim St** (see map 8). Notice all the graffiti and posters – the many different ultraorthodox sects inhabiting the area don't necessarily see eye to eye on all issues, and the walls of the neighbourhood are busy with propaganda, denunciations and ripostes. At the top of Harav Shmuel Salant St (the first left coming from Shivtei Y'Israel St) is the site of the former **Jerusalem Gate**, one of the six gates of the original settlement. At night these gates were locked to keep out bandits. Today only an iron bar remains and potential intruders are instead warded off with a barrage of warnings about immodest dress, mixing of the sexes and the unwelcome nature of gawping tourists.

The undeterred who press on will enter a warren of narrow alleys. Mea She'arim is a tight collection of small communities, each of which was designed to be a self-contained unit. The blocks of housing all face inwards, focused on one large building which serves as the religious teaching centre, synagogue and communal hall. One such building, **Beit Avraham** (Abraham's House), lies about 100m north-west beyond the Jerusalem Gate (straight on along the narrow alleyway and take the second left). If you cut north, back onto Mea She'arim street, walk west for 50m then head down the short flight of stairs on your right, you enter **Batei Ungarin** (Hungarian Houses), one of the best preserved of the area's *kolel* – neighbourhoods comprised of residents from one particular country or city in Europe and administered by a committee.

Jewish holidays are always the best time to visit Mea She'arim, as the entire area throws itself into the celebra-

ISRAELI MINISTRY OF TOURISM

A resident of the orthodox neighbourhood of Mea She'arim

tions with an enthusiasm not to be witnessed anywhere else in the city.

Bukharan Quarter

Established towards the end of the 19th century by Jews from the Central Asian khanates (now cities) of Bukhara and Samarkand, this was one of Jerusalem's most wealthy and exclusive districts. Unlike neighbouring Mea She'arim, an area dedicated to cramped communal dwelling and humility, the Bukharan Quarter was laid out on a spacious grid of wide tree-lined streets, with a collection of regal and elegant one-family mansions.

Shabbat Square

At one time this was just an unnamed major traffic junction where busy Mea She'arim St met blaring Strauss St. Now, it has acquired the informal name of Kikar Shabbat (Shabbat Square) and on one day every week it is completely quiet as for 24 hours it becomes off-limits to all motorised vehicles.

Observant Jews are forbidden from operating machinery on the Sabbath, a ruling that precludes driving. Not content simply to leave their own cars parked for the duration, the uncompromising ultraorthodox go so far as to insist that no one, practicing Jew or not, drives a vehicle in their part of town. To enforce their will, during the 1980s they held weekly Shabbat demonstrations at the junction in question, barraging errant motorists with cries of 'Shabbes! Shabbes!' and the occasional hurled missile. The end result was the complete closure of the junction, together with neighbouring Mea She'arim St, from sundown Friday to sun up Saturday.

In summer 1996, militant orthodox groups resumed their demonstrations, demanding further road closures. Nightly TV news reports showed black-hatted haredim in violent clashes with mounted riot police. It may not be long before Shabbat Square is supplemented with the likes of 'Stone Throwers' Alley' and 'Water Canon Ave'. ■

Many of these houses were used purely as summer residences – more often than not used only every second summer because the trip to Jerusalem and back was too long to make annually. In the aftermath of the Russian Revolution, Central Asia's Jews were stripped of their wealth and prevented from travelling. The sumptuous homes in Jerusalem were either lost or had to be rented out. The Quarter began a slide into decline. The change in character was further hastened when the ultra-orthodoxy of Mea She'arim moved in to fill the vacuum.

Though neglected and decaying, the Bukharan Quarter is still worth a visit. Most impressive of all is **Beit Yehudayoff** at 19 Ezra St, a great birthday cake of a building designed by an Italian architect for a particularly well-off Bukharan family. Known locally as 'the Palace', it has more than 30 rooms and once served as the headquarters of the Ottomans in Jerusalem. A reception for General Allenby and his victorious officers was also held in this mansion when the British took Jerusalem in 1917. It now houses two girls' schools. Also of note are the pagoda-roofed **Davidoff House** and the **Mosheioff House**, built by one of the Quarter's founding families.

REHAVIA & TALBIYEH

Built in the earlier part of this century by Jewish intellectuals (Rehavia) and wealthy Christian Arabs (Talbiyeh), these are among the city's more fashionable neighbourhoods – although the steadily increasing number of ultraorthodox Jewish residents is said to be changing that.

Rehavia stands in strict opposition to the conservative religious Jewish enclaves such as Mea She'arim and Batei Ungarin. It has traditionally been home to the like of intellectuals, Zionists and politicians – it is still home to the residences of both the prime minister and president. Much of the local architecture reflects the neighbourhood's progressive origins – at No 6 Balfour Street, for example, is the **Schocken Library**, designed by the modernist German architect Erich Mendelsohn (who fled to Jerusalem to escape the Nazis).

The houses of Talbiyeh (also known as Komemiyut) are more traditional in nature, but in many cases also wonderfully self-indulgent – take a look at No 17 Alkalay St, a house called **Beit Jalad**, built by an Arab contractor with a fondness for the imagery of *The Thousand and One Nights*.

Place de France & Ramban St

Place de France (also known as Zarfat Square) marks the junction of the city centre with Rehavia. It's dominated by the bulk of the **Terra Sancta** building, an underused college built by the Catholic Church in 1927. Just 100m west along Ramban St is the **Rehavia windmill**, one of two in Jerusalem (the other is in Mamilla). This was a functioning mill last century and it stood in an area of wheat fields. In the 1930s it became the home and offices of the architect Erich Mendelsohn while he designed the Hebrew University and Hadassah Hospital buildings on Mt Scopus. It is now part of a shopping complex.

Jason's Tomb

It's not worth the long walk to get here because there really is nothing to see but a cave barred by a rusting iron gate in a leafy suburban street. For archaeologists, however, this was one of the city's most interesting tombs because it provided a wealth of historical information. Built in the early 1st century BC by someone called Jason, it contains two or three generations of his family. The tomb told archaeologists about 1st century concepts of the afterlife – lighting and cooking pots,

EDDIE GERALD

The Museum of Islamic Art

complete with food, were provided in the individual graves, and some dice were found – gambling in heaven? The porch's charcoal drawings of a warship in pursuit of two other vessels suggest that Jason or a son was a naval officer.

If you're in the neighbourhood you may want to visit the tomb, which is on Alfasi St; look through the iron grille to see the burial chamber. Eight shaft graves can be seen through the small opening on the left.

LA Mayer Museum of Islamic Art

Housed in a modern, purpose-built structure at 2 HaPalmach St in Talbiyeh, this is a far better Islamic museum than that on the Haram ash-Sharif/Temple Mount. The collection here includes some beautiful Mogul miniatures, Persian tiling and various items of weaponry and jewellery from several different eras. All the exhibits are well labelled and attractively presented.

The museum (☎ 566 1291/2) is open Sunday, Monday, Wednesday and Thursday from 10 am to 5 pm, Tuesday from 4 pm to 8 pm, Friday from 10 am to 4 pm, and Saturday from 10 am to 2 pm. Admission is 8 NIS (students 6 NIS). To get here take bus No 15 from King George V St in the city centre.

MAMILLA

Bordering the Old City walls from Jaffa Gate up to Zahal Square and rolling across the valley to busy HaMelekh David St, Mamilla links old and new Jerusalem (see

EDDIE GERALD

The YMCA, famous for its architectual design

maps 9 and 10). At the beginning of this century it was a busy commercial district shared between Arabs and Jews, but the fighting in 1948 resulted in the border being drawn through Mamilla, and for 19 years the place existed as a sniper-targeted no-man's-land.

Such prime real estate wasn't going to lie fallow for too long, however, and since reunification numerous new developments have either been completed or are well under way. The most high profile of these is **David's Village**, a cluster of prestige residential blocks across the valley from Jaffa Gate. The sales pitch for these apartments is appropriately enough 'for those who can afford to live like a king' – except the village is not named, as you might assume, for the biblical King David but for the developer behind the project, David Taic. Adjacent to the village is a luxury **Hilton hotel**, expected to open in 1997, and there's also a shopping centre, parks and new highways to come.

HaMelekh David St, which runs south from the New City centre down to the railway station, escaped the fighting relatively unscathed and is home to several important landmarks, including the architecturally noteworthy **Hebrew Union College** building, the King David Hotel and the YMCA. The road leads to Herod's Family Tomb, the Yemin Moshe neighbourhood and Liberty Bell Gardens.

St Vincent de Paul Hospice

On HaEmek St (also known as Mamilla Rd) down from Jaffa Gate, this large convent is another of those wonderful Jerusalem buildings that gets lost in the crowd. It's an orphanage built in the late 19th century by the Sisters of Charity, a Paris-based order of nuns.

Note also the house at No 33 HaEmek St that bears a plaque recording that **Dr Theodor Herzl**, the founder of political Zionism, stayed here during his visit to Palestine in 1898.

The YMCA & the King David Hotel

Designed by the architect of New York's Empire State Building and completed in 1933, Jerusalem's YMCA building on HaMelekh David St is an appealing mix of Romanesque and Orientalism. The vaulted lobby is especially attractive and it's worthwhile poking your nose inside. Although for a time closed to the public after being used for an attempted suicide, the building's distinctive tower is open again, Monday to Saturday from 9 am to 2 pm, closed Sunday. Admission is 3 NIS. At the YMCA is the well-appointed Three Arches Hotel (see the Places to Stay chapter for details).

The stadium behind the main building used to be home to Jerusalem's football team but it's now moved to a new, modern ground (the Teddy Stadium) beside the Kanyon shopping centre in the west of the city.

Opposite the YMCA, and obscuring its view of the Old City, is the ungainly bulk of the King David Hotel (see the Places to Stay chapter). What the Savoy is to London and Raffles to Singapore, so is the King David to Jerusalem. Designed in 1930 by a Swiss architect, Emil Vogt, for an Egyptian Jewish family, the hotel has been host to Winston Churchill, Anwar Sadat, the last five US presidents, Elizabeth Taylor and Kirk Douglas, to name but a few. Home to the British military high command during the Mandate, in 1946 the hotel's southern wing was blown up by the Irgun, the underground militia led by the future prime minister Menachem Begin.

Herod's Family Tomb

Discovered in 1892, archaeologists believe that this may be the tomb of the family of King Herod because of its size and grandeur. Unfortunately, little was found inside to back up this theory, as tomb robbers had been there first. Herod himself is not buried here but at Herodian, near Bethlehem. The tomb is at the northern edge of Bloomfield Gardens on Aba Sikra St, just south of the King David Hotel.

Yemin Moshe & the Windmill

The small Yemin Moshe neighbourhood can be identified immediately by its windmill, one of the very first structures to be built outside the secure confines of the Old City.

The windmill was part of a scheme developed by Sir Moses Montefiore, an English Jewish philanthropist who wanted to ease the overcrowding within the city walls. He built a single block of 24 small apartments, buttressed either side by a synagogue, and called it **Mishkenot Sha'ananim** or 'Dwellings of Tranquillity'. The windmill was to have provided the basis for a flour industry. This aspect of the scheme failed (not enough wind) and the windmill is now an eccentric landmark serving as a museum dedicated to the life and work of Montefiore. It's open Sunday to Thursday from 9 am to 4 pm, and Friday from 9 am to 1 pm, closed Saturday.

Even if the windmill proved inappropriate, the idea of living outside the city walls was a success, and Yemin Moshe came into being in the 1890s. Despite being in the firing line, many of its residents clung on through the partition years of 1948 to '67, only to be turfed out after reunification as part of the municipality's gentrification plan for the area. Yemin Moshe is now one of the city's most desirable addresses.

The Mishkenot Sha'ananim complex is now a guesthouse for 'creative' visitors to Jerusalem, and past tenants have included Simone de Beauvoir, Isaiah Berlin, Marc Chagall, Milan Kundera and VS Naipaul.

Arts & Crafts Lane (Khutsot HaYotser)

Originally a small settlement of Sephardic Jews, Khutsot HaYotser was rebuilt in the 1920s as an Arab market and workshop complex. From 1948 on it sat abandoned in the middle of no-man's-land, and it was only when the barbed wire was removed in 1967 that reconstruction could begin. Today, it's a curious arcade (curious in that the arcade leads from nowhere to nowhere) of art galleries, craft workshops and a couple of cafes (see the Shopping chapter). It's not really worth a special trip but you might conceivably pass this way walking from the Old City to the Cinematheque or Talbiyeh.

Liberty Bell Gardens

Just west of the Montefiore Windmill, across traffic-logged David Remez St, are these gardens, which cover three hectares and have as their central point an exact

EDDIE GERALD

The attractive streets of Mishkenot Sha'ananim

replica of the Liberty Bell in Philadelphia. The gardens are often a venue for public events and are popular with picnickers.

St Andrew's Church

Also known as the Scottish Church, St Andrew's was built in 1927 in memory of the Scottish soldiers lost in the campaign to capture Palestine in WWI. It's owned by the Church of Scotland and the floor features an inscription to the memory of Robert the Bruce, who requested that his heart be buried in Jerusalem when he died. Sir James Douglas made an attempt at fulfilling Bruce's wish but en route he was killed in Spain, fighting the Moors. The heart was recovered and returned to Scotland where it's now buried at Melrose.

Jerusalem Film Centre & Cinematheque

Perched on the valleyside below Hebron Rd, with great views across to Mt Zion and the Old City, this complex (☎ 671 5398) houses several cinema screens, a small museum, a library and archives relating to the film industry. It's open Sunday and Monday from 10 am to 3 pm, Tuesday and Thursday from 10 am to 7 pm, and Friday from 10 am to 1 pm. Also part of the complex is the Cinematheque (see the Entertainment chapter) and a popular vegetarian restaurant.

EDDIE GERALD

Liberty Bell Gardens, a popular area for picnics

Sultan's Pool

Now a unique open-air amphitheatre used for a variety of concerts, this was originally a city reservoir created by the Mamluk Sultan Barquq in the 14th century and later renovated by Sultan Suleyman the Great. Its location, nestled below the walls of the Old City, makes it a spectacularly atmospheric venue: check the listings in *The Jerusalem Post* or ask at the tourist information office on Jaffa Rd in the New City, and if anybody is performing here (Stevie Wonder and Neil Young were playing during our last visit), get a ticket.

Sultan's Pool lies between Yemin Moshe and Hativat Yerushalayim, and beside the road above it is a beautiful 16th century sabil (drinking fountain), erected during the reign of Suleyman.

THE GERMAN COLONY

South of Talbiyeh, the German Colony (in Hebrew, HaMoshava HaGermanit) was founded in 1873 by a group of Templers, a Protestant sect, from rural southern Germany. The community arrived with the idea of founding in Jerusalem 'a small kingdom of heaven upon earth', which they modelled along the lines of a typical German village. The Germans were initially admired by the Jews for their work ethic and efficiency, but relations soured when the existence of a branch of the Nazi Party was uncovered in the Colony during the mid-1930s. In 1939 the Templars were deported by the British, who also took over their property. With the end of the

---

The Pool of Abomination
Jerusalem's first public swimming pool lies at No 13 Emek Refa'im St in the German Colony. Its construction, undertaken in the 1960s, prompted violent demonstrations by the city's ultraorthodox communities who venomously denounced the venture as an 'abomination' because it allowed men and women to swim together. ∎

Mandate the abandoned homes were filled by Jewish immigrants. The area has subsequently undergone a process of gentrification and is now one of the city's classier neighbourhoods.

TALPIOT

Talpiot (divided geographically into Talpiot, East Talpiot and North Talpiot) is one of Jerusalem's new suburbs. Lying astride the Bethlehem and Hebron Rds, and incorporating a large industrial estate, other than the few highlights described below it has nothing to offer apart from a multiplex cinema.

Haas Promenade

This terraced promenade was created to take advantage of some of the most spectacular views of the Old City and surroundings. A little difficult to get to without a car, it is nonetheless always busy, even at night when Jerusalemites flock here to sit at the outdoor cafes or dine in the picture-windowed restaurants. In Hebrew it's sometimes referred to as the Tayelet. Adjoining it is the similar Sherover Promenade. To get here take bus No 8 from Jaffa Rd and get off at the Kiryat Moriah stop.

Hill of Evil Counsel

A little to the east and below the Haas Promenade is the Hill of Evil Counsel. It's an alternative possibility for the location of the house of Caiaphas, the high priest who paid Judas to betray Jesus. Since 1933 it has also been the site of **Government House,** built as the residency of the British High Commissioner for Palestine during the Mandate, and now the headquarters of the United Nations in Israel – a beautiful building but sadly closed to the public. In Hebrew the place is known as Armon HaNatziv (the Palace of the Commissioner).

Agnon House (Beit Agnon)

The former residence of Nobel Prize-winning author SY Agnon, the house contains his library plus sundry exhibits and a video screening on the man and his work. There are guided tours in English; phone for details (☎ 671 6498). The house is open Sunday to Thursday 9 am to 1 pm and Saturday 10 am to 1 pm. It's at 16 Joseph Klausner St (see Map 1); take bus No 7 from the city centre.

GIVAT RAM & MUSEUM ROW

West of central Jerusalem and due south of the central bus station is the green swathe of Givat Ram (see map 17), which over the last 30 years or so has developed as the institutional heart of the city. As well as being home to the Knesset (the seat of the Israeli parliament) and the several museums mentioned below, it is also the site of the **prime minister's office** (usually easily identified by the placard-wielding protesters outside), the headquarters of the **Bank of Israel** and the Supreme Court building. You can get here from Jaffa Rd on bus No 9, 24 or 28 (to the university).

Israel Museum

The country's leading museum, this is a purpose-built grouping of several buildings on a specially created, landscaped site. It includes the excellent **Bezalel Art Wing**, which brings together work that ranges from Islamic calligraphy to Francis Bacon and is, as would be expected, strong on Jewish artists, including Chagall and Soutine. There's also the **Bronfman Biblical & Archaeological Wing**, exhibiting finds made in the Holy Land from prehistoric artefacts through to Roman and Byzantine remains, and a hall devoted to the Jewish community and ethnography.

Indisputably the museum's biggest drawcard, however, is the **Shrine of the Book**, the distinctive potlid shaped building at the north of the site. In the dimly lit subterranean chamber are displayed some of the 2000 year old Dead Sea Scrolls that were found in caves at Qumran, near the Dead Sea in 1947.

Aside from all the above there's a **sculpture garden** with work by Henry Moore, Picasso and Rodin, among others, as well as a **Youth Wing** for children. There are always several temporary exhibitions at any one time, as well as programmes of concerts, lectures and films.

The museum is open Sunday, Monday, Wednesday and Thursday from 10 am to 5 pm, Tuesday from 4 to 10

EDDIE GERALD A

AUSTRALIA-ISRAEL CHAMBER OF COMMERCE B

EDDIE GERALD C

EDDIE GERALD D

A: The Knesset
B: Dancers at the Hebrew University
C: The Supreme Court Building
D: The Shrine of the Book

pm, Friday from 10 am to 2 pm, and Saturday from 10 am to 4 pm. Admission is 20 NIS (students 15 NIS). Telephone ☎ 670 8811 for recorded information or check the tourist information office and *The Jerusalem Post* for details of special exhibits and events.

Guided tours in English are included in the museum admission price. They start from the main entrance and deal with a specific area rather than the whole complex. There's a good museum highlights tour daily (Saturday and Tuesday excepted) at 11 am and also Sunday, Monday, Wednesday and Thursday at 3 pm. On Sunday at 11 am it is given in French.

The Bible Lands Museum

One of the latest additions to the New City's cultural scene, this museum is billed as 'a nondenominational centre for the appreciation of the history of the Bible'. Dating from 6000 BC to 600 AD and presented chronologically, the exhibits include some 2000 artefacts. These range from mosaics and other art pieces, seals, ivories and bronzes to simple household items from all over Asia, Europe and Africa.

The Bible Lands Museum (☎ 561 1066) is on Granot St, adjacent to the Israel Museum. It's open Sunday, Monday, Tuesday and Thursday from 9.30 am to 5.30 pm, Wednesday from 9.30 am to 9.30 pm, Friday from 9.30 am to 2 pm, and Saturday from 11 am to 3 pm. Admission is 18 NIS.

The Knesset

A few minutes walk from the Israel Museum is HaKirya (The City), the government centre, dominated by the Knesset, Israel's parliament building. Belonging to the multistorey car park school of architecture, the building was inaugurated in 1966 – previously the parliament had met in what is now the Ministry of Tourism on King George V St. At least the modern Knesset is a lot more attractive inside than out, and it has a foyer decorated with three tapestries and a mosaic by Marc Chagall.

The building is open to the public on Sunday and Thursday from 8.30 am to 2.30 pm, when free guided tours are given. Bring your passport. You can also see the Knesset in session on Monday or Tuesday from 4 to 7 pm, and Sunday and Thursday from 11 am to 7 pm. The proceedings are conducted mainly in Hebrew and occasionally in Arabic. For further information call ☎ 675 3333.

Next to the bus stops opposite the Knesset is a bronze **menorah**, a gift from British supporters of the State of Israel. It's decorated with panels representing important figures and events in Jewish history. Just north of the menorah is the **Wohl Rose Park**, with over 10,000 bushes representing some 650 varieties of the plant.

Supreme Court Building

Not an obvious tourist attraction, the Court (dedicated in 1993) nevertheless attracts many visitors who come to admire what is reckoned to be one of the most important and impressive architectural creations in Israel. It's open to the public Sunday to Thursday from 8.30 am to 2.30 pm with free guided tours in English given on Sunday and Wednesday at 11 am. For further information and to confirm tour times, call ☎ 675 9612.

The Bloomfield Science Museum

Part of the Hebrew University (see below), this museum is devoted to aiding the understanding of the natural and technological worlds through a series of hands-on exhibits. It's designed primarily with the young in mind and it's a great place to take kids. The museum (☎ 561 8128) is open Monday, Wednesday and Thursday from 10 am to 6 pm, Tuesday from 10 am to 8 pm, Friday from 10 am to 1 pm and Saturday from 10 am to 3 pm. Admission is 12 NIS.

Hebrew University & Botanical Garden

The Givat Ram campus was created after 1948 when the original Hebrew University on Mt Scopus was cut off from Israeli held Jerusalem by the Jordanian frontline. The **University Library** here is the largest in the Middle East. Other features of interest include the **Academy of the Hebrew Language**, which displays the library and furniture of Eliezer Ben Yehuda, who was responsible for the revival of the Hebrew language, and the **Rubin Academy of Music & Dance**, which has a collection of ancient and old musical instruments. It's open Sunday to Thursday from 10 am to 8 pm during the academic year only. The campus also features a strikingly designed puff-ball shaped synagogue. Free daily guided tours of the campus start at 9 and 11 am at the old Sherman building.

On the eastern slopes of Givat Ram and a part of the university, the **Botanical Garden** is one of the city's best hidden beauty spots, a 12 hectare haven of flowers, pools and trees. Admission is free and it is open from early morning to sunset every day of the week. For further details call ☎ 636 342.

Monastery of the Cross

This great walled compound looks like a desert monastery, and appears completely out of place in the middle of the large urban sprawl of the New City – up until this century the city lay a mile or more from this then isolated valley. Founded by King Bagrat of Georgia, the monastery was built to commemorate the tradition that the tree from which Jesus' cross was made grew here. The monastery is basically 11th century, although various additions have been made since then. The Greek Orthodox Church purchased the complex in 1685.

It's worth a visit just to appreciate the incongruity, which is even greater once inside, but there are also some interesting 17th century frescoes, a bit of 5th century mosaic floor in the chapel and a small museum. The monastery is open Monday to Friday from 9 am to 4 pm, closed Saturday and Sunday. Admission is 5 NIS. It can be reached by walking through Rehavia along Ramban St, crossing Khay'in Hazaz Ave (Hanasi Ben Zvi) and following the path down the hillside. From the city centre take bus No 31 or 32; from Jaffa Gate, bus No 19. Get off at the first stop on Harav Herzog St and follow the path down.

WEST OF THE NEW CITY

For the locations of all the following places see map 1 on the inside front cover.

Model of Ancient Jerusalem

About 2.5 km south-west of Givat Ram in the grounds of the Holyland Hotel (☎ 643 7777) is a huge 1:50 scale model of Jerusalem as it was in 66 AD, at the end of the Second Temple period. While the model is fantastic and the attention to detail is incredible, it's a long way out of town and only those with a keen interest in Jewish history or archaeology are going to find the trip worthwhile.

The model is open for viewing Sunday to Thursday from 8 am to 8 pm, and Friday and Saturday from 8 am to 5 pm (closing daily at 4 pm during the winter months). Admission is 10 NIS (students 6 NIS). Take bus No 21 or 21A.

MAP 5

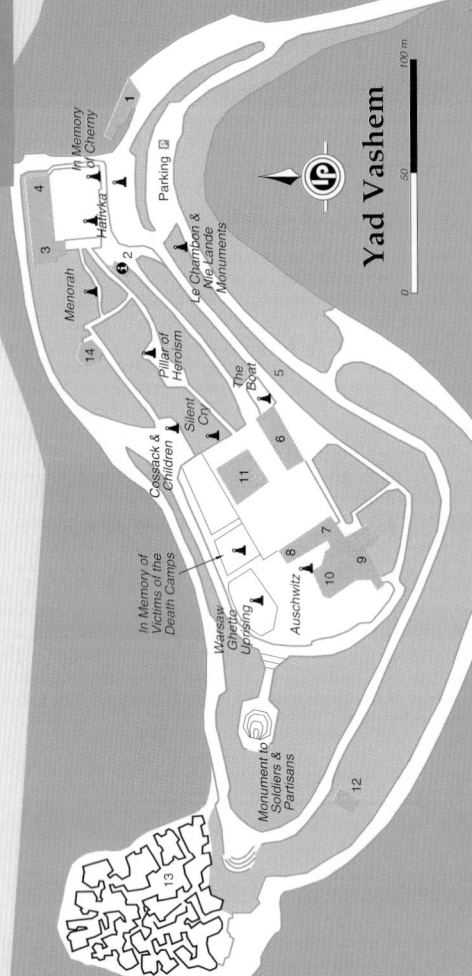

Yad Vashem

To Mt Herzl, Herzl Museum & Buses

0   50   100 m

Parking

In Memory of Cherry
Menorah
Hatryka
Le Chambon & Nie-Lande Monuments
Pillar of Heroism
Cossack & Children
Silent Cry
The Boat
In Memory of Victims of the Death Camps
Warsaw Ghetto Uprising
Auschwitz
Monument to Soldiers & Partisans

1 Cafeteria & Toilets.
2 Information Kiosk & Bookshop.
3 World Holocaust Teaching Centre.
4 Offices & Archives.
5 Avenue of Righteous Gentiles. This and the surrounding gardens are a memorial to the non-Jews who risked their lives to save Jews. The trees bordering the avenue bear plaques in remembrance of named individuals.
6 Historical Museum. A comprehensive and harrowing presentation of the events of the Holocaust presented through documents, photographs, artefacts and short films.
7 The Hall of Names. Containing over three million pages of testimony by Holocaust victims who have registered here.
8 Synagogue.
9 Art Gallery. A collection of work produced under some of the most unbearable conditions imaginable.
10 Auditorium.
11 Hall of Remembrance. A vast empty floor space marked simply with the names of the 21 largest concentration and death camps. On Holocaust Day (see Public Holidays in the Facts for the Visitor chapter), the Martyrs & Heroes Remembrance Day Assembly is held here and attended by the President of Israel and other national leaders.
12 Boxcar Monument of the Transportations.
13 Valley of the Destroyed Communities. Commemorating the European Jewish communities that were wiped out during WWII.
14 Children's Memorial.

New Biblical Zoo

Also known as the Tisch Family Zoological Gardens, since 1993 this has replaced the much reviled old Biblical Zoo that once existed in the north of the city. While fairly small, the new zoo (☎ 643 0111; 643 0122) is attractively landscaped with lakes, streams and grassy picnic areas. The animals seem to be well looked after with few cramped cages in evidence. One major aim of the zoo is to breed and reintroduce into Israel various species that through references in the Bible are known to have once inhabited this region – biblical quotes accompany the traditional Latin names and descriptions (in English as well as Hebrew and Arabic) tagged to the pens. The zoo is open Sunday to Thursday from 9 am to 7.30 pm and Saturday from 10 am to 6 pm. Admission is 20 NIS, or 15 NIS for children. The zoo is out in the Manahat (or Malkha) district; to get there take bus No 26, westbound, from the central bus station.

Mt Herzl

In November 1995 world leaders from over 86 nations assembled here to pay their respects to the assassinated prime minister Yitzhak Rabin. He was laid to rest beside the graves of other former holders of the office, including Levi Eshkol, Golda Meir and Menachem Begin. Also buried here is the founder of political Zionism, Theodor Herzl, the man after whom this pleasant parkland area is named.

The **Herzl Museum** (☎ 511 108) includes a replica of Herzl's Vienna study, library and furniture. It's open Sunday to Thursday from 9 am to 5 pm, and Friday from 9 am to 1 pm, closed Saturday. Admission is free. Take bus No 13, 18, 20, 23 or 27.

Yad Vashem

Anyone who spends much time in the country will soon become aware of just how much the spectre of the Holocaust continues to haunt Israeli society. The modern Jewish state was born out of the tragic experiences of persecution, flight and the death camps, and from the desire to make sure that such horrors would never be repeated. As a columnist in the *Jerusalem Report* put it, in effect the Holocaust is the civil religion of Israel. If that is so, then Yad Vashem is its greatest shrine. It's telling that while the Western Wall doesn't necessarily make it on to the programme, nearly all visiting heads of state are taken on an official visit to Yad Vashem.

While admittedly it's not going to make for the cheeriest day of your vacation, there's good reason to come here. The history and tragedy documented at the site speaks of far more than the Nazis and the nation of Israel.

Yad Vashem (taken from Isaiah 56:5, meaning 'A Memorial and a Name') (☎ 675 1611) is open Sunday to Thursday from 9 am to 4.45 pm, and Friday from 9 am to 1 pm, closed Saturday. Admission is free. There are free guided tours on Sunday and Wednesday at 10 am. Take bus No 13, 18, 20, 23 or 27.

Ein Kerem

Now enveloped by the expanding New City whose ugly apartment blocks threaten to blight the terraced valley slopes, this picturesque village contains several attractive churches commemorating the traditional birthplace of John the Baptist.

It's a very pleasant walking area, and although bus No 17 from Jaffa Rd comes directly to the village, you might instead take No 5, 6, 18 or 21 to reach Ein Kerem via the Jerusalem Forest. Get off at the Sonol petrol station on Herzl Blvd, continue walking in the same direction and take the first right onto Ye'fe Nof and the second left, Pirhe Chen, to enter the forest. Head for the Youth Centre in the middle of the forest and from there the village is visible most of the way.

Church of St John This church is owned by the Franciscans and built over the grotto where St John is believed to have been born (Luke 1:5-25, 57-80). Steps lead down to the grotto, with its remains of ancient structures and a Byzantine mosaic.

The church is open Sunday to Friday from 9 am to noon and 2.30 to 5 pm (closing an hour earlier in winter), closed Saturday. Admission is free. It's on the street to the right of the main road.

Church of the Visitation This church is also Franciscan and was built on the traditional site of the summer house of Zecharias and Elizabeth, the parents of St John. The church commemorates the visit to their home by the Virgin Mary, who was at that time carrying Jesus (Luke 1:39-56). Note also the ancient cistern and, in an alcove, the stone behind which John supposedly hid from Roman soldiers. Upstairs is the apse of a Crusader church. It's open daily from 8 to 11.45 am and 2.30 to 6 pm, and admission is free. You'll find it on the street to the left of the main road, opposite that leading to the Church of St John. The spring which gives the village its

---

Chagall

Marc Chagall was never a resident of Jerusalem (or even Israel), but he is possibly the artist closest to the heart of the city. Born in a small city in what is now Belarus in 1887, Chagall had a devoutly Jewish upbringing. This Jewishness permeates many of his paintings, which are dreamy semi-folkloristic scenes incorporating fiddlers on rooftops and heavily bearded rabbis. His greatest physical legacies to Jerusalem are the tapestries he designed for the foyer of the Knesset building and the 12 stained glass windows he created for the synagogue of the Hadassah Medical Centre (illustrated in the following two pages). Works by Chagall also hang in the Israel Museum in Givat Ram. ■

---

name is nearby. The wall bears the words of the prophet Isaiah, 'Ho everyone who thirsts, come to the waters' (Isaiah 55:1).

Russian Church & Monastery Higher up the steep slope, this monastery (☎ 622 2565, 565 4128) can only be visited by appointment.

Hadassah Medical Centre & the Chagall Windows

Often confused with its namesake on Mt Scopus, the Hadassah Medical Centre is the Middle East's largest hospital. However, it's far more well-known internationally for its synagogue featuring stained-glass windows by Jewish artist Marc Chagall. His 12 colourful abstract panels each depict one of the tribes of Israel, based on Genesis 49 and Deuteronomy 33. Created in 1960-61 and installed soon after, four of the windows were shattered during the 1967 War and had to be repaired by the artist who, as a testimony to the event, left a single symbolic bullet hole in the lower part of the green window.

The windows and tourist centre (☎ 641 6333, 644 6271) are open for viewing Sunday to Thursday from 8 am to 3.45 pm, and Friday from 8.30 am to 12.30 pm, closed Saturday. Admission is 9 NIS (students 4.50 NIS), which includes a guided tour (held every hour on the half hour until 12.30 pm). Take bus No 19 or 27 and get off at the last stop. You can also reach here by walking up from Ein Kerem.

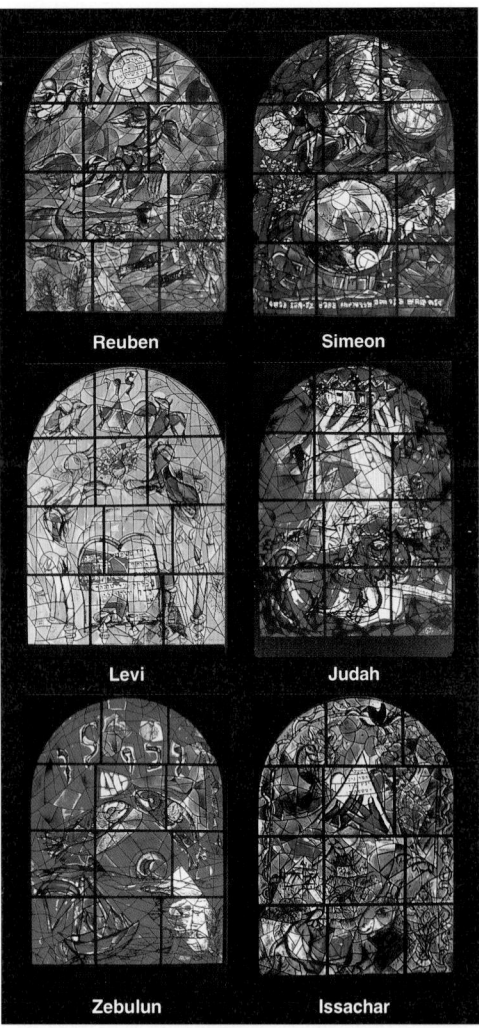

The 'Twelve Tribes of Israel'
stained glass windows by Marc Chagall,
Hadassah Medical Centre

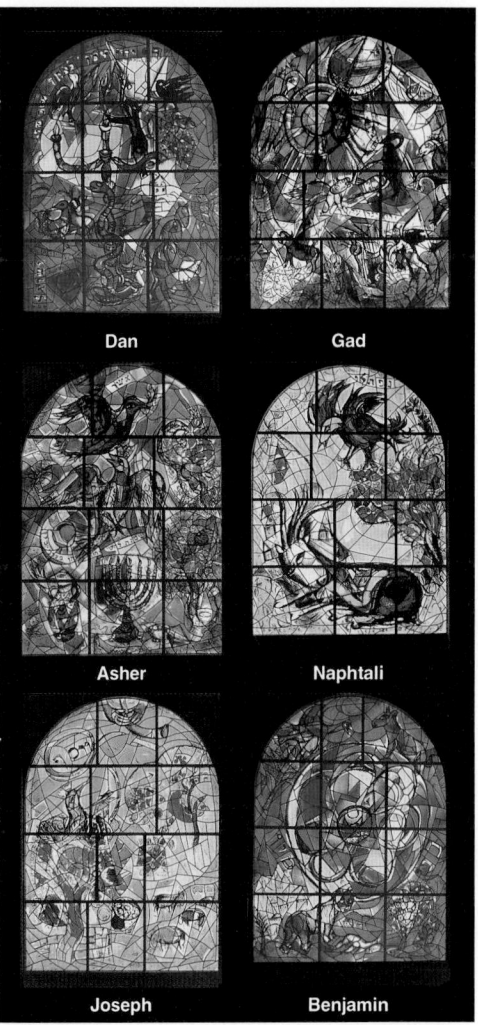

Dan

Gad

Asher

Naphtali

Joseph

Benjamin

ACTIVITIES

Jerusalem panders to the spiritual and the cerebral; for more earthly forms of recreation it's usually necessary to look elsewhere. Hiking and climbing are possible in the nearby Jericho and Dead Sea regions (see the Excursions chapter), while beach culture and water sports thrive in Tel Aviv, only a 45 minute bus ride away with departures from Jerusalem's central bus station every 15 minutes throughout the day.

Air Tours

Kanfei (☎ 583 1444; fax 583 1880) is an air tour company offering 30 minutes in a small plane over Jerusalem and its environs for 120 NIS per person, or a 60 minute whirl down to Masada and back for 225 NIS per person. Reservations must be made a few days in advance.

Archaeological Digs

Definitely not for gold-diggers, most archaeological digs require that you pay to work. In January of each year the Israeli Antiquities Authority (IAA), part of the Ministry of Education & Culture, publishes a list of the archaeological excavations open to volunteers for the coming year. To get a copy, contact the IAA at the Rockefeller Museum (☎ 629 2627; fax 292 628), PO Box 586, Jerusalem 91004. The requirements are that you be over 18 years old, fit and fully insured.

The busy archaeological season is May to September, when universities are not in session and the weather is hot and dry. No previous excavating experience is usually necessary, but volunteers should be prepared to participate for a minimum of one or two weeks, depending on the individual digA fee for food and accommodation (varying from sleeping bags in a field to three star-type hotels) is required. Some expeditions do provide volunteers with an allowance for food, accommodation and/or travel expenses within Israel. The Institute of Archaeology at the Hebrew University of Jerusalem (fax 582 5548), Mt Scopus, Jerusalem 91905, takes volunteers for week-long digs at a cost of US$180, including room and meals, lectures and field trips.

For those interested in trying archaeology one day at a time, there's a tourist-oriented 'Dig for a Day' programme operating during July and August and involving a three hour excavation, seminars and a tour. It costs about US$20. Contact Archaeological Seminars

(☎ 627 3515; fax 627 2660), PO Box 14002, 34 Habad St, Jerusalem 91140.

Cycling

The Jerusalem Cycle Club (☎ 561 9416) based at 2/18 Makhal St, off HaShalom Rd just south of Ammunition Hill, organises Saturday morning cycle rides around the environs of Jerusalem. The excursions usually last about four hours and the club can rent out bicycles. Call for details. See also the Getting Around chapter.

COURSES

Bible Studies

St George's College (☎ 894 704/5; fax 894 703), PO Box 19018, 20 Nablus Rd, Jerusalem, describes itself as a centre for fieldwork, study and reflection in the Holy Land, allowing you to study the Bible in its appropriate geographical setting. The college offers courses that include Bible study and field trips throughout the Holy Land and to the Sinai, lasting from 16 days (US$1500) to three (US$1720), four (US$2250) and 10 weeks (US$5100). Course headings include The Bible and the Holy Land Today, The Palestine of Jesus, and The Bible and its Setting. Food and board are included.

Language

The *ulpanim* (language schools) network caters for new Jewish immigrants and generally doesn't welcome non-Jews. Contact the Ulpan Office, Division of Adult Education (☎ 254 156), 11 Beit Ha'am, Bezalel St, Jerusalem 94591.

Places to Stay

Jerusalem has a wide range of accommodation with plenty of scope for both the big spender and the budget traveller. Before you convert all your currency into shekels, remember that by paying in dollars – where the option exists – you avoid the 17% VAT; in such cases the rates are given in dollars rather than shekels.

The best location to stay really depends on your requirements. The Old City and East Jerusalem tend to have the cheapest places and the best atmosphere, and of course they're the most convenient for the major sites nearby. However, some hostels and hospices have strict curfews, and being at least a good 20 minute walk from the nightlife of the New City centre, they aren't so great for those who want to stay out late (the Old City and East Jerusalem completely close down at dusk).

Hostels

Jerusalem has dozens of privately-run hostels, mainly clustered in the Old City and just outside Damascus Gate, in addition to five (at last count) large establishments administered by Hostelling International. Nonmembers can stay at HI hostels for usually only a handful more shekels than card holders, so it isn't worth buying a card especially. For a list of HI hostels countrywide or for any further information, contact the Israel Youth Hostels Association (☎ 625 2706; fax 625 0676), 3 Dorot Rishonim St, Jerusalem 91009 – Dorot Rishonim is in the city centre, just off Ben Yehuda St, and the office is open to visitors Sunday to Thursday from 8.30 am to 3 pm and Friday from 9 am to noon.

Christian Hospices

Various Christian denominations have accommodation in the vicinity of their religious sites. They are often the best value in the low to moderate price range, with cleanliness seemingly the top priority. You do not need to be a Christian to stay in most of these hospices, but you must be prepared to abide by the rules, which usually involve a strict curfew, an early check-out time and no double rooms for unmarried couples. Some hospices, however, are extremely informal and are more like regular guesthouses or hotels. ■

PETER JOUSIFFE

There are plenty of cheap hotels in Jerusalem, many close to transport and major sites

Hotels

In comparison to the number of lower and mid-price beds available, Jerusalem has a disproportionately high percentage of luxury accommodation – but this is the country in which the Minister of Tourism told a 1995 international travel trade conference that Israel 'does not want budget travellers'. In fact, the Israeli state goes as far as to sponsor and subsidise the construction of new upmarket hotels. Except during the high season (see When to Go in the Facts for the Visitor chapter), prices at these hotels compare favourably with those in other parts of the world and, attuned as they are to a predominantly North American clientele, the facilities and level of service are top class.

Note that the Israeli Ministry of Tourism no longer operates a star system, so in this book we use terms like five star-type and three star-type in a purely descriptive sense.

Renting

Anyone intending to spend two months or more in Jerusalem might want to consider renting a room or an apartment. If you look around you should be able to pay less rent than you would in a hostel (the going rate for a room in a shared flat is around 750 NIS or US$250 per calendar month), and you will have privacy and independence.

To find a cheap room or studio, or someone who needs an extra person to share an apartment, scan the 'In Jerusalem' section of Friday's *The Jerusalem Post*, or better still, get someone who reads Hebrew to take a look with you at the classifieds in *Kol Ha'Ir*, a local weekly. The notice boards at the two campuses of the Hebrew University, at the Israel Centre on the corner of Strauss and HaNevi'im Sts, and at the Sefer VeSefel and Tmol Shilshom bookshops, both in the New City centre, can also be good places to look.

She'al (☎ 622 6991), at 21 King George V St, is a property agency that keeps lists in English, although it charges a small fortune to let you look at them. It is open Sunday to Thursday from 8.30 am to 1 pm and 4 to 7 pm, and Friday from 8.30 am to 1 pm, closed Saturday.

PLACES TO STAY – BOTTOM END

Old City

Most of the Old City's budget accommodation is found near Jaffa and Damascus gates, which is convenient because they are the main access points and well served by buses; from outside the central bus station, across the other side of Jaffa Rd, take bus No 13 or 20 for Jaffa Gate and bus No 23 or 27 for Damascus Gate.

In the vicinity of Damascus Gate (see map 12) *Al-Arab Hostel* (☎ 628 3537) on Souq Khan as-Zeit St is a definite backpackers' favourite. As well as large airy, cat-prowled dorms (beds 14 NIS), there are beds on the roof (12 NIS) and a couple of private double rooms at 40 NIS. Showers and toilets are shared by all and are perhaps too few, but it has a kitchen with free tea, a table tennis room, and each night videos are shown in the cushion-strewn common room. Curfew is 1 am. Be warned, though: at the Al-Arab beds are usually paid for on checking out; if you buck the trend and pay on checking in it may not always be recorded and things then get nasty when it comes time to leave. Get a receipt for any money you hand over.

The other main contender in the popularity stakes is the *Tabasco Hostel* (☎ 628 3461) on Aqabat at-Takiya St (you can see the sign from Souq Khan as-Zeit St). This place is noisy, cramped and incredibly dirty but it has a lively atmosphere, a busy notice board and no curfew, and downstairs is the Old City's most partyin' venue. Plus it's cheap – dorm beds are 12 NIS, a mattress on the roof is 10 NIS, while a mattress on the roof enclosed by four shanty walls (it hardly justifies being called a 'room') is 35 NIS.

Far cleaner, far quieter and a much better option altogether is the *New Hashimi Hostel* (☎ 628 4410; fax 628 4667). The dorms have only eight beds (15 NIS), and each room has its own shower and toilet, as do the very attractive private doubles at 90 NIS. There's a large common area with plenty of tables and chairs and a well-equipped kitchen. Reception is open 24 hours a day. The New Hashimi is just two doors along from Al-Arab on Souq Khan as-Zeit St.

Right next to the mosque on Al-Wad Rd is the *Al-Ahram Youth Hostel* (☎ 628 0926), another fairly quiet and reasonably clean place that seems to attract an older crowd. Dorm beds are 15 NIS – less for a comfortable mattress up on the roof terrace. There is an enforced midnight curfew. Across from the Al-Ahram, on the corner of the Via Dolorosa, is the *Austrian Hospice* (☎ 627 1466). Secluded behind high walls, this place is almost monastic in its asceticism and sobriety. However, you may find it redeemed by the wonderful garden terraces which overlook the streets below. Dorm beds are 30 NIS and doubles start at 120 NIS (married couples only). There's a 10 pm curfew but a deposit gets you the keys.

Turn left up the Via Dolorosa off Al-Wad Rd and then take the second on the left, Aqabat Darwish St, to get to the *Black Horse Hostel* (☎ 628 0328). The location isn't so great: it's very isolated and to get to it at night involves walking along some dark, lonely alleyways.

In the Jaffa Gate area (see map 14) is, unsurprisingly, the *Jaffa Gate Youth Hostel* (☎ 627 6402), a popular, occasionally crowded place with a kitchen and cosy TV lounge. Dorm beds are 25 NIS, doubles 90 NIS, and there's a midnight curfew. It's behind the Christian Information Centre.

The *Petra Hostel* (☎ 628 2356) has a superb location on Omar ibn al-Khattab Square, so if you can get a room with a balcony overlooking the action it's great. Otherwise give it a miss – the Petra is squalid, with poor facilities, and the staff are not particularly friendly and not above taking advantage of a fresh face. Dorm beds cost 15 NIS, or a place on the roof is 12 NIS. Equally missable is the *New Swedish Hostel* (☎ 589 4124, 627 7855), some 100m down into the bazaar at 29 David St. It's a wonder the Scandinavians haven't sued for defamation of character. Beds in grubby dorms are 22 NIS while shoebox-size doubles, in which it isn't possible to stand upright (spend more than three nights here and Amnesty International will take up your case), are 44 NIS.

For a couple of better hostels, head into the bazaar along David St from Omar ibn al-Khattab Square, take the first right and then turn left immediately onto St Mark's Rd. The *Citadel Youth Hostel* (☎ 628 6273) is 50m down here on the right. The reception and the small double rooms (50 to 70 NIS) on the ground floor look like they've been burrowed into stone, as does the tight narrow stairway which leads up to some clean and comfortable dorms (beds are 20 NIS), a small lounge, a kitchen, and access to the roof with views over the Old City. Just beyond the Citadel Youth Hostel, on the opposite side of the street, is the *Lutheran Hospice* (☎ 628 2120, 628 5105; fax 628 5107), the closest thing we've ever seen to a 'five star' hostel. It is beautiful. There are shady cloisters, a huge spotless kitchen and a palm garden with a fountain and views of the Dome of the Rock. The dorms are single sex and beds are 22 NIS. The hospice is closed from 9 am to noon and has a strict 10.45 pm curfew, though you may stay out later if you tell the front desk when you'll be back.

At the end of a narrow winding street which begins across from the Lutheran Hospice is the *HI – Old City Youth Hostel* (☎ 628 8611), which has great facilities but, being more expensive than the competition (dorms are 30 NIS), is usually filled with Israeli school groups rather than travellers.

East Jerusalem

(See map 11.) 'Hostel Row' is the stretch of HaNevi'im St across from Damascus Gate, beside the service taxi rank. There are four possibilities here, the best of which are the two nearest the Old City walls. The *Faisal Hostel* (☎ 627 2492) is the closest at 4 HaNevi'im St, and it has a good terrace on which guests can laze around and watch the activity around the gate. There's a kitchen with free tea and coffee and a common room. Dorm beds (a bit cramped) are 12 or 15 NIS depending on the room and there are a few doubles at 50 NIS. There's a flexible 1 am curfew.

The *Palm Hostel* (☎ 627 3189), next door to the Faisal at 6 HaNevi'im St, has a great common room with plants and a glass roof. There's also a kitchen with a fridge stocked with cold beers, and videos are shown most nights. There is no curfew. Beds in large, spacious dorms are 16 NIS, and there are a few private rooms at 60 NIS.

Much harder to recommend are the *New Raghadan Hostel* (☎ 628 3348) and the *Ramses Hostel* (☎ 628 4818), a few doors up at 10 and 20 HaNevi'im St, respectively.

Around the corner from the Ramses and just north of the Nablus Rd Arab bus station is the *Cairo Hostel* (☎ 627 7216) at 21 Nablus Rd. It's a bit soulless and not partic-

PETER JOUSIFFE

Shopping in Jerusalem can be a visual feast

ularly friendly, but there's a large lounge with satellite TV, and free coffee and tea in the kitchen. Dorm beds are 15 NIS, and there are also some private rooms for 60 NIS that take three or maybe four people.

New City

(See map 9.) Although it is way more expensive than the Old City and East Jerusalem hostels, the *Jerusalem Inn Hostel* (☎ 625 1294) at 6 HaHistradrut St, just off pedestrianised Ben Yehuda St right in the centre of the New City, is recommended. It's a converted apartment building with dorms on three floors, all kept immaculately clean. It further endears itself to some by having a strictly enforced no smoking policy (and you don't want to mess with Olga, the manageress). There's no kitchen, but at the reception/bar area you can get breakfast, snacks, tea, coffee and beer. The place has a midnight curfew but a deposit will get you a front door key. Dorm beds are 42 NIS and singles are 96 NIS, while doubles start at 120 NIS. The Jerusalem Inn's near neighbour the *King George Hostel*, around the corner on King George V St, used to be very popular but it was closed at the time of our last visit and nobody knew whether it was due to reopen or not.

Another good one is the *Jasmine Ben Yehuda Hostel* (☎ 624 8021; fax 625 3032) up on the 3rd Floor at 23 Ben Yehuda St. Again, this place is very clean and well run and the management are friendly. It doesn't have a kitchen, but there are tea and coffee and breakfast if you want them. There's no curfew. Dorm beds are 30 NIS.

It's possible to get cheaper beds in the New City but only if you're not too concerned about how much you sleep. At the *Capitol Hostel* (☎ 623 4582) a dorm bed is only 20 NIS, but the hostel is right above the Underground, one of the city's busiest discos, and next door to the equally sonorous Q Bar. The trick, possibly, is to get yourself insensibly drunk and so remain oblivious to the party overspill in the hostel corridors. However, that doesn't help next morning when you are confronted with sinks clogged with vomit and cigarette butts, toilet cubicles minus doors and showers well short of anything resembling water.

The *Hotel Nogah* (☎ 625 4590 mornings only, or 566 1888) is something different altogether, a clean family-owned apartment in a quiet part of town alongside the Bezalel School of Art. The comfortably furnished rooms share a well-equipped kitchen and bathroom. Singles/doubles are 75/90 NIS, and there's also a triple for 120 NIS and a quad for 144 NIS. There's no curfew, as guests get their own front door key. The Nogah is at 4 Bezalel St, off Shmuel HaNagid St, but reservations must be made in advance; ask for Mr or Mrs Kristal.

There are several HI-affiliated hostels in the New City, three of which are central. The best is the *Beit Shmuel Hostel* (☎ 620 3466) at 6 Shama St, next to the Hebrew Union College near the junction of HaMelekh David and Agron Sts. This place is highly recommended. It's a beautiful building, more like a hotel than a hostel, and it's only a few minutes walk from both the Old City and the central area of the New City.

The *Bernstein Youth Hostel* (☎ 622 8286) is at 1 Keren HaYesod St, at the junction of Agron and King George V Sts, not far from the Sheraton Plaza Hotel. It's a 10 to 15 minute walk to Jaffa Gate and the central New City area. The *HaDavidka Youth Hostel* (☎ 625 2706; fax 625 0676) is at 67 HaNevi'im St, at the junction of HaNevi'im St and Jaffa Rd. It's just a few minutes walk from the city centre and a bus ride (Nos 23 and 27 stop outside on their way to Damascus Gate) from the Old City. The Bernstein and HaDavidka both have good facilities and are well maintained, but neither is very friendly and they're often busy with Israeli school groups. In all the above HI hostels, dorm beds are around 40 NIS (50 NIS at Beit Shmuel) and there are usually also private singles and doubles for around 90/120 NIS, breakfast included in all cases.

The *Louise Waterman Wise Hostel* (☎ 642 3366) is out at 8 Pisyah Rd in the Beit Gegan area, about 30 minutes by bus from the New City centre (take bus No 18 or 20 to Mt Herzl), while the *Ein Kerem Youth Hostel* (☎ 641 6282) is off Ma'ayan St in the village of the same name (take bus No 17 to Ein Kerem and get off at the last stop). Meals are served at both. Last buses from town out in this direction are at 11.15 pm, except on Friday when they stop in the mid-afternoon. Prices are comparable to those at the city centre HI hostels.

PLACES TO STAY – MIDDLE

Old City

Most of the Old City's mid-range accommodation is offered by the Christian hospices in the Jaffa Gate area (see maps 11 and 13). These tend to be quiet, sober places from which unmarried couples are likely to be turned away. They all have curfews. The *Christ Church Hospice* (☎ 627 7727; fax 627 7730) at Omar ibn al-Khattab Square, opposite the Citadel entrance, has pleasant staff and is very clean, quiet and comfortable, with a pretty courtyard and nice public rooms (see Christ Church in the Things to See & Do chapter for more information). Singles cost from US$35 to US$42, and doubles from US$64 to US$72. As well as its cheap dorm beds, the very popular *Lutheran Hospice* (see Bottom End for directions and description) has an attached guesthouse in which singles/doubles go for US$40/60, with breakfast provided.

The *Casa Nova Pilgrims' Hospice* (☎ 628 2791), run by the Franciscans with the help of some officious Arab staff, is clean and has vaulted ceilings and massive marble pillars in the dining room. The food is great and the rooms, mainly twins with bathrooms and central heating, are pleasant. The hospice is often full with

European pilgrims. Singles/doubles are US$35/60. It's at 10 Casa Nova St; from Jaffa Gate take the second left, Greek Catholic Patriarchate Rd, and follow it until it becomes Casa Nova St. The hospice is on your left.

The *Greek Catholic Patriarchate Hospice* (☎ 628 2023) is a bit unfriendly, but the basic singles/doubles (US$32/48) are comfortable and breakfast is included. It's on St Dimitri's Rd; from Jaffa Gate take the second left (Greek Catholic Patriarchate Rd which becomes St Dimitri's Rd) and the hospice is on the right on the bend.

Although owned by the Greek Orthodox Church, the *New Imperial Hotel* (☎ 628 2261), on your left as you enter Jaffa Gate, has few religious trappings. It was built in the late 19th century, and Kaiser Wilhelm stayed here when he visited in 1898. The hotel retains an air of dusty, faded grandeur, although the rooms have all been cleaned up and are very comfortable. Singles/doubles are a bit of a bargain, starting at US$20/35.

Up behind the New Imperial on Latin Patriarchate Rd, the *Gloria Hotel* (☎ 628 2431/2; fax 628 2401) is very modern inside and has large, quiet rooms, with nice views across the Citadel from the dining room. Singles/doubles cost from US$48/70 with breakfast, and there's no curfew.

Deep in the Muslim Quarter (see Map 13) on the Via Dolorosa, 50m west of the junction with Al-Wad Rd, is perhaps the most comfortable of the Christian-run establishments; the *Armenian Hospice* (☎ 626 0880; fax 626 1208) has recently been renovated and now offers immaculate double rooms with en suite bathroom and TV for \$US50. Around 100m further along the Via Dolorosa, on the left, is the *Convent of the Sisters of Zion* (☎ 627 7292), run by the Sisters of Zion. It's very clean, with a study area and kitchen. Singles/doubles are US$25/40 with breakfast. The hospice is closed from 10 am to noon and there is an 11 pm curfew.

East Jerusalem

This was where all the pilgrims to the Old City would stay when Jerusalem was a divided city, so most of these hotels (found mainly on or around Salah ad-Din St – see map 11) date from the 1950s and 1960s – and the majority are still firmly stuck there. The facilities are generally not as good as those in the New City hotels of comparable prices, but the East Jerusalem places tend to be more friendly.

One of the best accommodation deals in the city, *St George's Cathedral Guesthouse* (☎ 628 3302; fax 628 2253) is at 20 Nablus Rd, part of the St George's Cathedral

EDDIE GERALD

Vaulted ceiling in the YMCA Three Arches Hotel

compound, just 10 minutes walk from the Old City. It's a delightful cloistered building with an attractive garden. The atmosphere is very relaxed and friendly, with no curfew. The comfortable rooms, most with private bathroom, cost US$40/60 for singles/doubles with breakfast.

On the same street but a little closer to Damascus Gate is the *YMCA East-Aelia Capitolina Hotel* (☎ 589 4271) at 29 Nablus Rd, next door to the US Consulate. The decor is dowdy but there are good facilities, including a swimming pool and squash and tennis courts; singles/doubles are US$55/75.

Of the more conventional hotels, the *Pilgrims' Palace Hotel* (☎ 627 2135, 627 2416; fax 589 4658) definitely has the prime location, on Sultan Suleyman St facing the Old City walls, but it's also next to the bus station so rooms on that side suffer from chronic noise pollution. It's one of East Jerusalem's nicest hotels though; singles cost US$80, doubles US$100. Not much further from the Old City (just a few minutes walk from Damascus Gate), the *Jerusalem Hotel* (☎ 627 1356), just off Nablus Rd facing the bus station, is not a bad option. It's a beautiful building with an attractive courtyard and it's also well looked after; singles are priced from US$35, doubles from US$50.

Many of the other hotels in East Jerusalem suffered badly from a lack of trade in the intifada years and are now seriously in need of some money being spent on them. A case in point is the *Rivoli Hotel* (☎ 628 4871; fax

627 4879) at 3 Salah ad-Din St, on the corner of Sultan Suleyman St. It has rooms that are adequate if a little dingy, and what was once quite a nice lounge. Singles/doubles here are US$35/55.

Over the road and 50m along at 6 Salah ad-Din St, the *Metropole* (☎ 628 2507) is another down-market down-at-heel place where singles cost US$25 and doubles US$45. Do not confuse it with the adjacent *New Metropole Hotel* (☎ 628 3846; fax 627 7485) at 8 Salah ad-Din St, which is a much better place. It has a roof garden with views of Mt Scopus, the Mount of Olives and the Rockefeller Museum. Comfortable air-con singles/doubles with good facilities cost US$40/65.

Continuing north up Salah ad-Din St, No 18 is the aged *Lawrence Hotel* (☎ 589 4208; fax 627 1285), which has basic singles from US$30 and doubles from US$50, while over the road is the more modern *Capitol Hotel* (☎ 628 2561), with a bar and well-equipped air-con rooms with balconies which face the Mount of Olives. The hotel is popular with tours from Europe. Singles/doubles are US$55/85.

From the Capitol Hotel, continue north up Salah ad-Din St and turn right onto As-Zahra St, where you'll find the *National Palace Hotel* (☎ 627 3273; fax 628 2139), which is rather characterless but does well from the pilgrim trade, packing them into singles/doubles at US$70/96. Equally unexceptional though smaller and more private are the *Victoria Hotel* (☎ 627 3858; fax 628 5551) at 8 Al-Masoudi St (round the corner to the right of the National Palace), which has singles/doubles at US$45/64, and the *Christmas Hotel* (☎ 628 2588), off Salah ad-Din St opposite St George's Cathedral, which has clean and comfortable singles from US$40 and doubles at around US$70.

New City

(See maps 8 and 9.) A wonderful location outside one of the Old City gates (and just 10 minutes walk from the city centre) help make the guesthouse at the *Notre Dame of Jerusalem Centre* (☎ 627 9111; fax 627 1995) one of the city's absolute best mid-range accommodation options. The rooms have three star-style facilities, while the majestic surroundings and views are just excellent. Singles cost US$65 and doubles US$85, breakfast included.

Similarly enchanting is the *YMCA Three Arches Hotel* (☎ 625 7111; fax 625 3438), probably the best-looking YMCA in the world. Guests have free use of the pool, gym and squash and tennis courts. Singles are US$90, doubles US$110. The YMCA is on HaMelekh David St and can be reached on bus No 7, 8, 21 or 30. If you are walking, it will take you 10 minutes to reach Jaffa Gate, while the city centre area is some 15 minutes away.

Another place of great character is *St Andrew's Hospice* (☎ 673 2401; fax 673 1711) which, belonging to the church of the same name, has a friendly Scottish country house atmosphere – very comfortable and peaceful. Singles/doubles are US$55/75 with breakfast included. However, despite its appealing location near Bloomfield Gardens, overlooking Mt Zion and the Old City, the hospice is a little far away from the action. It's a 15 to 20 minute steep walk to Jaffa Gate and more than that to the New City centre. During the day take bus No 5, 7, 8, 21 or 30 to get here; later at night you may find yourself having to resort to pricey taxis.

If you value being in the middle of it all then there are several extremely central options, the best of which, in our opinion, is the *Jerusalem Inn Guesthouse* (☎ 625 2757; fax 625 1297), which has an almost Scandinavian looking interior with masses of open space and a large lounge and bar/restaurant. Prices are US$52/58. It's at 7 Horkenos St; from Zion Square head north up Eliyshar St (look for MacDavid's on the corner), up the steps at the end and it's on the left.

Right across from Zion Square at 44 Jaffa Rd is the *Hotel Ron* (☎ 625 3471; fax 625 0707). It's from one of this building's balconies that Menachem Begin, former underground leader and future prime minister, made his first major public speech. The rooms are large and reasonably pleasant, although those facing the front may be a little noisy; singles/doubles are US$49/59. Around the corner from the Ron is the less appealing *Hotel Kaplan* (☎ 625 5754; fax 623 3513) at 4 HaHavazelet St, which has rooms without toilets at US$28/38 or with shower and toilet at US$40/60.

For anyone looking for something at the cheaper end of the mid-range hotels, then the best bet is the *Eyal Hotel* (☎ 623 4161), which is at 21 Shamai St, one block south of Zion Square. It has a good central location and is up to three star standard but prices are from just US$28 per person. The Eyal also has a good, smarter sister hotel in the *Zion* (☎ 623 2367; fax 625 7585), which is as central as it gets, lying between Jaffa Rd and Ben Yehuda St on Luntz St, one of the small cafe-filled pedestrian alleys. It's very attractive inside, but because it is surrounded on all sides by some of Jerusalem's liveliest all-night streets, some people might have problems with the noise. Singles are from US$51 to US$72 while doubles are US$69 to US$80.

PLACES TO STAY – TOP END

Jerusalem is top-heavy with luxury hotels. Most are in the New City, with just one or two in East Jerusalem and none in the Old City. Sometime in 1997, however, the Hilton chain is set to open what promises to be the city's brashest and most glitzy hotel, located in Mamilla, a champagne cork's arc away from the Old City walls.

Indisputably the country's top hotel, the *King David* (☎ 625 1111; fax 623 2303) at 23 HaMelekh David St has been given the seal of approval by a stream of visiting kings and queens, presidents and prime ministers. While the place does have the benefits of a distinguished history, a superb high-class restaurant and excellent, uninterrupted views of the Old City from its eastern side, it's difficult not to suspect that the major attraction of the King David is its pure snob appeal. Singles cost upwards of US$229, while doubles start at US$255.

Not far behind the King David in the luxury stakes is the *Laromme Jerusalem Hotel* (☎ 675 6666; fax 675 6777) at 3 Ze'ev Jabotinsky St, beside the Liberty Bell Gardens and overlooking the Old City. Owned by El Al, this place has excellent standards of service and is again an occa-

---

The Colony

The *American Colony Hotel* (☎ 628 2421, 627 9777; fax 628 3357) is East Jerusalem's counterpart to the King David. Both places have served as unofficial no-man's lands, playing host to the key players and observers in recent Middle Eastern history. But while the King David has been graced with the leaders and the representatives of state, the Colony has been the favoured haunt of journalists, writers, diplomats and spies. Past guests have included TE Lawrence, John Le Carre, Graham Greene, Lord Allenby and, intriguingly, Lauren Bacall.

Built between 1865 and 1876 by a Turkish pasha, who lived there with his four wives, it is the city's only top-class Arab hotel. Despite being English-owned and Swiss-managed, the Israelis used to refer to the Colony as the PLO hotel because of alleged links between staff and the Palestinian movement.

The place is graced by some beautiful Oriental decor, a lovely swimming pool, a popular garden terrace and serves non-kosher food, including a renowned lunch-time buffet on Saturday. Singles cost from US$124 to US$169 while doubles range from US$150 to US$208. The American Colony is at 1 Louis Vincent St, off Nablus Rd. ■

AUSTRALIA-ISRAEL CHAMBER OF COMMERCE

The Hyatt Regency overlooks the Old City

sional host to heads of state. Singles cost from US$182 to US$229 and doubles from US$200 to US$247.

Next in ranking is the *Sheraton Plaza Hotel* (☎ 625 9111; fax 623 1667) at 47 King George V St, overlooking Ha'Atzmaut Park, although the upper floors of this 18 storey slab enjoy views across the whole city. The Plaza is very convenient for the New City and about 15 minutes walk from the Old City. Singles cost from US$185 to US$229 and doubles from US$203 to US$247.

The other two five star-style hotels that are within an easy walk of the Old City are the *King Solomon* (☎ 624 1433; fax 624 1774) and the *Radisson-Moriah Plaza* (☎ 623 2232; fax 623 2411). The Solomon was originally built for the Sheraton chain and it maintains their high standards. Visit the foyer for a look at the enormous sculpted bronze globe and the view *up* into the swimming pool. Rooms here are US$116 to US$126 for singles and US$127 to US$138 for doubles. The King Solomon is at 32 HaMelekh David St, just south of the King David Hotel. The Radisson-Moriah Plaza is one block west at 39 Keren HaYesod St and prices here are US$135 to US$150 and US$175 to US$195.

Jerusalem's other top rank hotels suffer badly from unfavourable locations. The village-size *Hyatt Regency* (☎ 533 1234; fax 581 5947) at 32 Lehi St has excellent facilities and the Hyatt reputation ensures the hotel's popularity with US visitors; however, the hotel is stuck out over towards Mt Scopus (see map 1), miles from anywhere of interest and impossible to get to by public transport; singles cost around US$140 and doubles about US$160. Similarly isolated, *Seven Arches* (☎ 627 7555; fax 628 5384) is up on the Mount of Olives (see map 17). It has a classic view over the Old City but once that's savoured and the nearby churches have been explored there's a long way to go to get anywhere else. Business has not been great here and singles/doubles are a low US$78/104.

There are also several hotels west of the New City centre in the Givat Ram area (see map 17), quite a bus ride from the Old City. The *Holiday Inn Crown Plaza* (☎ 536 151; fax 538 0575) was originally a Hilton and has five star specifications, but because of the awful location (behind the conference centre, which is the great glass block facing the bus station) prices are as for a four star-style establishment; singles/doubles are priced from US$148/174.

Even further afield (see map 17) are the *Park Plaza* (☎ 528 221; fax 528 423), the *Paradise Jerusalem* (☎ 565 5888) and the *Jerusalem Renaissance* (☎ 528 111; fax 511 824), all good top class hotels with, in the case of the last two, pools, health clubs, restaurants and all the trimmings. They are hindered, however, by being located to the west of Givat Ram virtually on the outskirts of the city. As a result room rates are very low for the quality of hotel – in the region of US$80 for singles and US$100 for doubles.

For good value *and* a central location we recommend the *Kings Hotel* (☎ 620 1201; fax 620 1211), close to the Sheraton Plaza at 60 King George V St – it's just over the road from a late night Supersol supermarket. Singles are from US$105, doubles from US$130. Even more central but with inferior facilities to the Kings, the *Jerusalem Tower* (☎ 625 2161; fax 625 2167) is a three or four star-style hotel at 23 Hillel St, the street parallel with Ben Yehuda. It's very popular with package tour operators. Singles are in the US$60 to US$72 range while doubles are US$74 to US$92.

One final good place is the modest *Mount Zion* (☎ 672 4222; fax 673 1425) at 17 Hebron Rd just south of the Cinematheque (see map 10). It has an unusual design in that it's built into the side of the valley and the street level reception area is actually on the top floor. Most rooms have good views of the Old City; singles are US$100, doubles US$135.

Places to Eat

Despite the exotic and varied international ingredients that go into making up Jerusalem's society, much of the food on offer in the city's restaurants and cafes is disappointingly bland. It's often indifferently prepared, and invariably overpriced. The reliable exception is the city's Oriental cuisine. 'Oriental' in the Israeli sense means Middle Eastern (Oriental Jews are those originating in the Maghreb and Spain, Iraq, Yemen and other Arab countries). The dishes rely heavily on salads doused in olive oil, accompanied by dips of *houmos* (cooked chickpeas ground into a paste and mixed with garlic and lemon) and *tahina*, a thinner paste made from sesame seeds. Pickled vegetables are also prevalent, as is the use of eggplant. The accompanying meat is almost always grilled on skewers or the spit and is typically lamb or turkey – both Islam and Judaism forbid pork, while beef is uncommon.

The other pleasure is fruit, of which Israel with its varied climate produces a wide range, including oranges, apples, mangoes, guava, melons, persimmons, pomegranates, figs, dates and avocadoes. Mahane Yehuda Market, in the New City, is the most plentiful and cheapest source of fruit and other foodstuffs. The best bargains are to be had towards the end of the day (packing up time is about 8 pm Sunday to Thursday), particularly on a Friday (go between 3 and 4 pm).

Look out for the *sabra*, a cactus fruit that looks like a hand grenade, which was imported to Palestine from Mexico a few centuries ago. Israeli-born Jews are nicknamed 'sabra' after the fruit: tough and prickly on the outside, soft and sweet on the inside. Sabra is sold on the streets everywhere when in season, but it's an acquired taste. The seeds give the locals another chance to use their unsurpassed spitting skills.

Most places to eat are in the central area of the New City, especially on or around Ben Yehuda St and in the Nahalat Shiv'a quarter.

VEGETARIAN & HEALTH FOOD

(See map 9.) Established for over 30 years, *The Village Green* restaurants at 10 Ben Yehuda St, and also at 1 Bezalel, both in the New City centre, are reliable places for good-value vegetarian food and refreshment. Also worth a visit is the attractive stone and foliage-filled

Big Mac Attack

According to Judaism, every meal is a religious rite and so has to be *kosher* – which roughly translated means 'ritually acceptable'. Defining what is and is not kosher, however, is not so simple.

Genesis 1:29 permits all fruit and vegetables, and 'clean' animals (7:2). 'Clean' is taken to mean animals that chew the cud and have wholly cloven hooves (Leviticus 11; Deuteronomy 14). Clean birds, according to the Mishnah, must have a crop, a gizzard and an extra talon – for example chicken and turkey – while only fish that have at least one fin and easily removable scales are acceptable.

There are other rules that specify exactly how an animal must be slaughtered and which parts may be eaten. But of all the rules of *kashrut* (the noun from kosher), the most intriguing is that forbidding the mixing of meat and dairy products. Exodus 23:19 states that 'you shall not seethe a kid in its mother's milk', which is interpreted by orthodox Jews to mean that they cannot cook or eat meat and milk (including all dairy products) together. So, no chicken in cream sauce, no fish in batter, no tea with milk in a meat restaurant. American-style fast food chains have failed in the past in Israel because they cannot put cheese or mayonnaise on top of hamburgers.

Despite the largely secular nature of modern Israeli society, a 1995 survey found that 90% of Jewish Israelis observe at least some of the requirements of the dietary laws. It makes sense then for local restaurants to be kosher. To gain official recognition as such they have to submit to regular check-ups carried out by rabbinical inspectors. Kosher criteria don't stop at the kitchen either; in recent years one Jerusalem restaurant found itself threatened with the removal of its kosher licence for having a Christmas tree on the pavement outside.

That said, on Shamai St in central Jerusalem, a large cheeseburger-selling McDonald's opened in 1995 and it is always crowded. A spokesperson for the restaurant has said that its meat is kosher and anybody is free not to eat cheese with their burger. This has failed to placate the orthodox community, which has responded by fly-posting denunciations of the company and exhorting all good Jews to stay off the Big Macs. ■

Alumah Natural Food Restaurant, (☎ 625 5014) close to the first Village Green at 8 Yaabez St. Main dishes are 25 to 35 NIS but they do cheaper takeaways. It's open Sunday to Thursday from 10 am to 11 pm, Friday until 2 pm only, closed Saturday.

The kosher laws of Judaism ensure that Israel is a dream for vegetarians, with numerous dairy-only res-

ISRAELI MINISTRY OF TOURISM

You don't have to love olives to visit Jerusalem,
but it helps

taurants. *Tavlin* at the bottom of cafe-lined Yoel Salomon
St is dairy and vegetarian, serving dishes like mushroom
lasagne and cheese pie in stomach-straining portions at
prices in the 25 to 30 NIS range. Other places offering
similar fare are *Ticho House Cafe* and *Cacao* (see map 10),
the latter at the Cinematheque (see Cafes for details on
both).

The 7th Place (☎ 625 4495) is a Southern Indian-style
restaurant with a dairy and vegetarian-only menu.
Prices are very reasonable, with most of the menu under
20 NIS. It's at Beit Agron, 37 Hillel St, just east of the
junction with Yoel Salomon St (see map 9). It is open
Sunday to Thursday from 8 am to 1 am, Friday until 3
pm, and Saturday from sunset until 1 am.

FELAFEL, SHWARMA & HOUMOS

Felafel, shwarma and houmos are the three staples of
Jerusalem 'fast food'. Felafel is ground chickpeas
blended with herbs and spices, shaped into a ball and
then deep-fried in oil. It's not particularly tasty, but
covered in tahina and served with an assortment of
salads in a pitta bread (a type of unleavened bread), it's
palatable, fairly substantial and cheap. The most
popular way to eat meat is as shwarma, also known
elsewhere as doner kebab. This is lamb, or sometimes
turkey or chicken, sliced from a revolving vertical spit
and stuffed, along with salad, into a pitta or rolled in a
plate-sized piece of laffa bread.

Old City & East Jerusalem

Considering that felafel originates in the Arab world, there is surprisingly little of it to be found in the (predominantly Arab) Old City – and what you will find isn't particularly good. The most popular place to get it is a stall just down from Damascus Gate, at the point at which the road forks. For good houmos head down Al-Wad Rd and, by the 5th Station of the Cross, where the Via Dolorosa turns west (right), is *Abu Shukri*, on the left hand side (see map 13). A good houmos platter is 8 NIS, but stay off the fuul (mashed fava beans) and felafel, which are terrible here. Heading up the Via Dolorosa towards Souq Khan as-Zeit St, on the left near the top is *Linda's Restaurant* (see map 12), which also does good houmos served with pitta and maybe olives or onions.

Most shwarma and grilled meat shops are along Souq Khan as-Zeit St, but sadly they're not very good, and they overcharge, possibly as a result of the large numbers of tourists around. For better cheap food, head out of Damascus Gate and try the places on Sultan Suleyman St (see map 11). Down towards the junction with Salah ad-Din St, *Al-Quds* and neighbouring *Candy's* both do superb shwarma and shashlik (chunks of meat grilled on a spit). For those with skip-size appetites, they sell roasted chicken, whole or half, hot off the skewer.

Something of a cult among houmos freaks is the *Abu Ali Restaurant*, although it may be greeted with something less than enthusiasm by the hygiene conscious. It's hidden away off Salah ad-Din St; head north from Herod's Gate and turn right along an alley at the sign for 'Ibrahim Dandis'; it's downstairs on your left. Abu Ali is open daily from 6 am to about 2 pm.

New City

(see map 9.) Most New City felafel is sold on King George V St between Jaffa Rd and Ben Yehuda St – just follow the trail of tahina and squashed felafel balls on the pavement. Many of the places selling felafel also have shwarma. None of them stands above the others in price or quality, but one of the most popular with locals is *King of Felafel & Shwarma* on the corner of King George V and Agrippas Sts. If you want to sit while eating go to 6 Ben Hillel St (no sign in English), the pedestrianised street running between Ben Yehuda and King George V Sts.

Houmos is available in most Oriental restaurants (see the Oriental Jewish section, later in this chapter), and is

---

Bagels & Bread

Jerusalem has a delicious selection of breads, both Jewish and Arabic. Not surprisingly, bagels are very popular. Originally from Eastern Europe, Jerusalem's bagels are different to most others, being crisper and drier. A traditional way to end a night out is to visit the bagel factory and pick up a hot bagel or two – *Bonkers* on Zion Square is open 24 hours daily. *Hallah*, a softer style of bread, is baked for Shabbat. Jewish bakeries produce sweet breads, too. Glazed with sugar syrup, filled with currants or chocolate, they vary in quality but can be great. *Matza* is the unleavened bread eaten by Jews during Passover.

Arabs mainly bake pitta or a kind of bagel thickly covered with sesame seeds or sprinkled with *za'atar*, a mixture of herbs (mainly oregano) and spices. ■

---

reputably very good at *Ta'ami* (no English sign) at 3 Shamai St, parallel with and to the south of Ben Yehuda St, and at *Rahmo*, beside the Mahane Yehuda Market, on the corner of Ha'Armonium and Agrippas Sts.

CAFES

Old City

For breakfast, *Cafeteria St Michael* on Omar ibn al-Khattab Square at Jaffa Gate (see map 14) does a decent omelette, bread and jam, and tea or coffee spread. A door away, *Abou Seif* also serves breakfast and has various Middle Eastern snacks such as grilled cheese and felafel or houmos platters. It's open daily except Sunday from 8 am to 8 pm. Across the square, the *Coffee Shop*, next to the Christian Information Centre (see map 14), is a lovely place – clean, and decorated with Christian-theme Jerusalem tiles on the tables and walls. It features a modestly priced all-you-can-eat salad bar with soup and bread. It's open daily except Sunday from 10 am to 6 pm.

A popular meeting point for travellers and proud of it, the *Backpacker Tearooms* at 100 Aftimus St, in the Christian Quarter's Muristan area (see map 14), offers all-day cheap food and beer as well as nightly videos. In the sanitised New York-accented Jewish Quarter (see map 15), *Tzaddik's Old City Deli* fuels hungry diners with heavily loaded submarine rolls, plus things like chilli dogs and draught beer. It's open Sunday to Thursday until 8 pm, and Friday until mid-afternoon.

The Coffeehouse
The Arab version of the cafe is the coffeehouse, or *qahwa* (the word also means coffee). These places are generally much plainer than their European-originated counterparts, often no more than a collection of battered chairs and tables in a sawdust-strewn room open to the street. The drink served is bitter Turkish-style coffee, often flavoured with *hehl* (cardamom). Tea, or *chay*, is also popular, served in a glass, black, very sweet (if you don't want sugar say so when you order – minREEYA sukar) and often with *na'ana* (mint), which is extremely refreshing even on a hot day.

The hubbub of conversation is sometimes accompanied by the incessant clacking of slammed domino and backgammon pieces and, inevitably, by the bubbling sound of smokers drawing hard on their nargilehs (the cumbersome waterpipe, also known as a sheesha). Rarely will a Palestinian woman enter a qahwa but there's no reason, however, why a western women shouldn't.

Most of Jerusalem's qahwas are in the Old City; there's a particularly popular and long-established place at the top of Al-Wad Rd, just on the left when entering from Damascus Gate, and a couple on Bab as-Silsila St. ■

East Jerusalem

Decorated with pink lacy curtains and embroidered 'God Bless Our Home' pennants, and with a waiter who switches effortlessly between Arabic and half a dozen different European languages, the *Cafe Europe* seems way out of place in the heart of blaring, wailing Arab East Jerusalem (see map 11). The menu is similarly quirky but the food is superb and offers some of the best-value quality eating in the whole of the city, East, New and Old. The platters are particularly recommended, and the ice cream cocktails are excellent too, although a little pricey. The Europe is at 9 As-Zahra St, east of Salah ad-Din St. It's open daily from 10 am to 10.30 pm.

New City

The Nahalat Shiv'a quarter and the pedestrianised areas around Ben Yehuda St (see map 9) are crowded with cafes. Take your pick; there's little to distinguish between most of them. The majority offer basic hot dishes and salads as well as cakes, ice cream and beverages. Coffee here comes black and strong, and if what you want is something like a Nescafe then ask for 'milk

ANDREW HUMPHREYS

A bakery near the Damascus Gate

coffee' or 'nes'. Beware the cappuccino, which usually resembles something like a warmed up icecream sundae.

If tea is your preference, the cushion-strewn, would-be bohemian *Tea House* at 12 Yoel Salomon St offers 20 or more herbal teas. It's popular with local young hippy types and is open Saturday to Thursday from 7 pm to 2 am, and Friday from 9 am to late afternoon.

Tmol Shilshom is a furniture-crowded cafe with ambitions to be a bookshop. Its walls are lined with shelves of second-hand titles, although we suspect that these add far more to the ambience than to the cash till. The place gets packed at lunch times but it's quieter early on and there's a good breakfast spread, including waffles with homemade jam. It's at 5 Yoel Salomon St, round the back. Conversely, *Sefer VeSefel* (meaning 'Mug and Book') is an excellent bookshop which sidelines as a cafe. It serves only basic beverages, but there's a pile of UK and US magazines for patrons to browse through. Sefer VeSefel is upstairs at 2 Yaabez St. It's open Sunday to Thursday from 8 am to 8 pm, Friday from 8 am to 2.30 pm, and Saturday from the end of Shabbat to 11.30 pm.

Another good place to sit and read (bring your own book) is the tranquil *Ticho House Cafe*. The house provides cool and pleasant surroundings, or you can sit out in the tree-shaded garden. Ticho House is off the top end of Harav Kook St, and the cafe is open Sunday to Thursday from 10 am to midnight, Friday from 10 am to 3 pm, and Saturday from sunset to midnight.

Despite the name, *Strudel* is a pastry-free zone – the name comes from the Hebrew term for the '@' common to all e-mail addresses. It's an Internet cafe/wine bar, with tables for dining, a sofa area and three computer stations in alcoves. It has a menu of homemade soups, salads and sandwiches and an impressive array of beers and wines. Strudel is at 11 Mounbaz St in the Russian Compound area. It is open from noon until late, closed Sunday.

Away from the city centre, *Cacao*, the vegetarian cafe at the Cinematheque (see map 10), has great views from its terrace of the Old City, Mt Zion and the Judean Desert. It's open seven days a week from 10 am until after midnight.

BURGERS & PIZZA

Jerusalem has an enormous *McDonald's* on Shamai St one block south of Ben Yehuda St, but anyone wanting a good burger would do better to head for *Babel*, 50m shy of the golden arches at 19 Hillel St (see map 9). It's more expensive (25 NIS and up) but Babel burgers actually taste like meat and they come accompanied with fries and salad. The meal-size sandwiches are great too – try a Reuben: grilled corned beef, Swiss cheese and sauerkraut. It's open Monday to Wednesday from 7.30 am to 1 am, and nonstop from 7.30 am Thursday until 1 am Sunday morning.

About the best place to eat in the Old City is *Abu Shanab* at 35 Latin Patriarchate Rd, Jaffa Gate (See map 12). It specialises in excellent pizza, made on the premises, which comes in three sizes: filling (7.50 NIS), very filling (15 NIS) and 'do you want half of this?' (25 NIS). Abu Shanab also does hot sandwiches, salads, lasagne

Late Night/Early Morning

Fat Dannys is an American-style diner open 24 hours seven days a week. It serves burgers, hot dogs, chicken, pancakes and an all-day (and all-night) breakfast special of grilled sausage and eggs. It's at the top of Yoel Salomon St, next door to the Underground Bar. Two doors up, on Zion Square, *Bonkers* keeps the same all-hours as Fat Dannys, but serves only bagels and coffee. *Babel* (see Burgers & Pizza), not far from Nahalat Shiva on Hillel St, also remains open overnight Thursday and Friday.

For more general provisioning, the large *Supersol* supermarket on Agron St near the junction with King George V St is open until late, and again serves 24 hours over the weekend. ■

and spaghetti, all about 15 NIS. It's open daily from 9 am until midnight.

For a very different pizza-eating experience visit the *Green Door Bakery*, a large, empty cave of a room in which Mohammed Ali tends a furnace-like oven and bakes for the local neighbourhood. For travellers, he rustles up crude cheese, egg and tomato pizzas – although the pleasure is more in watching them being prepared than it is in the eating. The pizzas cost just a few shekels and he will happily use any ingredients that you care to bring along. The bakery is open daily from early morning to late at night. It's on Aqabat ash-Sheikh Rihan just left off Al-Wad Rd at the bottom of the slope from Damascus Gate (see map 12).

ORIENTAL JEWISH

Best exemplified by Jerusalem's many Yemenite restaurants, Oriental kitchens are especially renowned for offal dishes. Turkey testicles, cow's udder, spleen and heart all taste a lot better than they sound. Non-vegetarians should not miss trying the city's speciality, meorav Yerushalmi – literally 'Jerusalem meats'. This is a mix of chopped livers, kidneys, hearts and beef with onions and spices sizzled on a great hot plate and scooped into pockets of bread. The best place to try it is on Agrippas St, in the vicinity of Mahane Yehuda (see map 9), where there are dozens of restaurants frying from early evening through until early morning.

One of the tastiest aspects of Oriental Jewish cooking is the art of stuffing vegetables and meat with rice, nuts, meat and spices. Most Yemenite restaurants have a

EDDIE GERALD

The Yemenite Step in Nahalat Shiva'a

varied selection of stuffed vegetables as starters, but one or two on their own make for an ample meal.

For basic Oriental favourites like salads, soups and stuffed vegetables, try *Chen*, a busy lunch time stop-off point in the New City where you can eat well for under 25 NIS. Israel's President Chaim Herzog is said to have favoured this place. It's at 30 Jaffa Rd, across from the main post office (no English sign; it's next to two pastry shops – see map 9), and is open Sunday to Thursday from 8 am to 6 pm and Friday from 8 am to 3 pm, closed Saturday. *Ma'adan* at 35 Jaffa Rd is a similar sort of place, where a full meal including soup or salad starts at around 20 NIS. The menu is wider than that at Chen and Ma'adan is open until late.

Up-market Orientalism is best represented by *The Yemenite Step* at 10 Yoel Salomon St (see map 9), open from 10 am to midnight. The mainstay of the menu is malawach (a thin, flaky-pastry bread) stuffed with meat, mushrooms or other savouries. It's extremely filling, though a little monotonous eaten on its own.

EASTERN EUROPEAN JEWISH

What most people think of as typically 'Jewish food' is Eastern European, typified by such dishes as goulash, schnitzel, klops (chopped meat) and gefilte fish. Most of the Israelis we met completely denied enjoying the last of these, which basically consists of ball-shaped pieces of fish heads and tails served chilled. Much more appetising are blintzes, a type of heavy pancake typically filled with something savoury such as mushrooms

PETER JOUSIFFE

A sweet shop in the Muslim Quarter

or cheese – though never meat because of kosher laws. On Shabbat, most secular Jews join the religious and follow the traditional rule of no cooking. For many, this will mean eating cholent, a heavy stew prepared before sunset on Friday.

Probably the best place to sample some of the above is *Feferbergs*, at 53 Jaffa Rd just east of the junction with King George V St (see map 9). This is a Jerusalem institution which has been around for more than 50 years. You can sit down to eat or there's takeaway. It's open Sunday to Thursday from noon to 10 pm, Friday for lunch only and Saturday after Shabbat.

Csardas, a fairly cheap though gloomy Hungarian restaurant at 11 Shlomzion HaMalka St, also serves a menu of Jewish specialities, including a lot of roasts. It's open more or less the same hours as Feferbergs. Romanian restaurants are particularly good for steaks and liver, and one of the best is *Gilly's*, on the corner of Yoel Salomon and Hillel Sts (see map 9). It is quite pricey though, with main dishes in the 24 to 50 NIS price range.

In the Jewish Quarter of the Old City, just up from the Western Wall on Tiferet Y'Israel St (see map 15), the self-service *Quarter Cafe* (upstairs) has decent, reasonably priced kosher food in pleasant surroundings, with a great view across to the Dome of the Rock and the Mount of Olives from the upper level. It's open Sunday to Thursday from 8.30 am to 6.30 pm, and Friday from 8.30 am to 4 pm, closed Saturday.

PALESTINIAN ARAB

Felafel originates from the Arab world, as does tahina and its close cousin, houmos (see Felafel, Shwarma & Houmos above). These three, with accompanying vinegary salads and bread, form the backbone of most menus at the cheap sit-down Arab restaurants, along with fuul (pronounced 'fool') – mashed fava beans. More up-market places will also serve grilled chicken, shwarma and shashlik and, if you're lucky, mansaf, a Palestinian dish of rice with small pieces of lamb, nuts, lemon juice and herbs. Other Palestinian dishes include melok, a soup made from greens, and kubbe, minced spiced lamb or beef mixed with burghul (cracked wheat) and deep fried. If you are offered mezze, this is a selection of starters which typically includes houmus, brain salad, eggplant purée, stuffed vine leaves, olives and pickles.

At the cheaper end of the range are places like *Al-Quds* (see the Falafel, Shwarma & Houmos section above) and, in the Old City on Al-Wad St close to Damascus Gate (see map 12), the *Jerusalem Star*, which serves basic grilled meat dishes. Half a grilled chicken with potatoes and salad costs 15 NIS. There are often special offers – check the door. It's open daily until 9.30 pm.

For top quality Arab food there's the *Petra* at 11 Al-Rashid St, parallel to and east of Salah ad-Din St (see map 11). It's worth dining here just for the decor, especially if you can get a seat in the back room beside the

---

Arab Sweets & Pastries

Usually soaked in honey and full of sugar, these edible highlights of Arab cuisine can't be good for you, but who cares? *Baklava* is like toasted shredded wheat, stuffed with pistachios or hazelnuts and drowned in honey, while *katayeef* and *kanafe* are concoctions of cheese, wheat, sugar and honey.

Souk Khan as-Zeit St is the honey-soaked sweet street in the Old City (see Map 12) and of all its syrupy confections the best are made at *Zalatimo's*, just back from the stairs leading up to the 9th Station of the Cross. The speciality of this unremarkable looking little bakery is *moutabak*, made to order by Abu Ali Hawash, the baker here for over 20 years. Super light pastry is kneaded and rolled over and over with a fresh cheese filling and served straight from the traditional oven with hot sugar syrup. If you fancy some get there early, as by about 11 am the pastry is finished and Abu Ali has locked up and gone home for the day. ■

fountain. Expect to pay 25 to 35 NIS for a main course and salad. The *Philadelphia Restaurant* (☎ 628 9770), at 9 As-Zahra St off Salah ad-Din St in East Jerusalem (see map 11), is one of the city's best Arab restaurants. Named after Amman, as it was known in ancient times, the restaurant specialises in mezzes as well as grilled lamb dishes and seafood. It's open seven days a week from noon to 10 pm.

ARMENIAN

Near Jaffa Gate in the Old City is the *Armenian Tavern*, at 79 Armenian Patriarchate Rd (see map 14), which has a beautiful tiled interior with a fountain gently splashing in one corner. The strongly flavoured meat dishes (25 to 35 NIS) are without exception excellent and it is recommended you try the khaghoghi derev, a spiced mince meat mixture bundled in vine leaves. There is another similarly priced but not as good Armenian restaurant, *The Yerevan*, close to the New Gate in the Christian Quarter.

ITALIAN

There are several Italian-oriented places in Nahalat Shiv'a, but despite their popularity many of these places are unapologetically mediocre. Instead, we recommend *Spaghettim* at 8 Rabbi Akiva St, off Hillel St (see map 9). Occupying the ground floor of a villa, Spaghettim has a spacious, cool, bare stone interior which is refreshingly uncluttered compared to most Jerusalem restaurants. The menu is spaghetti only, but it's served in over 50 different ways, from the predictable bolognaise through to ostrich in hunter sauce. Prices are 20 to 30 NIS and it's open from noon to 1 am. *Mamma Mia* is also extremely good. The pastas here, all homemade, cost between 27 and 35 NIS, and it does a great calzone for 30 NIS. It's at 38 King George V St at the back of the car park, 100m south of the junction with Hillel (see map 9), and is open Sunday to Thursday from noon to midnight, Friday from noon to 4 pm, and Saturday from sunset to midnight.

INTERNATIONAL

The Wild Bull (Shor HaBar) (☎ 624 4395) at 3 Yaabez St is a good South African-run steak restaurant which we'll upgrade to 'excellent' at lunchtime because of its cheap and filling business lunches; burgers and steak sandwiches with heaps of potato wedges and salad, starting

EDDIE GERALD

Sample French crepes Jerusalem style at Zion Square

from 15 NIS. Similarly substantial is the fare at *Norman's Bar & Grill* (☎ 566 6603), an American-style restaurant specialising in burgers, steaks and chicken. It also offers good value lunch specials – best eaten out on the lovely tree-shaded patio. The only drawback is the location, way down in the German Colony at 27 Emek Refa'im St. It's open Sunday to Thursday from noon to 11.30 pm and Saturday from sundown to 1 am.

One of the city's great kitchens is to be found at the *Notre Dame of Jerusalem Centre* opposite New Gate (see map 9). The Vatican-owned complex features a terrace coffee shop, open all day, and a restaurant with excellent food served in grand surroundings. It's open daily to non-residents for lunch and dinner; expect to pay about 40 NIS per head.

CREME DE LA CREME

As well as the vast array of fine wines and spirits, the semi-legendary *Fink's* bar (see the Entertainment chapter) serves a menu of consistently excellent Austro-Bavarian food. A speciality is the goulash soup, described as a 'Jewish ploughman's lunch'. With less than a dozen stools at the bar and only six tables, reservations are advisable. Fink's (☎ 623 4523) is found on King George V St, 50m north of the junction with Ben Yehuda St (see map 9). It's open Saturday to Thursday from 6 pm until midnight, closed on Friday.

The food served in the elegant surroundings of the *American Colony Hotel* (☎ 628 2421, 627 9777) (see map 11) is also said to be superb.

EDDIE GERALD

Dine in style at the King David Hotel

The *Mishkenot Sha'ananim* (☎ 625 1042, 625 4469), below the Montefiore Windmill (see map 10), serves award-winning French cuisine combined with a few Moroccan appetisers. It also claims to possess one of the largest and best restaurant wine cellars in the world. Whether or not its cellar is that good (we are sadly unqualified to comment), the views of the floodlit Old City walls are undeniably terrific. It's open seven days a week from 11 am to 1 am.

Opened only in summer 1996, *Rungsit* (☎ 561 1757) offers superior Thai/Japanese food in opulent Oriental (Far Eastern as opposed to Middle Eastern) surroundings. It's a sister restaurant to the Rungsits in New York and Bangkok. In Jerusalem it's to be found at 2 Jabotinsky St, opposite the Laromme Hotel in Talbiyeh. It's open Sunday to Thursday from noon to 11.30 pm, Friday from 12.30 to 3 pm, and Saturday from the end of Shabbat to 11.30 pm.

For superior seafood, head for the *Ocean* (☎ 624 7501), a restaurant described by the London *Times* Jerusalem correspondent as 'unhappily pretentious' but also as having fresh fish on a par with anything served in any European capital. The Ocean is at 7 Rivlin St (see map 9) and is open daily from 1 to 4 pm and 7 to 11 pm.

Entertainment

Well, despite the best attempts of the religious element, things have picked up a little since then. Those in search of 'amusement' in present-day Jerusalem can enjoy classical recitals or jazz jamming sessions, catch the latest Hollywood bubble gum or some obscure Swedish brain squeeze at the cinema, watch 22 men sweat it out on a football field or do plenty of perspiring themselves hammering the dance floor at some all-night rave. Pick up *The Jerusalem Post*, in particular the Friday edition, for an up-to-date and comprehensive list of events, and also stop by the Jaffa Rd tourist information office for a free copy of the current *Your Jerusalem* brochure. The *Traveller* newspaper, available free in bars and hostels, also has a good bar and nightlife guide.

CINEMAS

Central Jerusalem is very poorly served by cinemas. The two or three that existed, around the Shamai and Hillel St area, have been closed down and the premises converted to other uses. Instead, in most cases, the movie-goer now has to travel some distance out to the suburbs to one of the big new multiplexes. Standard Hollywood fare prevails. Films are nearly always left in their original language and subtitled into Hebrew. Tickets cost about 22 NIS. The city's centrally located cinemas are listed below.

Cinematheque (☎ 672 4131) shows a variety of classics, avant-garde, new wave and off-beat films, and presents a festival each July. It's a membership cinema but usually a sufficient number of tickets are available just before the performance. The complex of the cinema, cafe, archives and museum is tucked below Hebron Rd, down from St Andrew's Church.

Gil 1-10 (☎ 678 8440) is out at the Malkha shopping mall; take bus No 6, 24 or 31 from Jaffa Rd.

Kfir (☎ 624 2523) is at 97 Jaffa Rd, at the junction with HaNevi'im St, in the Klal building.

Rav-Chen 1-7 (☎ 679 2799) is at 19 Ha'Oman St in the Rav Mecher building, way down in Talpiot near the Haas Promenade.

Semadar (☎ 561 8168) is at 4 Lloyd George St, in the German Colony, south of the Liberty Bell Gardens.

Films are also shown at the Jerusalem Sherover Theatre in Talbiyeh (see below, under Theatre) and at the Israel Museum, in Givat Ram. French films are screened regularly at the Alliance Francaise (☎ 625 1204, 625 7167) on Agron St (see map 9).

BARS & CLUBS

While East Jerusalem and the Old City close up completely at sunset, with just *Abu Shanab*, the *Tabasco Tearooms* and the *Backpacker Tearooms* providing any alternative to beer and a book back at the hostel, the New City stays buzzing till sunup. Yoel Salomon and Rivlin Sts, the two parallel main streets in Nahalat Shiv'a (see map 9), are lined with enough late night bars and cafes to defeat even the most alcohol-absorbent of pub-crawlers. Down at the bottom of Rivlin St, *The Tavern* was the original Jerusalem pub and it attracts a mainly ex-pat, bar-propping, beer drinking crowd. *The Blue Hole*, down a little side alley about midway along Yoel Salomon St, is a similar sort of place to The Tavern but considerably more dingy. Like most of the bars it has a popular happy hour, only in the case of the Blue Hole it's a whole 3½ hours long.

Possibly Jerusalem's most popular nightspot is the *Underground*, at 1 Yoel Salomon St, more or less on Zion Square. It's a crowded pub on the ground floor with a

---

Israeli Beers

The Israelis are not big drinkers, which is reflected in their relative disinterest in the brewing business. One company, the National Brewery Ltd, controls 98% of the beer market – a position of dominance attained not through aggressive marketing or competitive prices, but simply through lack of any competition. At the bottom of the range is the little-seen Nesher (3.8% alcohol), which is not served by most bars or cafes but, when found, is the cheapest beer on the market. Goldstar (4.7%) is the most popular beer with travellers, both bottled and draught, while Maccabee (4.9%) is the Israeli favourite, considered up-market and the only beer that Israel exports.

A relative newcomer is Taybeh, the product of a small, private Palestinian-run brewery in the West Bank town of the same name. We didn't get to sample any but we're informed it's available bottled in Jerusalem and at restaurants in places like Bethlehem. ■

EDDIE GERALD

The Jerusalem Sherover Theatre complex, home to the
Jerusalem Symphony Orchestra

EDDIE GERALD

The Khan Theatre and nightclub

disco downstairs – not recommended for those who
enjoy breathing. The stairs to the left of the
Underground's entrance lead up to the *Q Bar,* another
place dominated by its dance floor. Both of these places
don't get going until around 10 or 11 pm and are open
until everyone's way past caring what time it is.

Right around the corner, *Arizona* is the favoured
travellers' haunt. It's another bar/disco, but the beer
prices are lower than average, there are nightly happy
hours and the music tends towards rock. It's between
Zion Square and the Steimatzky bookshop.

Fink's

True bar-hopping aficionados will appreciate the unique ambience at the legendary *Fink's*, rated in a 1994 *Newsweek* article as one of the world's best bars. Opened some 61 years earlier, Fink's was the favourite watering hole for British military and police officers during the Mandate, and Jewish underground fighters would frequent the bar to hear the gossip. Since that time it has been a regular refuge for international statesmen and correspondents taking time out from the turmoil that brought them to the city.

The present landlord is a model of quiet professionalism. An apology proffered by a friend and I for our rum-fuelled and particularly rowdy behaviour the night before was met with a shrugged acceptance: 'Gentlemen, this is not a pharmacy. We serve alcohol here.'

Fink's, God bless it, is found on King George V St, 50m north of the junction with Ben Yehuda St. It's open Saturday to Thursday from 6 pm until midnight, closed on Friday. ■

The other main concentration of bars is in the Russian Compound area, crowded around the upper part of Heleni HaMalka. These places are less congested with travellers and visitors and tend to be where the local Israelis hang out. Best of the lot are the suitably laid back *Cannabis* on Mounbaz St and the ever-popular *Glasnost*, which features live music four nights a week – see below. Also worth dropping by is *Strudel*, the Internet cafe/wine bar at 11 Mounbaz St.

Decent Guinness (18 NIS but 9 NIS during happy hour, which goes from 4 to 7 pm) is served at the *Champs*, a lone English-style pub midway between the New City centre and the Old City walls at 19 Jaffa Rd, opposite the new City Hall complex. It's open from 4 pm to 5 am.

Gay & Lesbian

At the time of writing, the Q Bar (see above) is about the closest thing Jerusalem has to a gay venue, although the clientele is still predominantly straight. During our last visit a new bar in the Russian Compound area, *Metro Subway* (☎ 623 3087) at 15 Heleni HaMalka St, was promising a weekly gay night – drop by or call for details.

Live Music

For live music nightly – rock, folk and blues – squeeze in at *Mike's*, a tiny bar which, aside from the guy with the guitar and the bartender, has room for only about a dozen customers. It's on Horkenos St off Heleni HaMalka St in the Russian Compound area (see map 9). Up the hill, *Glasnost* at 15 Heleni HaMalka St has live music, varying from rock to reggae to jazz funk and samba, depending on what night of the week it is. There's a cover charge of 15 NIS. Neighbouring *Metro Subway* has Israeli pop artists performing one night a week, while there's usually a small jazz or blues outfit entertaining at one or another of the numerous bars in the area.

What to do on Shabbat
'Shabbat Shalom' for the unobservant and the non-Jew in Jerusalem need not be a password for boredom. For Jerusalem's large Arab population, Shabbat is just another day and nothing is closed in most of the Old City, Mt Zion, the Mount of Olives and East Jerusalem. The exception in the Old City is, of course, the Jewish Quarter, which completely shuts down for the day – wander over to the Western Wall to see the crowds, the singing and the dancing that welcome the Shabbat on Friday at sunset.

While the Egged buses are off the road the Arab bus network and service taxis still operate from the Damascus Gate area, and Shabbat is as good a time as any to head for Bethlehem, Jericho, Hebron, Ramallah or Nablus.

You might also try beating Shabbat by taking a bus down to the Dead Sea on Friday before the shutdown and staying somewhere overnight like Ein Gedi or Masada – the parks and reserves are all open seven days a week. You can return later in the day when the buses start running again. Even better, sign up for the all-inclusive Masada-Ein Gedi-Qumran-Jericho trip offered by many of the Old City hostels. This departs every morning, Shabbat included, at 3 am, and gets you back into Jerusalem at about 3 pm – in time for a quick snooze before sunset when the city comes back to life for its busiest night of the week.

If you do elect to stay in town on Friday night then you'll find that, much to the annoyance of observant Jews, most of the bars on and around Yoel Salomon and Rivlin Sts and the Russian Compound defy Shabbat and open as usual.

During the day on Saturday, with only slightly reduced hours, distraction is also offered by, amongst others, the Israel Museum and neighbouring Bible Lands Museum, the Bloomfield Science Museum, the Citadel (Tower of David) and the highly recommended LA Mayer Museum of Islamic Art. ∎

Elsewhere, *Tmol Shilshom* bookshop/cafe (see the Places to Eat chapter) in Nahalat Shiv'a occasionally has folky acoustic evenings. For jazz, ethnic and Arabic music, and the odd buzzsaw guitar band, check the schedule at the *Pargod Theatre* (☎ 623 1765) at 94 Bezalel St. Friday afternoons feature free jazz jamming sessions from 1.30 to 5.30 pm.

THEATRE

Israel has a pretty active theatre and dance scene, but as in many places today it faces an increasing struggle for funds and audience attendance. Most performances are in Hebrew, although there are occasional foreign-language productions.

Al-Masrah Centre for Palestinian Culture & Art and *Al-Kasaba Theatre* (☎ 628 0957) are on Abu Obeida St off Salah ad-Din St, behind the Tombs of the Kings in East Jerusalem (see map 11). Plays, musicals, operettas and folk dancing are performed here in Arabic, often with an English synopsis.

Jerusalem Sherover Theatre (☎ 561 7167) is at 20 David Marcus St in Talbiyeh (see map 10). This modern complex features the classics and modern works. Simultaneous English-language translation headsets are available for certain performances.

Khan Theatre (☎ 671 8281) is on David Remez St across from the railway station entrance (see map 10). A converted and refurbished Ottoman-era caravanserai, this complex features mainly Hebrew plays in its theatre. It also has a nightclub. Take bus No 6, 7, 8 or 30 to get here.

Train Theatre (☎ 561 8514) is in the Liberty Bell Gardens (see map 10). This is a converted railway carriage that now serves as a puppet theatre.

Tzavta (☎ 622 7621) is at 38 King George V St, behind the car park on the right if you're coming from Ben Yehuda St, opposite the start of Gan Ha'Atzmaut (Independence Park – see map 9). This small music-theatre club often features productions in English, and visiting entertainers are invited to audition for unscheduled performances.

Pargod Theatre (☎ 623 1765) is at 94 Bezalel St, just west of the New City centre. It mainly serves as a music venue, but there are occasional small scale productions put on here.

CLASSICAL MUSIC

Classical music lovers are well catered for in Jerusalem. The *Henry Crown Concert Hall* at the Jerusalem Sherover Theatre (see map 10) is home to the Jerusalem Symphony Orchestra while *Binyanei Ha'Umah Conference Centre* (☎ 622 2481), opposite the central bus station and adjacent to the Holiday Inn Crown Plaza (see map 17), is the national residence of the Israel Philharmonic Orchestra.

Free classical performances are held occasionally at a number of venues including the *YMCA Auditorium* on HaMelekh David St (see map 10); the *Mishkenot Sha'ananim* (see map 10), held on alternate Fridays; *Beit Shmuel*, part of the Hebrew Union College on HaMelekh David St (Saturday morning) (see map 9); and at the *Church of the Dormition* on Mt Zion (see map 14). Immigrant musicians also give performances at Ticho House every Friday morning.

FOLK/TRADITIONAL MUSIC

At the *International Cultural Centre for Youth (ICCY)* (☎ 566 4144/6, 563 0900, 566 9838) at 12A Emek Refa'im St in the German Colony, south of Talbiyeh (see map 10), the Pa'amez Teyman Folklore Ensemble regularly performs from a repertoire that includes Israeli folk dances and Yemenite, Hasidic and Arabic traditional dances, Israeli folk singing and Khalifa Arabic drummers. Tickets are sold at the door and at many hotels. You could also try the *Pargod Theatre* (see under Live Music in the Bars & Clubs section above).

SPECTATOR SPORTS

The two big sports are basketball and football. The city's main sporting venue is the Teddy Stadium (named for former mayor Teddy Kollek), which is out in Malkha district west of the city centre, adjacent to the Kanyon shopping mall; take bus No 6, 24 or 31. For dates and further details of what's on, check with the Jaffa Rd tourist office.

Shopping

The prime city centre shopping street is King George V St (see map 9), which has a couple of multistorey shopping malls and the large Hamashbir department store. Jerusalem has also succumbed to the out-of-town-mall malaise, and the Kanyon mall, out in the Malkha district (take bus No 6, 24 or 31 from Jaffa Rd), is the largest shopping centre in Israel.

For more interesting buys take a look around Nahalat Shiv'a (see map 9), which is full of arts and crafts boutiques or, for those with Rockefeller-like reserves, browse HaMelekh David St, the Jerusalem equivalent of Knightsbridge (see maps 9 and 10).

The bazaars of the Old City (see maps 12-15) are prime souvenir territory. Their tightly compacted stalls are completely devoted to filling the mantelpieces and wall units of the world with multi-denominational kitsch, from glitter-dusted prints of the Dome of the Rock and glow-in-the-dark crucifixes, to 'Shalom Y'All' plaques.

EDDIE GERALD

Espresso Bar in King George V Street, New City

Probably Jerusalem's best bookshop, however, is Sefer VeSefel, a creaky little place with floor to ceiling new and second-hand titles, both fiction and nonfiction. It also has a small balcony cafe. It's upstairs at 2 Yaabez St, which is a little alley off Jaffa Rd, one block east of King George V St (see map 9). It's open Sunday to Thursday from 8 am to 8 pm, Friday from 8 am to 2.30 pm, and Saturday from the end of Shabbat to 11.30 pm.

In the Old City, The Bookshelf at the southern end of Jewish Quarter Rd (see map 14) has piles of dog-eared thrillers, while the Moriah Bookstore on nearby Misgav Ladakh is the place for English-language material on Judaism. In East Jerusalem, Educational Books at 22 Salah ad-Din St (see map 11) carries an assortment of Palestinian-oriented publications.

French readers will find a limited selection of books in the Steimatzky stores but are much better catered for at Librarie Francaise on Jaffa Rd, across from the main post office.

For information about books written about Jerusalem, see under Books in the Facts for the Visitor chapter.

Periodicals If the contents of your wallet are equal to your craving, Steimatzky is also the place to pick up your copy of the *Economist*, *Paris-Match* or *Wired*. For a more varied and eclectic selection try Tower Records, on Hillel St behind McDonald's (see map 9), which has a wide range of UK and US style music and arts publications.

Ceramics

The tiling on the Dome of the Rock is the work of Armenian craftshops, as are the ceramic street name plaques that adorn the walls of the Old City. Tiles and plates fashioned in the same manner are one of the most attractive buys in Jerusalem. Probably the best sales studio to visit is Jerusalem Pottery on the Via Dolorosa next to the 6th Station. Commissions are also accepted. Also recommended are the two ceramic shops on Armenian Patriarchate Rd (see map 14) and Palestinian Pottery at 14 Nablus Rd, across from the US consulate in East Jerusalem (see map 11).

Handicrafts and Souvenirs

Oriental coffee pots, inlaid lapis boxes, *nargilehs* (hubble bubble pipes) and a bewildering array of other ornaments seem sometimes to be the raison d'être of the Old City. The backbone of the handicrafts industry are the 'Jerusalem candles', prettily patterned spherical things that become translucent when the wick is lit. They are genuinely attractive and go for between 15 and 30 NIS, depending on the size.

Olive wood is similarly ubiquitous, most commonly used to fashion crucifixes, camels, worry beads and carvings of biblical scenes and characters.

Excursions

AROUND JERUSALEM

Kibbutz Ramat Rachel

Its location between Jerusalem and Bethlehem made this kibbutz a scene of bloody fighting during the 1948 War. Today, that same location has helped the kibbutz develop itself as a full-scale tourist attraction. Its name means 'the Heights of Rachel', referring to Jacob's wife, whose tomb is in Bethlehem. Its tours offer visitors a glimpse of life on the collective farm, and there's a museum with exhibits on the 1948 War, open daily from 8 am to noon. It's also possible to stay at the *kibbutz guesthouse* (☎ 702 555; fax 733 155); rates are US$75 to $105 for a single, US$90 to $125 for a double. To get there take bus No 7 from Jaffa Rd or Keren HaYesod St in Talbiyeh.

Kennedy Memorial

South of the Hadassah Medical Centre and about 11 km from the city centre, this fine memorial to John F Kennedy sits atop Mt Orah. Unfortunately, you may need a car to get here as the nearest buses (Nos 20 and 50) stop a good 30 minutes walk away.

Sorek/Avshalom Stalagmite & Stalactite Cave

The stunning Sorek, or Avshalom (Absalom's), cave is some 20 km west of Jerusalem along the road from Ein Kerem. The predominance of limestone in the region has caused these geological formations, which are floodlit for effect. Opening hours are Sunday to Thursday 8.30 am to 3.45 pm and Friday 8.30 am to 12.45 pm. Admission is 13 NIS for adults and 7 NIS for children. For more information on the caves, call ☎ (02) 911 117.

The pleasant scenery en route from Jerusalem is almost worth an excursion itself. No regular bus goes directly to the cave, but Egged Tours offers two half-day guided tours, each for around US$20. If you are driving there from Jerusalem, take the Beit Shmesh road via Ein Kerem. The caves are well signposted.

Shoresh Junction

West of this junction on the Jerusalem-Tel Aviv highway, the road descends into a gorge. On both sides you can see the rusted remains of vehicles that were part of the Jewish supply convoys attacked by the Arabs during the 1948 siege of Jerusalem. Some have been daubed with red paint and inscriptions, and they form a memorial to the Jews who were killed here.

Abu Gosh

This peaceful and picturesque Arab village (13 km from Jerusalem and off the main highway to Tel Aviv) is significant because it is the site of the biblical Kiriath-Jearim (Town of Forests) where the Ark of the Covenant was located for 20 years until David moved it to Jerusalem (I Chronicles 13:5-8). The village is known from the time Joshua conquered it. Before the new highway bypassed the village it was a popular beauty spot for Israelis, but now it sees fewer visitors.

There are two interesting churches here. **Notre Dame de l'Arche** (Our Lady of the Ark of the Covenant) was built in 1924 and is a local landmark, with its statue of St Mary carrying the baby Jesus. It belongs to the French Sisters of St Joseph of the Apparition, and they believe that it stands on the site of Abinadab's house where the Ark was kept (I Samuel 7:1). Ring the bell at the door of the adjacent building if no-one is about and the church is closed. The church is built on the same site as a larger Byzantine church, and you can see its mosaic floor inside and out. You reach the church from the top of the hill overlooking the village and facing Jerusalem. Turn right coming out of the Caravan Restaurant and head up the hill. It's open daily from 8 to 11.30 am and 3.30 to 6 pm. Admission is free.

The **Crusader Church & Monastery** is one of the country's best-preserved and most attractive Crusader remains. It was built about 1142 and destroyed in 1187. It is believed that the monastery stands on the remains of a Roman castle. A stone from the castle is displayed in the church and bears an inscription of the 10th Legion, a renowned Roman unit stationed in Jerusalem in the 1st century.

Used for many centuries as an animal shelter, the church was acquired in 1859 by the French government, who placed it under the guardianship of the French Benedictine Fathers. Since 1956 it has belonged to the Lazarist Fathers. In the subterranean section of the building is a small spring.

The complex is next door to the mosque, so look for the minaret in the valley. The sign outside reads, 'Eglise de Croisse – Crusaders' Church'. Ring the bell to enter. The monastery is open Monday to Wednesday, Friday and Saturday from 8.30 to 11 am and 2.30 to 5.30 pm, closed Sunday and Thursday. Admission is free, but donations are requested.

Getting There & Away Abu Gosh is most conveniently reached from Jerusalem on bus No 185 or 186, both of which depart frequently between 6 am and 11 pm from the central bus station.

Bethany

On the western slopes of the Mount of Olives, Bethany is renowned as the site of the resurrection of Lazarus (John 11:1-44). A Franciscan church commemorates the traditional site of the miracle performed by Jesus. Bethany is also named as the place where Jesus was anointed, much to the disapproval of his disciples (Matthew 26:6-13, Mark 14:3-9, John 12:1-8). The church features some impressive mosaics, one of which illustrates the resurrection. Built in 1954, this is the fourth church to occupy the area. The first was constructed in the mid-1st century, the second in the Byzantine period and the third by the Crusaders.

A Greek Orthodox church stands by the Tomb of Lazarus. In the 16th century, Muslims built a mosque here and Christians later dug their own entrance to enable them to worship. Local guides are often on hand and do a decent job of telling their interesting version of the local history. If you listen, you should tip a couple of shekels. The tomb is open daily from 8 am to noon and 2 to 6 pm. Admission is 2 NIS.

The church itself is only open to the public on the Feast of Lazarus, usually in early April. The Greek Orthodox convent, a 10 minute walk away from Jerusalem, boasts the rock upon which Jesus sat while waiting for Martha to arrive from Jericho. Ring the bell to enter.

Getting There & Away To reach Bethany you can take either of two Arab buses – the Bethany service, No 36 (there are two No 36 services, so ask for El-Azariya (Lazarus) before boarding) or No 28 to Jericho – and get off on the way through. Another option is to walk. If it's not too hot (or too wet), you can walk up and over the Mount of Olives and around the side to Bethany, or choose other routes. You can't really get lost, and you're

---

Latrun Monastery

Founded in 1890 by the French Trappist Order of monks as a contemplative monastery, Latrun Monastery is now widely renowned for its wine, as well as its lovely location, architecture and gardens.

The wine-making began in 1899. The monks reclaimed and cultivated the land and planted olive groves, grain fields and vegetable gardens, as well as vineyards. In the rocky areas pine trees and cypresses were planted. In WWI the monks were expelled by the Turks, but they were able to return, and in 1926 the present monastery was constructed.

Visitors are welcome to enjoy the gardens and the architecture and to buy the wine, spirits, vermouths and olive oil produced here. The shop by the gate is open Monday to Saturday from 8.30 to 11.30 am and 2.30 to 4.30 pm, closed Sunday. ■

---

never far from a busy road on which to hitchhike or hail a service taxi.

Latrun

About halfway between Jerusalem and Tel Aviv lies Latrun. Its popular wine-producing monastery enjoys views of many biblical sites: Emmaus, Ayalon, Bethoron, Gezer, Modin, Lydda and Sorec. Also nearby is Canada Park, a result of the tree-planting programme initiated by the Jewish National Fund. Latrun means 'Home of the Good Thief'; it is believed to have been the home of one of the thieves crucified with Jesus.

A modern highway cuts through the area, and to the west (the left-hand side heading towards Tel Aviv) is the attractive Latrun Monastery, while to the east is Canada Park and the ruins of the Emmaus Church.

In the 1948 War, the Arabs closed the road here, thus cutting off supplies to Jerusalem. It was not until the Six Day War that the Israelis took Latrun. Going further back in time, the area has seen its fair share of conflict. Greeks, Romans, Arabs, Crusaders, the British and the Ottoman Turks have all passed through en route to Jerusalem.

Emmaus Church Above the ruins rises the monas-
tery formerly belonging to the Beit-Haram Brothers, but now functioning as the French Prehistorical Research Centre. The church commemorates Christian tradition that this is where Jesus appeared to two of his disciples after his resurrection (Mark 16:12-13, Luke 24:13-31).

ISRAELI MINISTRY OF TOURISM

Bethlehem may be the birthplace of Jesus Christ, but it's also a Palestinian Arab town where there are as many minarets as church spires

Canada Park This park is one of the country's many beautifully forested areas, and you can wander around and picnic here. You can find a well-preserved Roman bath near the church, dating from around 640 AD. Various water holes, conduits and the remains of an amphitheatre are also to be found in the park.

Getting There & Away Latrun can be reached most easily by bus from Jerusalem, with a service every 30 minutes.

BETHLEHEM

Modern-day Bethlehem (see map 6) may be a cynic's delight, with Manger Square, Manger St, Star St, Shepherds' St, two Shepherds' Fields and an unheavenly host of 'Christmases', but for most travellers with even the remotest Christian background, a trip to Jerusalem without visiting the nearby site of the Nativity is unthinkable, even if only to please a pious relative back home.

Orientation & Information

With the Church of the Nativity on its eastern side, Manger Square is the centre of town and, ludicrously, also the town's main car park. Squeeze through the tour buses and taxis, and you'll find around the square the tourist office, police station, post office and various shops, hotels and eating places. Milk Grotto St heads off to the south-east, while Paul VI St heads uphill to the north-west, and the museum, outdoor market and more shops and hotels.

Manger St, which runs to the north of the square, is the main winding route through the new town. It eventually intersects with the Jerusalem-Hebron highway opposite the Jewish shrine of Rachel's Tomb.

Accommodation in Bethlehem is limited, especially at Easter and Christmas (some things never change) and it makes more sense to stay in Jerusalem.

Things to See

The **Church of the Nativity**, (see map 7) one of the world's oldest working churches, is built like a citadel over the cave where it is believed that Jesus was born. Happily, it's a suitably august and venerable building, which unlike Jerusalem's Holy Sepulchre or Nazareth's Basilica manages to avoid the 'holy site as sideshow' feel. Down Milk Grotto St is the **Milk Grotto Chapel**, a kitschy little shrine that owes its existence to the Virgin Mary's clumsy lactations (at least that's how the legend goes). North-west of the square, on Paul VI St, the **Bethlehem Museum** has exhibits of traditional Palestinian crafts and costumes; it's open Monday to Saturday from 10 am to noon and 2.30 to 5.30 pm, closed Sunday.

One of Judaism's most sacred shrines, also revered by Muslims and Christians, **Rachel's Tomb** is housed in a small white domed building on the edge of town at the intersection of Hebron Rd and Manger St.

Getting There & Away

Arab bus No 22 runs frequently from East Jerusalem and stops outside Jaffa Gate en route. It's about a 40 minute ride. Service taxis (costing 2 NIS) from outside Damascus Gate are more convenient; they tend to depart more frequently and make the journey in half the time of the bus.

As they are so close, walking from Jerusalem to Bethlehem is a popular option. At Christmas there's an official procession, but the two to 2½ hour, downhill-all-the-way hike is pleasant all year round.

JERICHO

Jericho is best known for the biblical account of Joshua and the tumbling walls. There are some ancient, well-visited ruins on the outskirts of town but these are surpassed by the shabby beauty of the surrounding landscape.

Orientation & Information

Service taxis from Jerusalem drop their passengers off in the main square with its shops, eating places, police station, taxi ranks and moneychanger.

To reach the sights, follow the six km loop formed by Qasr Hisham St and Ein as-Sultan St. Moving anti-clockwise is the popular choice: head north up Qasr Hisham St to Hisham's Palace, a walk (or cycle) of about 2.5 km, then west to the old synagogue and ancient Jericho.

With the distance involved between the town and the sights, cycling is a popular mode of transport. The roads are relatively flat and traffic free, so decide for yourself whether the heat is easier to bear on foot or on the saddle of a rented boneshaker. Zaki's bicycle shop is on the town square and he charges 3 NIS per hour. You may be asked to leave a passport or something similar as security.

Ancient Sites

Hisham's Palace is the impressive ruins of a 7th century hunting lodge and includes a beautiful Byzantine mosaic floor depicting a lion pouncing on one of a group of gazelle grazing beneath a great leafy tree. There's another mosaic floor – part of the ruins of a 5th or 6th century **synagogue** – passed on the way to the site of **ancient Jericho**, otherwise known as the Tel as-Sultan excavations. Only true archaeology buffs are likely to be

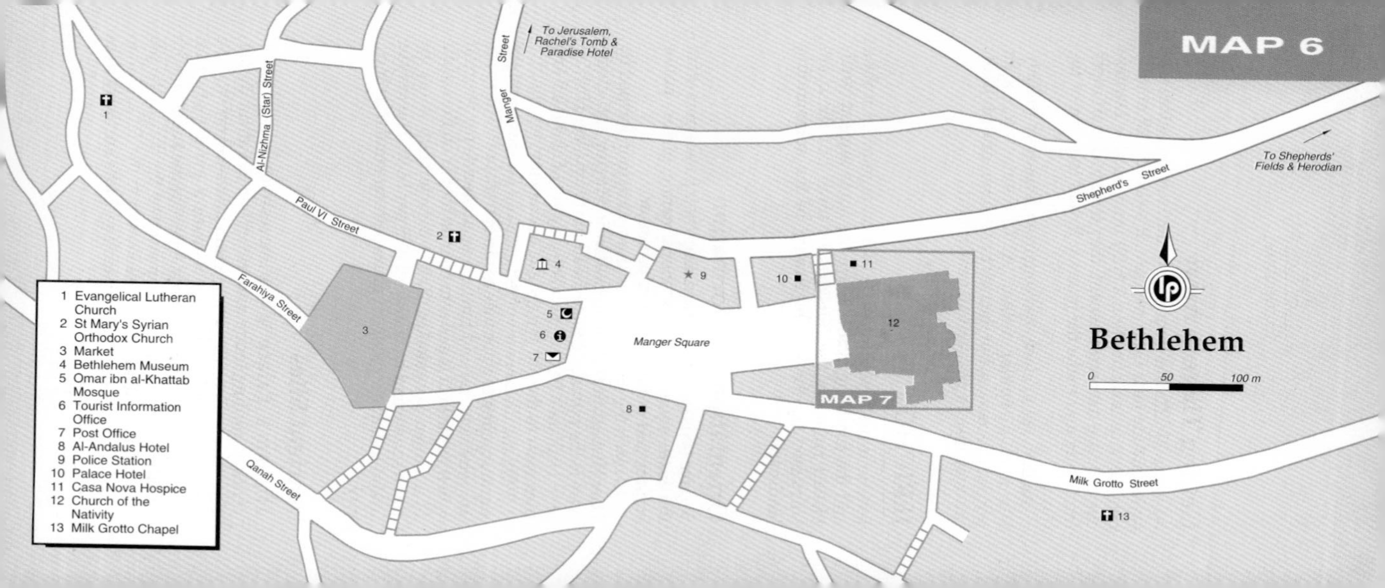

MAP 6

To Jerusalem,
Rachel's Tomb &
Paradise Hotel

To Shepherds'
Fields & Herodian

Bethlehem

0   50   100 m

1 Evangelical Lutheran
  Church
2 St Mary's Syrian
  Orthodox Church
3 Market
4 Bethlehem Museum
5 Omar ibn al-Khattab
  Mosque
6 Tourist Information
  Office
7 Post Office
8 Al-Andalus Hotel
9 Police Station
10 Palace Hotel
11 Casa Nova Hospice
12 Church of the
  Nativity
13 Milk Grotto Chapel

Al-Nizhma (Star) Street

Manger Street

Paul VI Street

Shepherd's Street

Farahiya Street

Manger Square

MAP 7

Qanah Street

Milk Grotto Street

Church of the Nativity

Not to Scale

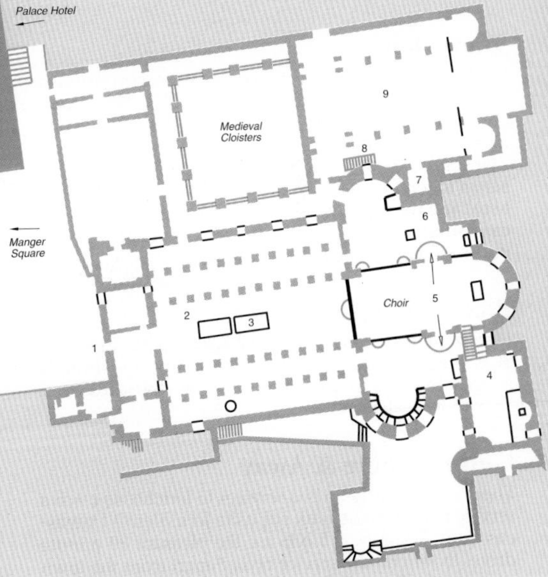

MAP 7

Palace Hotel

Medieval
Cloisters

9

8

7

6

← Manger
Square

Choir

5

2

3

1

4

O

1 Entry to the church is through the tiny Door of Humility. Originally the
   entrance was much larger but the Crusaders reduced its size to prevent
   attackers from riding in. Later, either during the Mamluk or Ottoman
   period, the portal was made even smaller. You can still see the outline
   of the original 6th century doorway and within it the pointed Crusader
   era arch.
2 The red limestone pillars may date back to the original 4th century
   church. Some of them are decorated with frescoes of saints, painted
   by artistically inclined Crusaders in the 12th century.
3 Wooden trapdoors are usually left open to reveal parts of Constantine's
   4th century mosaic floor.
4 Greek Orthodox Monastery.
5 Stairs down to the Grotto of the Nativity, supposed site of Jesus' birth.
6 Armenian Chapel.
7 Statue of St Mary.
8 Steps down to the caves.
9 The Franciscan Church of St Catherine was built in 1881. It's here that
   midnight mass is held every December 24th and broadcast around the
   world.

impressed here, and even visitors blessed with the most visionary imaginations are going to struggle to make anything of the signposted trenches and mounds of dirt.

The **Mt & Monastery of Temptation**, on the other hand, are well worth the steep climb. This 12th century Greek Orthodox monastery clings to the cliffside on the traditional site where the Devil tempted Jesus. It's closed on Sunday.

Wadi Qelt

Wadi Qelt is a nature reserve with a natural spring where you can swim in a pool under a waterfall and hike along an aqueduct to **St George's Monastery**, built into the cliff face of a canyon. The hike takes about four hours. The starting point is the Wadi Qelt turn-off on the Jerusalem to Jericho road (get the bus driver to drop you off here) and the finishing point is Jericho, from where you can continue sightseeing in the town or easily find transport back to Jerusalem.

Places to Stay

Hisham's Palace Hotel (☎ (02) 992 7282) on Ein as-Sultan St is the only place to stay in town, but we strongly suggest that you give it a miss and catch the last service back to Jerusalem.

Getting There & Away

There are currently no bus services to Jericho, so catch a service taxi from the rank opposite Jerusalem's Damascus Gate. The fare is 5 NIS for the pleasant 30 minute drive. In Jericho the service taxis depart from the town square, usually until about 7 pm. You can find taxis after this time, but with a shortage of passengers you may have to fork out for a higher fare.

THE DEAD SEA

It's the ultimate Israel cliché, the picture of the swimsuited bather lying in – almost on – the water, feet up and newspaper open, like a Sunday morning in bed. But unlike a camel ride at the pyramids or wrapping a *keffiyah* round your neck, this is one Middle Eastern cliché well worth indulging in. With a shoreline of some 90 km there is no one bathing spot, but you are advised to take your dip somewhere with shower facilities (the Dead Sea has a slightly slimy quality) – the beach at Ein Gedi is one of the most popular spots.

Dead Healthy?
Compared to regular sea water, the water of the Dead Sea contains 20 times as much bromine, 15 times as much magnesium and 10 times as much iodine – it is, in effect, 33% solid substance. Bromine, a component of many sedatives, relaxes the nerves, magnesium counteracts skin allergies and clears the bronchial passages, while iodine has a beneficial effect on certain glandular functions – or so it's claimed, especially by local health spa owners and the various Dead Sea cosmetic companies.

Due to the low altitude there is 10% more oxygen in the air than at sea level, and the lack of urban development has kept the air free of pollution. All of this increases the body's metabolic rate and has a bracing effect.

Healthy or not, soaking in the water of the Dead Sea can also be extremely painful. Wade in with any exposed cuts or grazes and you will gain instant enlightenment as to the meaning of the phrase to 'rub salt in your wounds'. We guarantee that you are going to discover scratches and sores that you never knew you had. The magnesium chloride in the water gives it a revolting bitter taste and if you swallow any then it's stomach pump time. Don't get the water in your eyes either as it will sting and inflame – if this happens then rinse them immediately with fresh water. ■

After the obligatory float, the next popular thing to do is to visit **Masada**, a place which readers consistently rate as Israel's number one attraction. A free-standing, sheer-sided plateau high above the Dead Sea, Masada was fortified by Herod the Great. In 66 AD the Jews rose up against the Romans in what's known as the First Revolt, and a group of them called the Zealots captured the lightly guarded Masada. After suppressing the uprising in the rest of the country, the Romans turned their attention finally to the mountain-top stronghold. When defeat was inevitable the 967 men, women and children atop Masada committed mass suicide with just a couple of survivors left to tell the tale. The event figures large in the Israeli national psyche, and the melodramatic utterance 'Masada shall not fall again' is a favoured pearl of political rhetoric. The site and views are superb, and you can reach the top by cable car or on foot.

Not as well known or as well frequented by travellers, the **Ein Gedi Nature Reserve** also deserves some exploration. One of the country's most attractive oases, Ein Gedi is a lush area of freshwater springs, waterfalls, pools and tropical vegetation nestled in the arid desert

ANDREW HUMPHREYS

A float in the Dead Sea is a must for any visitor to Israel

ANDREW HUMPHREYS

Jaffa, the world's oldest port

landscape of the lowest place on earth. It's a haven for desert wildlife, which hangs in there despite the terrifyingly raucous coach loads of kids that rampage through the reserves on an almost daily basis.

Ein Gedi sprawls over four km – the nature reserves, field school and youth hostel are to the north, on the west side of the road; one km further south are the bathing beach, restaurant and campsite. Another 2.5 km to the south is the turn-off for Kibbutz Ein Gedi, with the Hamme Mazor sulphur baths 2.5 km beyond. Avoid weekends and holidays when Ein Gedi is noisy and crowded.

North of Ein Gedi is **Qumran**, where the Dead Sea Scrolls were discovered. The site includes the settlement and caves of the Essenes, the Jewish sect who wrote the scrolls between 150 BC and 68 AD. The bus stops on the main road; follow the turn-off up the hill. There is a self-service *cafeteria* at the site. It's a hot climb up to the caves, so bring drinking water.

Tours

By far the cheapest way of sampling the Dead Sea region is to sign up for the 12 hour tour you'll see advertised in almost all the hostels in Jerusalem. It departs the Old City at 3 am each morning, getting you down to Masada in time to watch the sunrise over the desert. There's a visit to Ein Gedi Reserve and a float in the Dead Sea before photostops at Qumran and Jericho's Mt of Temptation. Despite the stopwatch-timed schedule, most travellers find that they get to see all they want. SPNI Tours operate a very similar programme but it's about three times more expensive.

Metzoke Dragot (☎ (02) 964 501/4; fax (02) 964 505) offers various tours and activities in the Judean Desert, either with or without accommodation. They are highly recommended by those who have experienced them.

Places to Stay

The *IH – Beit Sara Hostel* (☎ (07) 658 4165) at Ein Gedi charges 54 NIS for a place in an air-con eight bed dorm, or a double room is 138 NIS (nonmembers pay a few shekels more). In both cases breakfast is included. Dinner is also available in the evenings. Check-in is from 4 pm onwards and check out is 9 am. The hostel is about 250m north-west from the Ein Gedi Reserve bus stop.

At Masada, the *IH – Isaac H Taylor Hostel* (☎ (07) 658 4349) provides air-con dorms at 46 NIS per person, with breakfast included. Sleeping out on top of Masada is no longer permitted, but the hostel does have tent-pitching space.

Back up at Ein Gedi, the *Camping Village* (☎ (07) 584 4444; fax 658 4455) by the beach has tent space for 24 NIS per person and air-con cabins for US$64 for a double, plus US$10 for each extra person. There is a self-service restaurant, a mini-market for supplies and a clubhouse with a snack bar, TV and video lounge.

Surrounded by tree-filled gardens beside the Dead Sea, with a swimming pool and hot spa included in the price, the guesthouse at *Kibbutz Ein Gedi* (☎ (07) 659 4222; fax 658 4328) is one of the most popular in the country. Terms are half-board only; singles cost from US$76 to US$109 and doubles from US$113 to US$153. Booking in advance is recommended.

Getting There & Away

The entire west coast of the Dead Sea, about 90 km long, is served by a single main road (No 90) which comes off the Jerusalem-Jericho highway in the north and follows the shoreline southwards to Sodom, continuing to Eilat. The most comprehensive bus service is from Jerusalem's central bus station. Buses from there to Eilat and Beersheba go by Qumran (60 minutes; 14 NIS), Ein Gedi (90 minutes; 18 NIS) and Masada, and there should be something departing at least every hour or so.

TEL AVIV

Tel Aviv is a greatly underrated Mediterranean city, barely a century old, that thumbs its nose at the 3000 year history of Jerusalem. Forsaking synagogues for stock exchanges and tradition for fadism, the concerns of secular Tel Aviv are finance, business and fun. The city has an absorbing array of distinctive neighbourhoods, a result of the diverse backgrounds of its inhabitants, all of whom arrived in the last few generations with piles of cultural baggage intact. A short walk can encompass the spicy Orientalism of the Yemenite Quarter, the seedy vodka cafes of Russified lower Allenby St and the Miami chic of pastel pink and blue glass beachfront condominiums.

Possibly the major attraction is the lengthy stretch of fine white sand fringing the city centre area. When the sun is out (and it usually is) the beaches are a strutting ground for the local poseurs and a vast sandy court for pairs playing *matkot*, Israeli beach tennis. On summer nights the beaches remain crowded as they become impromptu sites for concerts and discos. Visitors should also make a point of visiting the **Diaspora Museum** up in the northern suburb of Ramat Aviv, and the former Arab port of **Jaffa**, now an unashamed till-ringing tourist attraction and popular Israeli venue for a candle-lit, waterfront seafood dinner.

For information on getting between Jerusalem and Tel Aviv, see the Getting There & Away chapter.

Glossary

HEBREW

Aliyah – immigration of Jews to Palestine: First Aliyah 1882-1903; Second Aliyah 1904-1918; Third Aliyah 1919-1923
Ashkenazim – Jews of German and East European descent
Atzmaut – independence

Bar Mitzvah – literally, 'subject to Jewish law', more commonly a coming of age ceremony for 13-year-old boys (bat mitzvah is the female equivalent)
Beit – house
Beit Knesset – synagogue

Diaspora – Jewish dispersion or exile from the Land of Israel; the exiled Jewish community worldwide

Egged – the national bus company

Halakic – based on Jewish law
Hared or Hasid – (pl **Haredim or Hasidim**) member of an ultra-orthodox Jewish sect
Hurva – ruin

IDF – Israel Defence Force, the national army
Iriya – city hall or municipality

Kabbalah – Jewish mysticism
Kosher – food prepared according to Jewish dietary law
Kibbutz – (pl **kibbutzim**) communal settlement, originally farms, but now involved in additional industries
Kibbutznik – member of a kibbutz
Kikar – city, town or village square
Kippa – another word for yarmulke
Klezmer – traditional Yiddish violin-based dance music
Kolel – neighbourhood where everyone comes from one place; administered by a committee
Knesset – Israeli Parliament

Magen David Adom – (Red Star of David) Israeli equivalent of the Red Cross
Mahkolet – grocery shop
Menorah – seven-pronged candelabra; an ancient Jewish symbol associated with the Hanukkah Festival
Mikveh – Jewish ritual bath

Mishnah – the legal codification of basic Jewish law – the Halakha
Moshav – co-operative settlement with a mix of private and collective housing and industry

Nahal – river; agricultural-military settlement

Olim – those who've made aliyah, immigrants to Israel

Payot – the side curls worn by Orthodox Jewish men

Sabra – native born Israeli
Sephardim – Jews of Spanish or Oriental descent
Shabbat – the Jewish sabbath and shutdown, observed from sundown Friday to sundown Saturday
Shechina – the divine presence which Jews believe inhabits the Western Wall
Sherut – shared taxi (fixed route)
Shuq – market

Talmud – part of the backbone of the Jewish faith: rabbinical interpretations of the scriptures, including the Mishnah
Tallit – Jewish prayer shawl
Tel – an ancient mound built up over centuries of urban rebuilding
Torah – the five books of Moses (the first five Old Testament books)

Ulpan – Hebrew school

Yad – memorial
Ya'ar – forest
Yarmulke – skullcap
Yeshiva (pl **yeshivot**) – Jewish religious seminary
Yerida – opposite of aliyah; to emigrate from Israel

ARABIC

Ablaq – the Mamluk technique of decorating buildings with bands of red and white stone
Ain/Ein – water spring or source

Caravanserai – see Khan

Fateh – Arafat's political party

Haj – annual Muslim pilgrimage to Mecca
Hamma – hot spring
Hammam – hot baths

Haram – holy sanctuary (literally 'forbidden')

Imam – Muslim preacher
Intifada – the Palestinian uprising against Israeli authorities in the Occupied Territories and Jerusalem (literally 'shaking off')

Keffiyah – the black & white checked Palestinian head scarf beloved of chic backpackers
Khan – also called caravanserai, a travellers' inn usually constructed on main trade routes, with accommodation on the first floor and stables and storage on the ground floor around a central courtyard
Khatib – low, railed wooden platform in a mosque where the khatib (reader) sits to recite from the Koran
Kfar – village
Koran – see Qur'an

Majdal – tower
Madrasa – theological school
Mihrab – prayer niche in a mosque, indicating the direction of Mecca
Minbar – pulpit used for sermons in a mosque
Muezzin – the man who sings the call to prayer, traditionally from atop a mosque minaret

Nargilah – water pipe for smoking

Qur'an – the Muslim holy book

Ramadan – the Muslim month of fasting

Sabil – public drinking fountain
Souk – market

Wadi – dried up river bed

FOOD

Blintzes – heavy pancakes filled with a savoury vegetarian stuffing
Cholent – a heavy stew prepared before sunset on Friday, eaten on Shabbat
Felafel – a deep-fried ball of ground chickpeas mixed with herbs and spices
Fuul – mashed fava beans
Gefilte fish – chilled balls made from fish heads and tails
Houmos – paste made from chick peas, tahina and seasonings

Kubbe – minced spiced meat mixed with cracked wheat and deep fried

Malawach – a thin flaky pastry bread, often stuffed

Mansaf – rice with small pieces of lamb, nuts, lemon juice and herbs

Melok – a soup made from greens

Meorav Yerushalmi – Jewish meats – a mixture of liver, kidney, hearts, beef, onion and spices served in pockets of bread

Mezze – a selection of starters, possibly including houmus, brain salad, eggplant dip, stuffed vine leaves, olives or pickles

Pitta – a type of unleavened bread

Sabra – a cactus fruit that looks like a hand grenade

Shashlik – chunks of meat grilled on a spit

Shwarma – sliced meat (usually lamb) cooked on a spit and served with salad in pitta bread

Tahina – thin paste made from sesame seeds

Index

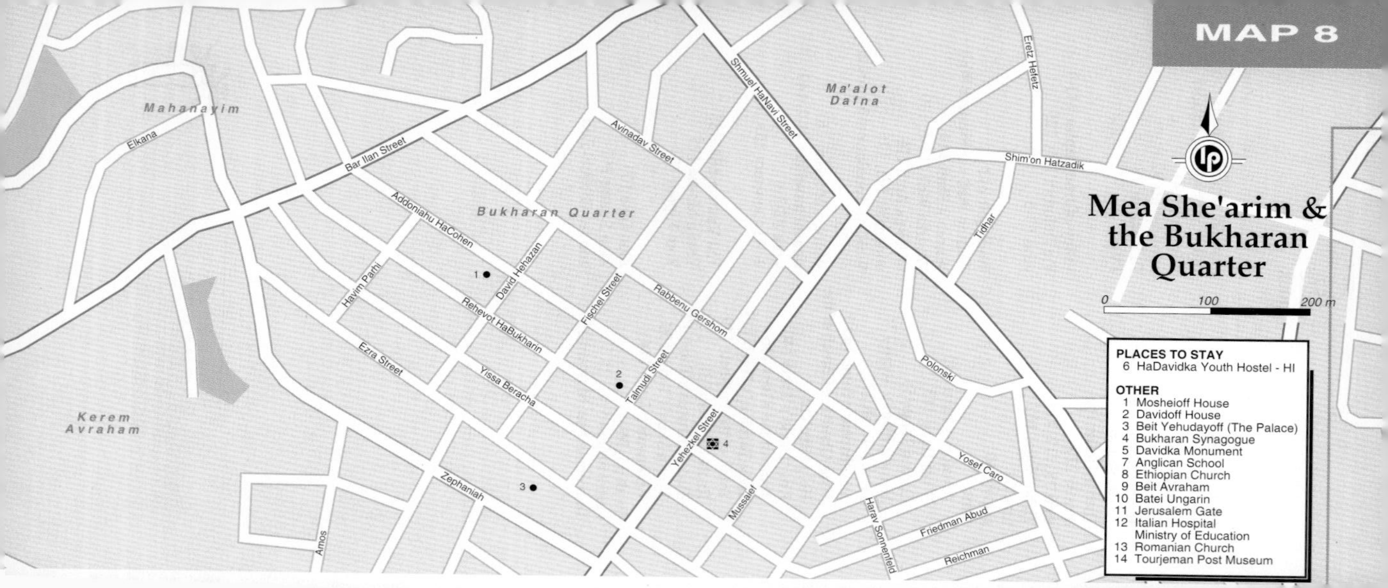

MAP 8

Ma'alot Dafna

Mahanayim

Bukharan Quarter

Kerem Avraham

0   100   200 m

PLACES TO STAY
6 HaDavidka Youth Hostel - HI

OTHER
1 Mosheioff House
2 Davidoff House
3 Beit Yehudayoff (The Palace)
4 Bukharan Synagogue
5 Davidka Monument
6 Anglican School
7 Ethiopian Church
8 Beit Avraham
9 Batei Ungarin
10 Jerusalem Gate
11 Italian Hospital
   Ministry of Education
12 Romanian Church
13 Tourjeman Post Museum
14

Street labels: Bar Ilan Street, Addoniahu HaCohen, Avinadav Street, Shmuel HaNavi Street, Erez Heletz, Shim'on Hatzadik, Lidhar, Haim Pann, Ezra Street, David HaNazan, Reliavot HaBukharin, Yossa Beracha, Prophet Street, Rabbenu Gershom, Talmud Street, Yehezkel Street, Minshel, Harav Sonnenfeld, Zephaniah, Amos, Friedman Abud, Reichman, Polonski, Yosef Caro

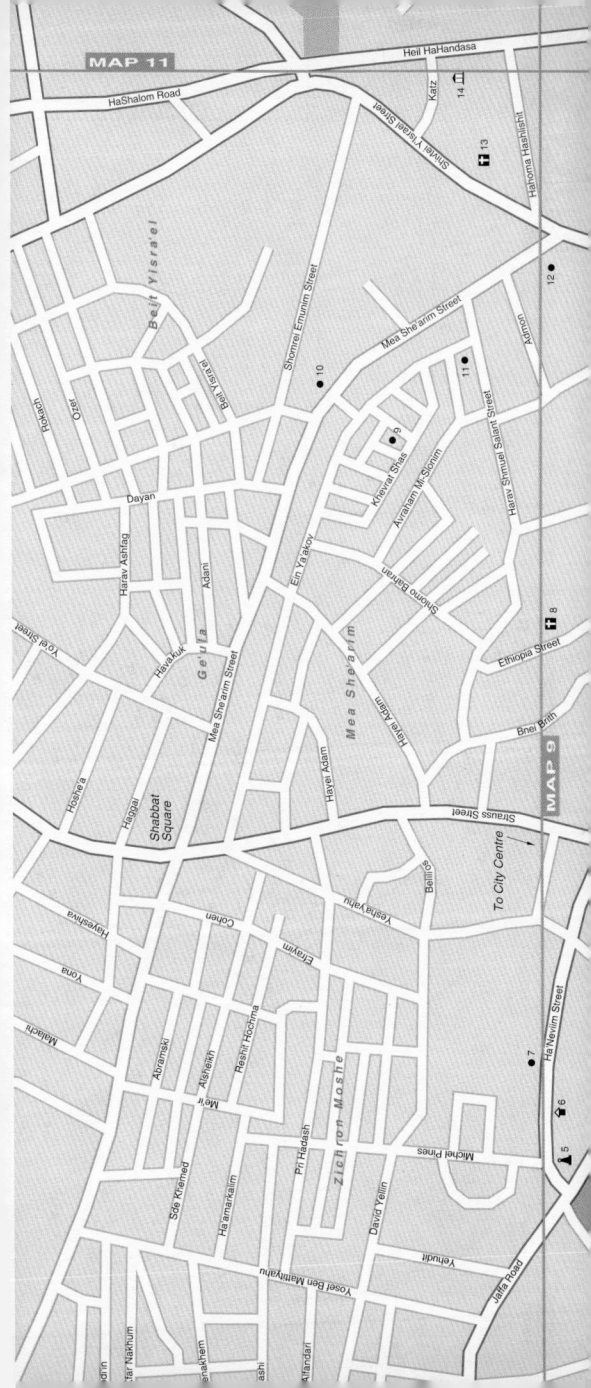

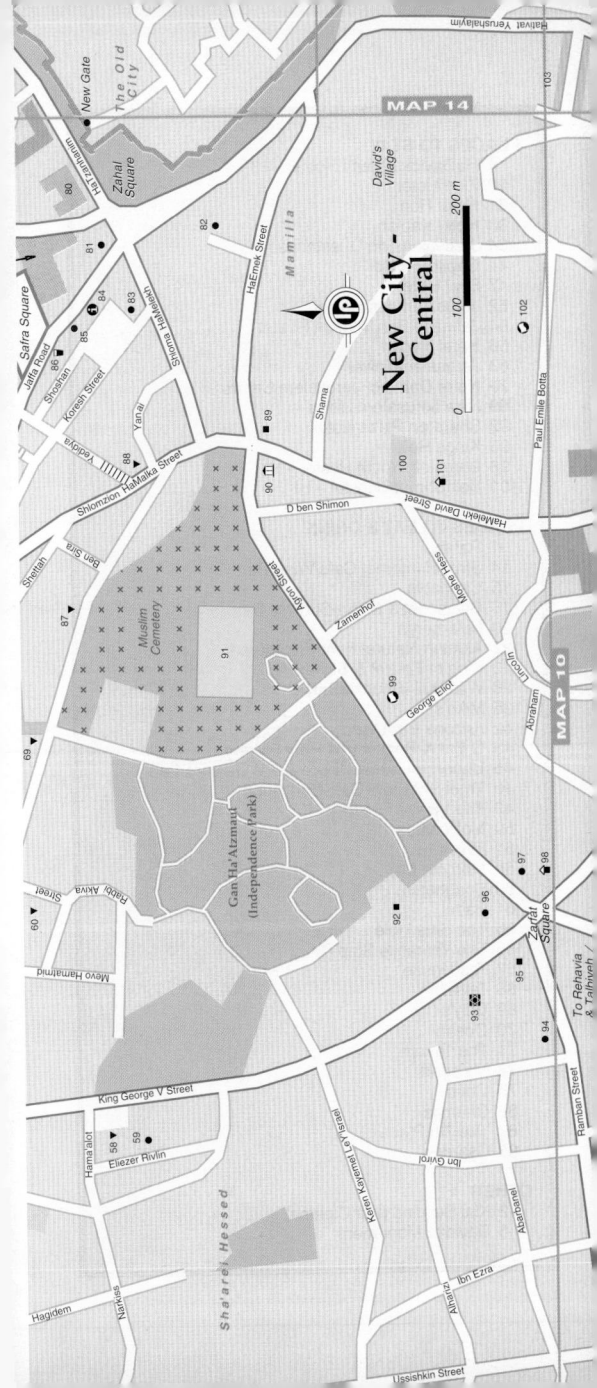

PLACES TO STAY
- 4 HaDavidka Youth Hostel – HI
- 28 Zion Hotel
- 31 Hotel Ron
- 33 Hotel Kaplan
- 34 Jerusalem Inn Guesthouse
- 44 Capitol Hostel
- 47 Eyal Hotel
- 52 Jerusalem Inn Hostel
- 54 Jasmine Ben Yehuda Hostel
- 56 Hotel Nogah
- 63 Jerusalem Tower
- 79 Notre Dame of Jerusalem Centre
- 89 New Jerusalem Hilton
- 92 Sheraton Plaza Hotel
- 95 Kings Hotel
- 98 Bernstein Youth Hostel – HI
- 101 Beit Shmuel Hostel – HI

PLACES TO EAT & DRINK
- 1 Rahmo
- 14 Strudel Internet Cafe/Wine Bar
- 15 Cannabis
- 16 Glassnost & Metro-Subway Bars
- 20 Feferbergs
- 22 Alumah Natural Food Restaurant
- 23 King of Felafel & Shwarma
- 26 Wild Bull (Shor HaBar)
- 35 Mike's
- 42 Arizona Bar/Disco
- 43 Q Bar & Bonkers 24 Hour Bakery
- 45 Underground Bar/Disco & Fat Danny's Diner
- 46 Tmol Shilshom Cafe/Bookshop
- 49 The Village Green
- 50 McDonalds
- 51 Fink's
- 58 Mamma Mia
- 60 Spaghettim
- 61 Babel
- 65 The Blue Hole
- 66 The Yemenite Step
- 67 Tea House
- 68 Tavlin
- 69 Gilly's
- 70 Ocean
- 71 The Tavern
- 73 Ma'adan
- 75 Chen
- 86 Champs
- 87 The 7th Place
- 88 Csardas

OTHER
- 2 Klal Building (Kfir Cinema)
- 3 Davidka Monument

5 Anglican School
6 Israel Centre
7 Holman Hunt House
8 Thabor House (Swedish Theological Institute)
9 Ben Yehuda House
10 Ethiopian Church
11 Italian Hospital (Ministry of Education)
12 Ethiopian Consulate
13 ISSTA Student Travel
17 Sergei Building (SPNI Office & Bookshop)
18 Beit David (Rabbi Kook Museum)
19 Ticho House & Cafe
21 Sefer VeSefel Bookshop
24 Steimatzky Bookshop
25 Israel Youth Hostels Association Office
27 Solan Telecom
29 Change Point
30 Egged Tours
32 The Jerusalem Post Bookshop
36 Central Police Station
37 Church of the Holy Trinity
38 Kodak Express
39 Change Point
40 Steimatzky Bookshop
41 American Express Office
48 Steimatzky Bookshop
53 City Tower
55 Ministry of Tourism Building
57 Bezalel School of Art & Artists' House
59 Tzavta Theatre
62 Tower Records
64 Synagogue & Museum of Italian Jewish Art
72 Tzipor Hanefesh Laundromat
74 Libraire Francaise
76 Main Post Office
77 Hall of Heroism
78 New City Hall Complex
80 St Louis Hospice
81 Old City Hall
82 St Vincent de Paul Hospice
83 Mazada Tours (Buses to Cairo)
84 Tourist Information Office
85 Jerusalem Municipal Gallery
90 Taxation Museum
91 Mamilla Pool
93 The Great Synagogue & Heichal Shlomo
94 Rehavia Windmill
96 Supersol Supermarket
97 Alliance Francaise
99 US Consulate
100 Hebrew Union College
102 French Consulate
103 Arts & Crafts Lane (Khutsot HaYotser)

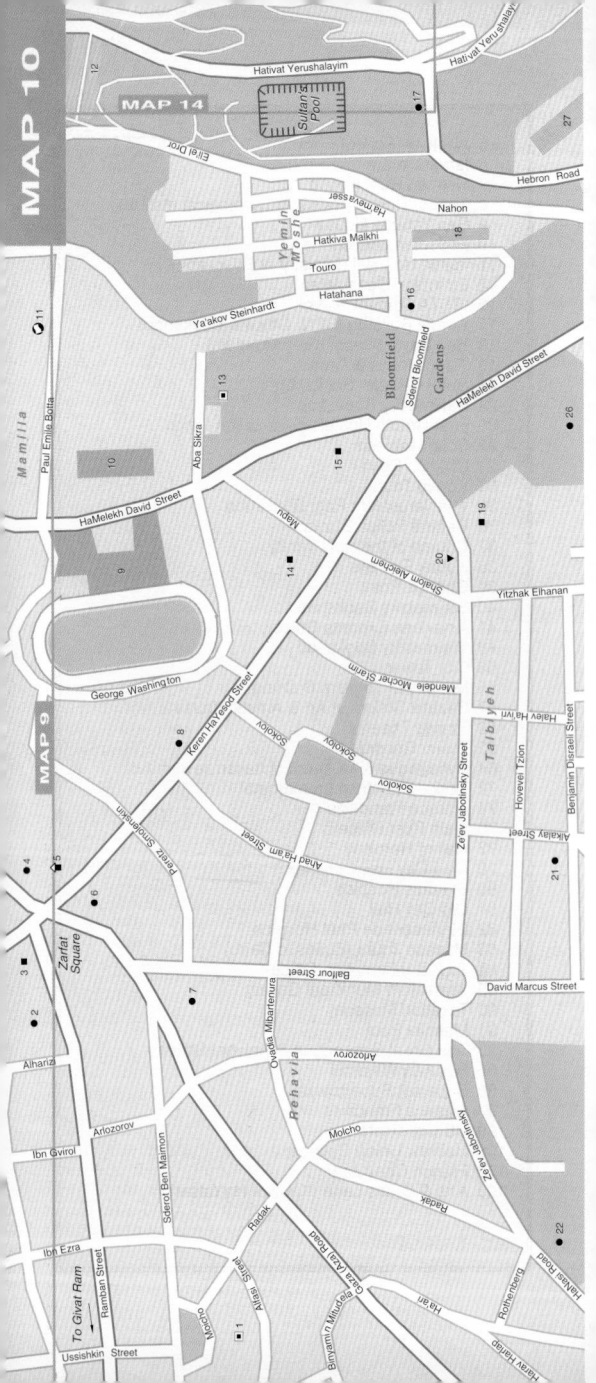

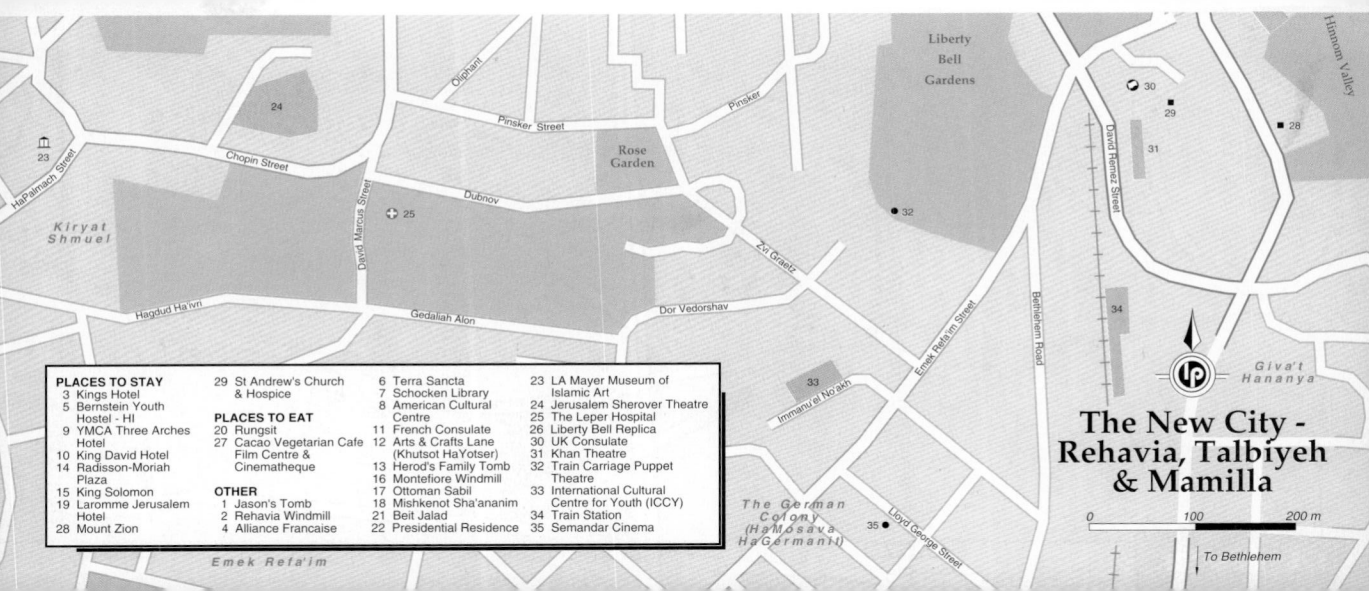

The New City – Rehavia, Talbiyeh & Mamilla

PLACES TO STAY
3 Kings Hotel
5 Bernstein Youth Hostel - HI
9 YMCA Three Arches Hotel
10 King David Hotel
14 Radisson-Moriah Plaza
15 King Solomon
19 Laromme Jerusalem Hotel
28 Mount Zion
29 St Andrew's Church & Hospice

PLACES TO EAT
20 Rungsit
27 Cacao Vegetarian Cafe

OTHER
1 Jason's Tomb
2 Rehavia Windmill
4 Alliance Francaise
6 Terra Sancta
7 Schocken Library
8 American Cultural Centre
11 French Consulate
12 Arts & Crafts Lane (Khutsot HaYotser)
13 Herod's Family Tomb
16 Montefiore Windmill
17 Ottoman Sabil
18 Mishkenot Sha'ananim
21 Beit Jalad
22 Presidential Residence
23 LA Mayer Museum of Islamic Art
24 Jerusalem Sherover Theatre
25 The Leper Hospital
26 Liberty Bell Replica
30 UK Consulate
31 Khan Theatre
32 Train Carriage Puppet Theatre
33 International Cultural Centre for Youth (ICCY)
34 Train Station
35 Semandar Cinema

Film Centre & Cinematheque

0   100   200 m

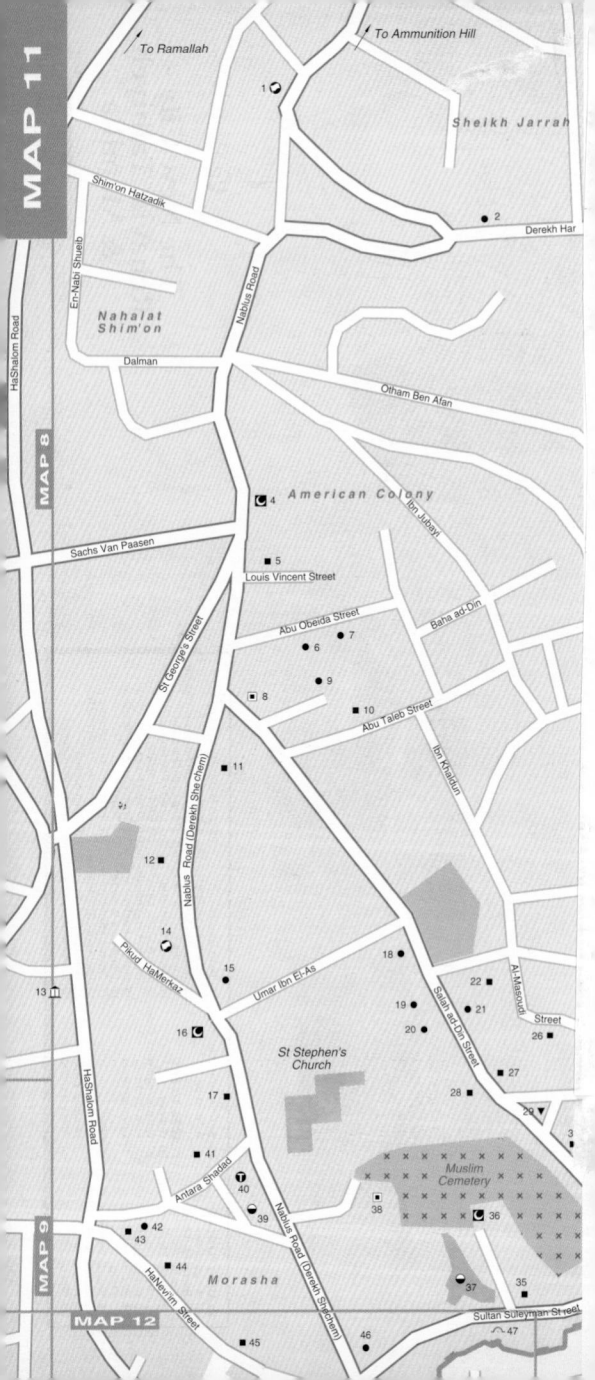

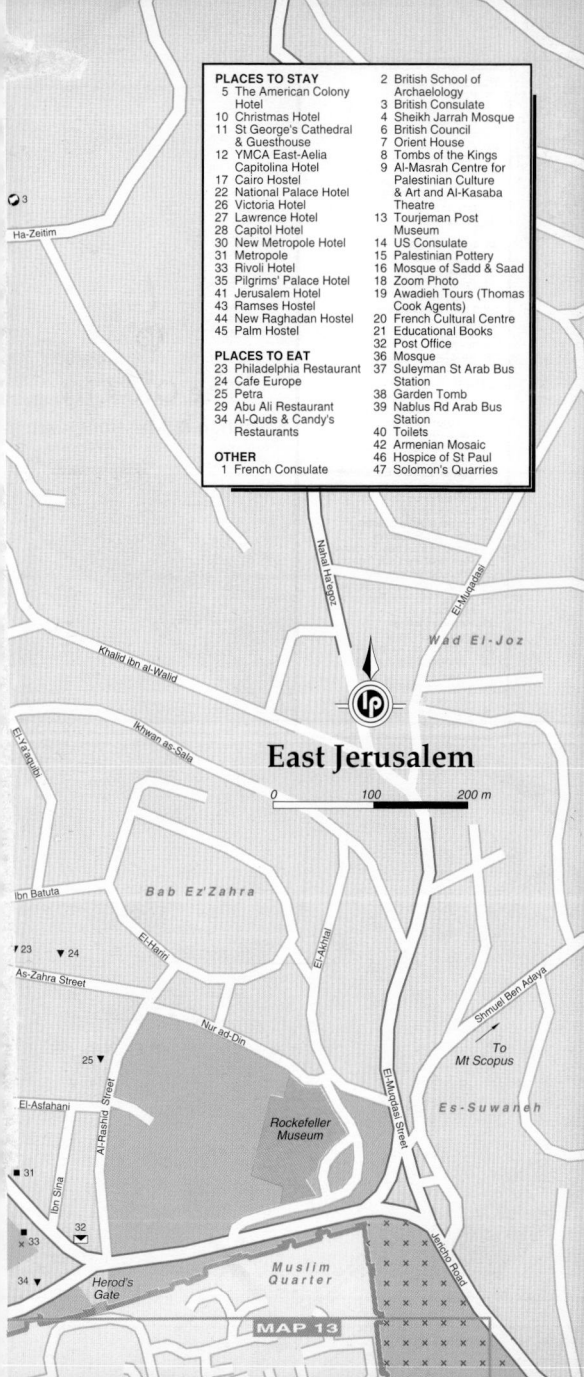

East Jerusalem

0   100   200 m

MAP 13

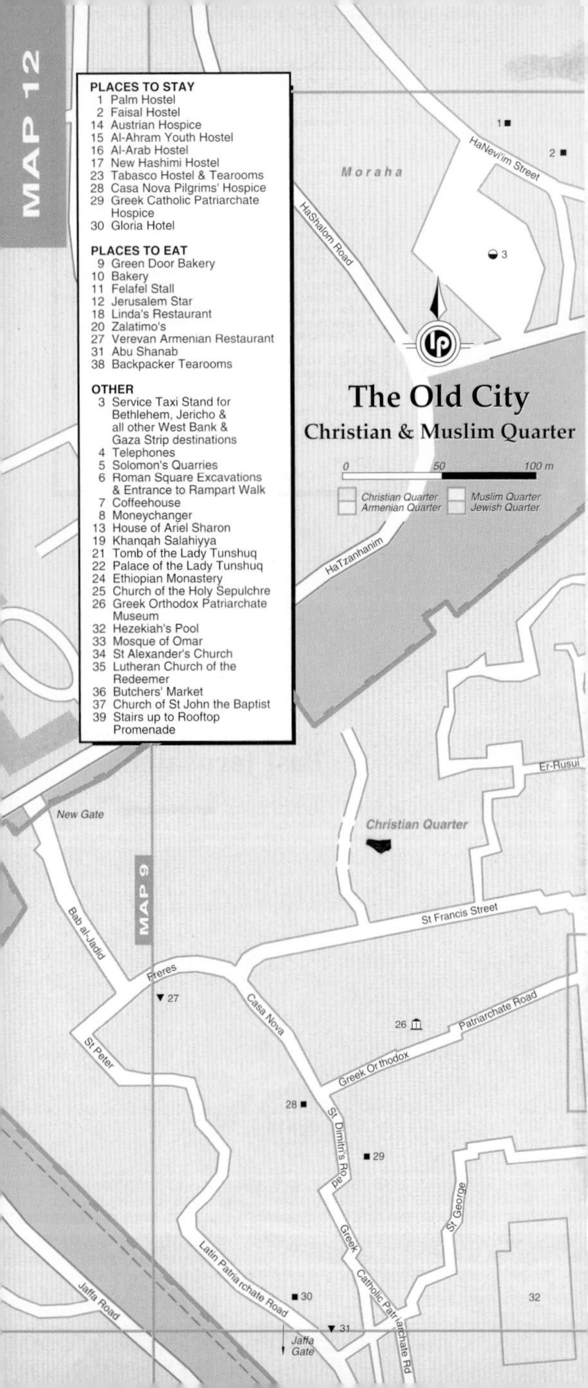

MAP 12

The Old City
Christian & Muslim Quarter

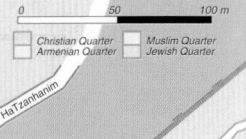

PLACES TO STAY
1 Palm Hostel
2 Faisal Hostel
14 Austrian Hospice
15 Al-Ahram Youth Hostel
16 Al-Arab Hostel
17 New Hashimi Hostel
23 Tabasco Hostel & Tearooms
28 Casa Nova Pilgrims' Hospice
29 Greek Catholic Patriarchate Hospice
30 Gloria Hotel

PLACES TO EAT
9 Green Door Bakery
10 Bakery
11 Felafel Stall
12 Jerusalem Star
18 Linda's Restaurant
20 Zalatimo's
27 Verevan Armenian Restaurant
31 Abu Shanab
38 Backpacker Tearooms

OTHER
3 Service Taxi Stand for Bethlehem, Jericho & all other West Bank & Gaza Strip destinations
4 Telephones
5 Solomon's Quarries
6 Roman Square Excavations & Entrance to Rampart Walk
7 Coffeehouse
8 Moneychanger
13 House of Ariel Sharon
19 Khanqah Salahiyya
21 Tomb of the Lady Tunshuq
22 Palace of the Lady Tunshuq
24 Ethiopian Monastery
25 Church of the Holy Sepulchre
26 Greek Orthodox Patriarchate Museum
32 Hezekiah's Pool
33 Mosque of Omar
34 St Alexander's Church
35 Lutheran Church of the Redeemer
36 Butchers' Market
37 Church of St John the Baptist
39 Stairs up to Rooftop Promenade

Moraha

HaNevim Street

HaShalom Road

0   50   100 m

Christian Quarter
Armenian Quarter

Muslim Quarter
Jewish Quarter

HaTzanhanim

Er-Rusul

New Gate

Christian Quarter

St Francis Street

Bab al-Jadid

Freres

Casa Nova

St Dimitri's Rd

St George

Greek Catholic Patriarchate Rd

Greek Orthodox

Patriarchate Road

26

St Peter

28

29

Latin Patriarchate Road

Jaffa Road

30

31

Jaffa Gate

32

27

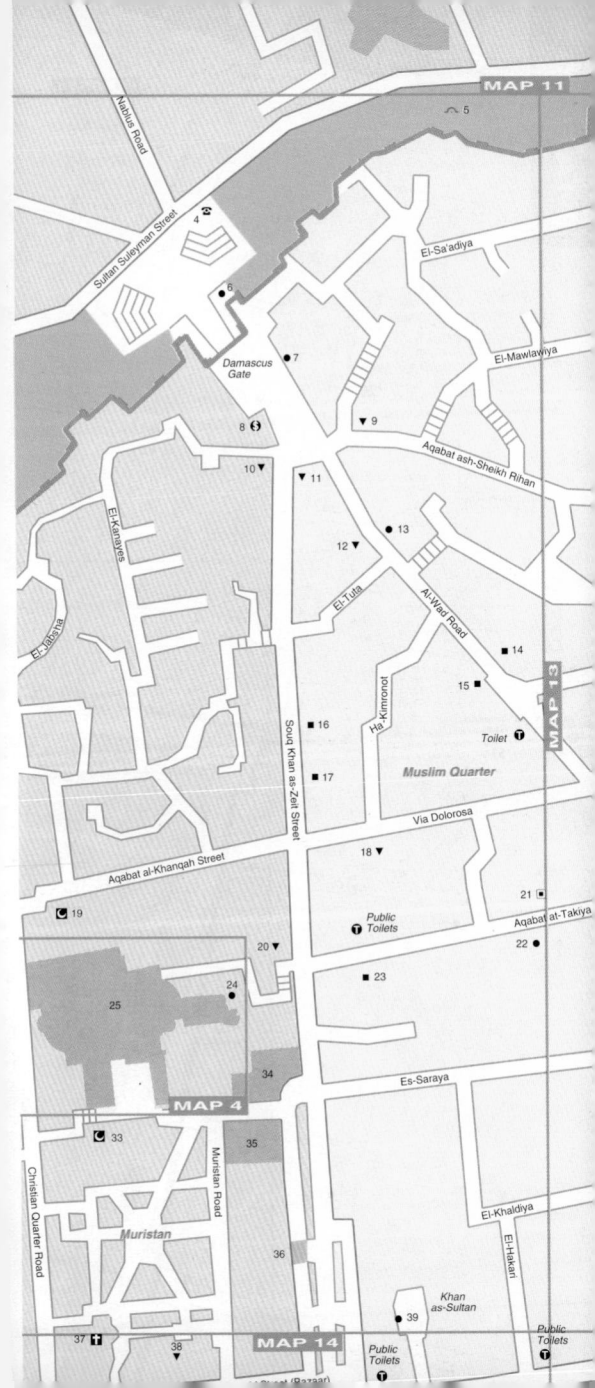

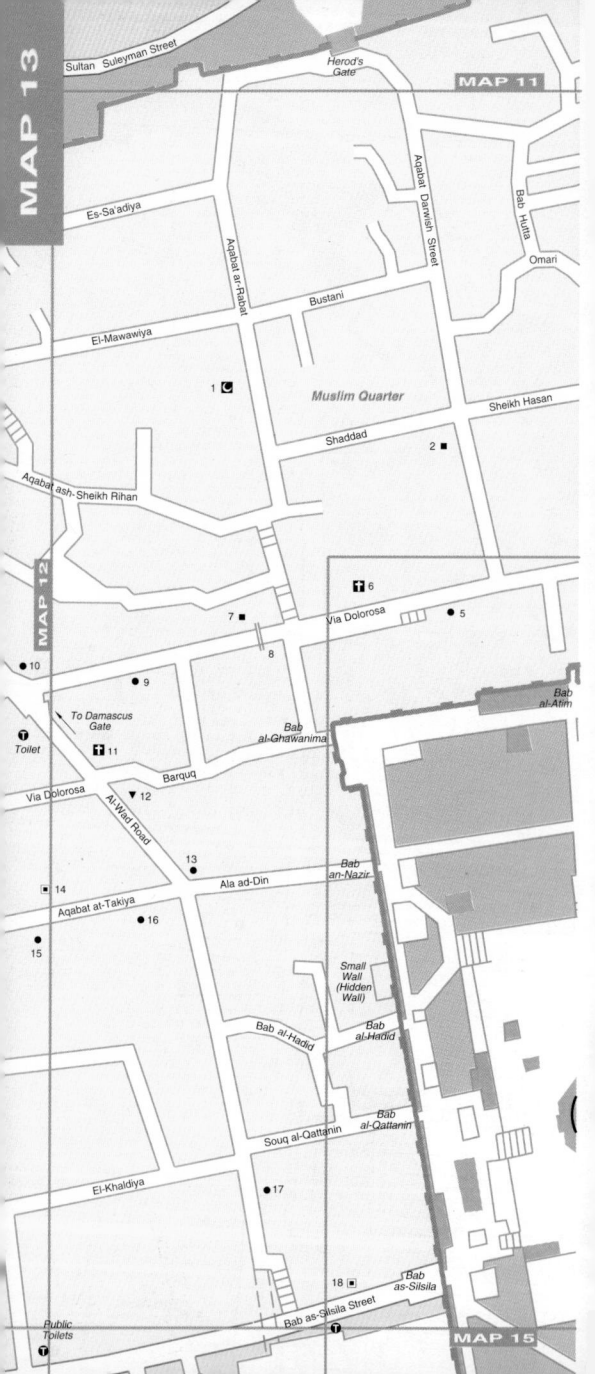

MAP 13

Sultan Suleyman Street

Herod's Gate

MAP 11

Es-Sa'adiya

Aqabat ar-Rabat

Aqabat Darwish Street

Bab Hutta

Omari

Bustani

El-Mawawiya

1

Muslim Quarter

Sheikh Hasan

Shaddad

2

Aqabat ash-Sheikh Rihan

MAP 12

6

7

Via Dolorosa

5

8

10

9

Bab al-Atim

To Damascus Gate

11

Bab al-Ghawanima

Toilet

Barquq

Via Dolorosa

Al-Wad Road

12

13

Ala ad-Din

Bab an-Nazir

14

Aqabat at-Takiya

16

15

Small Wall (Hidden Wall)

Bab al-Hadid

Bab al-Hadid

Souq al-Qattanin

Bab al-Qattanin

El-Khaldiya

17

18

Bab as-Silsila

Bab as-Silsila Street

Public Toilets

MAP 15

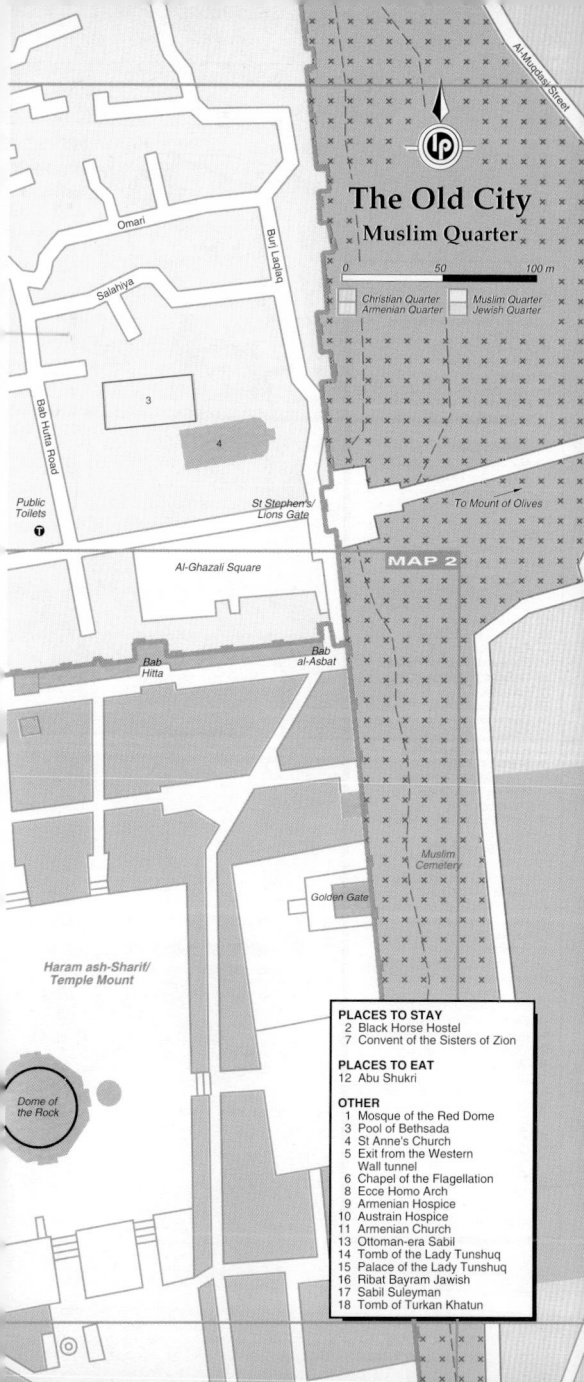

The Old City
Muslim Quarter

Al-Mujaheer Street

Omari

Burj Laqlaq

Salahiya

Bab Hutta Road

0   50   100 m

Christian Quarter
Armenian Quarter

Muslim Quarter
Jewish Quarter

Public Toilets

St Stephen's/
Lions Gate

To Mount of Olives

Al-Ghazali Square

MAP 2

Bab
Hitta

Bab
al-Asbat

Muslim
Cemetery

Golden Gate

Haram ash-Sharif/
Temple Mount

Dome of
the Rock

PLACES TO STAY
2 Black Horse Hostel
7 Convent of the Sisters of Zion

PLACES TO EAT
12 Abu Shukri

OTHER
1 Mosque of the Red Dome
3 Pool of Bethsada
4 St Anne's Church
5 Exit from the Western
   Wall tunnel
6 Chapel of the Flagellation
8 Ecce Homo Arch
9 Armenian Hospice
10 Austrian Hospice
11 Armenian Church
13 Ottoman-era Sabil
14 Tomb of the Lady Tunshuq
15 Palace of the Lady Tunshuq
16 Ribat Bayram Jawish
17 Sabil Suleyman
18 Tomb of Turkan Khatun

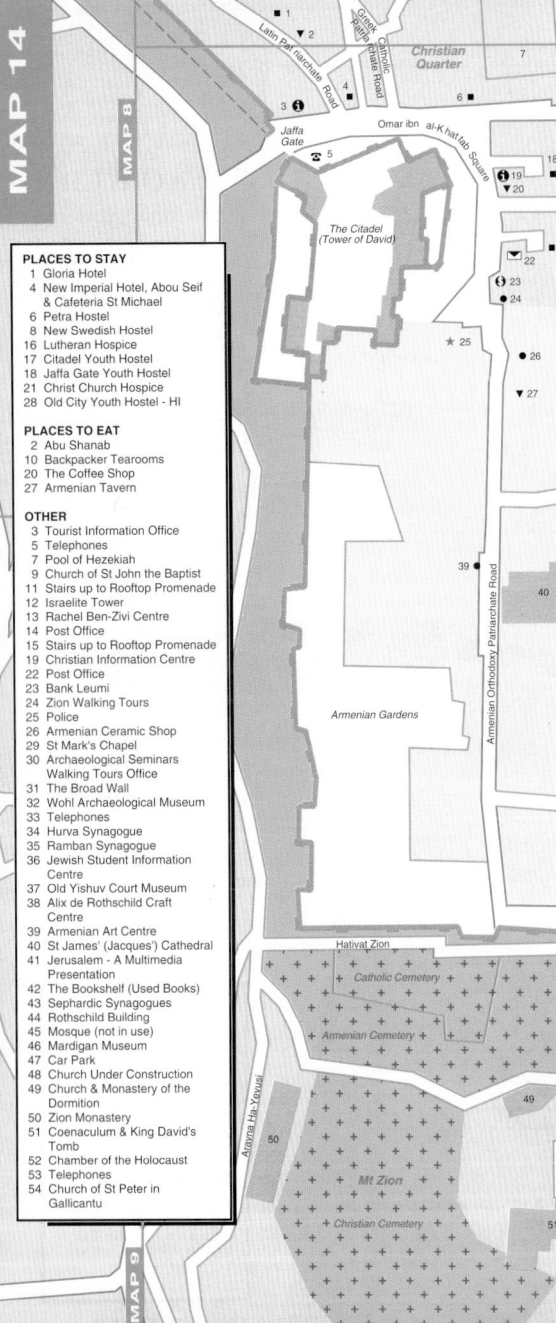

MAP 14

MAP 8

MAP 9

Latin Patriarchate Road

Greek Catholic Patriarchate Road

Christian Quarter

Omar ibn al-K̲ẖat̲t̲ab Square

Jaffa Gate

The Citadel (Tower of David)

Armenian Orthodox Patriarchate Road

Armenian Gardens

Hativat Zion

Catholic Cemetery

Armenian Cemetery

Aravva Ha-Yevusi

Mt Zion

Christian Cemetery

PLACES TO STAY
1 Gloria Hotel
4 New Imperial Hotel, Abou Seif & Cafeteria St Michael
6 Petra Hostel
8 New Swedish Hostel
16 Lutheran Hospice
17 Citadel Youth Hostel
18 Jaffa Gate Youth Hostel
21 Christ Church Hospice
28 Old City Youth Hostel - HI

PLACES TO EAT
2 Abu Shanab
10 Backpacker Tearooms
20 The Coffee Shop
27 Armenian Tavern

OTHER
3 Tourist Information Office
5 Telephones
7 Pool of Hezekiah
9 Church of St John the Baptist
11 Stairs up to Rooftop Promenade
12 Israelite Tower
13 Rachel Ben-Zivi Centre
14 Post Office
15 Stairs up to Rooftop Promenade
19 Christian Information Centre
22 Post Office
23 Bank Leumi
24 Zion Walking Tours
25 Police
26 Armenian Ceramic Shop
29 St Mark's Chapel
30 Archaeological Seminars Walking Tours Office
31 The Broad Wall
32 Wohl Archaeological Museum
33 Telephones
34 Hurva Synagogue
35 Ramban Synagogue
36 Jewish Student Information Centre
37 Old Yishuv Court Museum
38 Alix de Rothschild Craft Centre
39 Armenian Art Centre
40 St James (Jacques') Cathedral
41 Jerusalem - A Multimedia Presentation
42 The Bookshelf (Used Books)
43 Sephardic Synagogues
44 Rothschild Building
45 Mosque (not in use)
46 Mardigan Museum
47 Car Park
48 Church Under Construction
49 Church & Monastery of the Dormition
50 Zion Monastery
51 Coenaculum & King David's Tomb
52 Chamber of the Holocaust
53 Telephones
54 Church of St Peter in Gallicantu

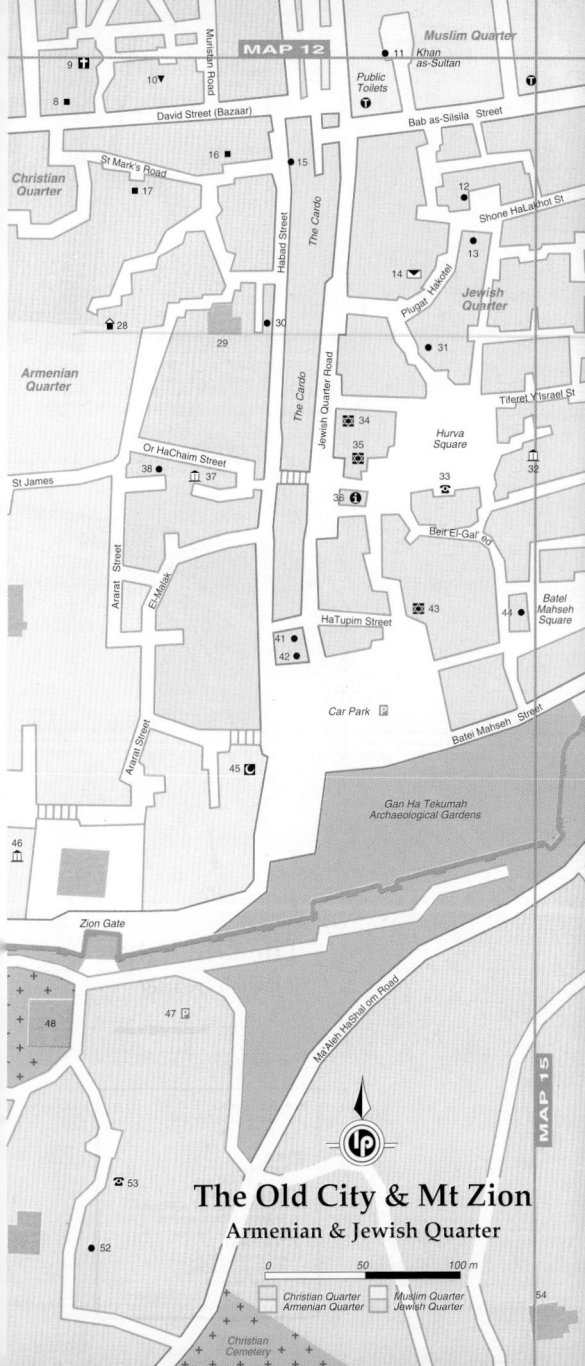

The Old City & Mt Zion
Armenian & Jewish Quarter

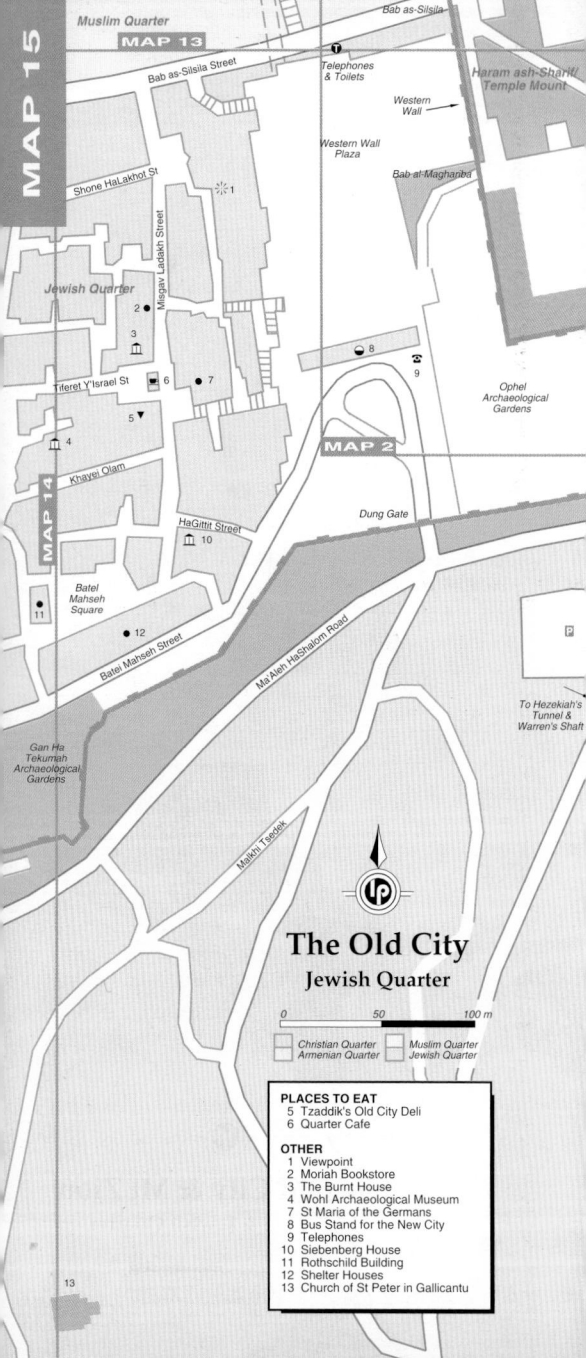

The Old City
Jewish Quarter

MAP 15

Muslim Quarter
MAP 13
Bab as-Silsila

Bab as-Silsila Street

Telephones & Toilets

Haram ash-Sharif/ Temple Mount

Western Wall

Western Wall Plaza

Shone HaLakhot St

Misgav Ladakh Street

Bab al-Magharba

Jewish Quarter

Tiferet Y'Israel St

Ophel Archaeological Gardens

MAP 14

MAP 2

Khayei Olam

HaGittit Street

Dung Gate

Batei Mahseh Square

Batei Mahseh Street

Ma'Aleh HaShalom Road

To Hezekiah's Tunnel & Warren's Shaft

Makhi Tsedek

Gan Ha Tekumah Archaeological Gardens

| 0 | 50 | 100 m |

Christian Quarter
Armenian Quarter
Muslim Quarter
Jewish Quarter

PLACES TO EAT
5 Tzaddik's Old City Deli
6 Quarter Cafe

OTHER
1 Viewpoint
2 Moriah Bookstore
3 The Burnt House
4 Wohl Archaeological Museum
7 St Maria of the Germans
8 Bus Stand for the New City
9 Telephones
10 Siebenberg House
11 Rothschild Building
12 Shelter Houses
13 Church of St Peter in Gallicantu